MW00441243

TOUCHDOWN UCLA

The Complete Account Of
Bruin Football

TOUCHDOWN UCLA

The Complete Account Of
Bruin Football

By
Hendrik Van Leuven

Original Edition Published 1982

Strode Publishers
Div. Circle Book Service
P.O. Box 626, Tomball, Texas 77375

Dedication

To my mother, Hallie Couch Van Leuven (UCLA '35), whose strength and perseverance in raising six children and indulgence for her last in all his creative efforts has been an ultimate inspiration, I most gratefully dedicate this book. She's a Bruin, folks, and one of the best.

ACKNOWLEDGMENTS

Mark Dellins, Gary Rausch and Vic Kelley of the UCLA Sports Information Department, William C. Ackerman, Robert Fischer, Peter Dalis, Angelo Mazzone, Jerry Long, Glenn Toth, Gary Considine, Greg Masters, Norm Schindler, Ann Sanders, Tommy Prothro, Ducky Drake, George Dickerson, Terry Donahue, Homer Smith, Bert LaBrucherie, Mike Frankovich, Loran Peak, Dick Wallen, Rick Purdy, John Sciarra, Paul Cameron, John Jackson, Chuck Cheshire, John Johnson, Kermit Alexander, Al Sparlis, Tom Ramsey, Bea Kass, Patt Troutman, Bill Schroeder, Braven "Buddy" Dyer, Jr., Jolie Oliver, Eileen Lawrence, Bill Rees, The Westwood Bruin Touchdown Club, Averil Paserow, and John Gunn.

Contents

CHAPTER 1
1918-1924

The records show UCLA fielded a football team in 1919. But at that time, the school was not UCLA, and its team was not the Bruins.

In 1918 Dr. Ernest Carroll Moore, head of the Los Angeles State Normal School (teachers colleges were called normal schools), was approached by Edward Dickson, the only University of California regent from the Southern California area. Dickson was exploring the possibility of establishing a branch of the university, tentatively in Los Angeles. From that meeting developed the presentation to the regents, a subsequent battle to see through, and the victory. The little school on Vermont Avenue in Los Angeles became the home of the first real branch of the state's university. The school's first name was the University of California, Southern Branch.

The old normal school had an existing athletic program, and the team name or "totem" was the Huskies. But when the Branch was created, falling under the aegis of the big U at Berkeley, all felt that a totem in relation to that school's name, the Golden Bears, would be more appropriate. The Normal School Huskies were transformed into the Southern Branch Cubs. (As the school was also referred to as the Southern Branch of the University of California, it was noticed that those initials, SBUC, were "Cubs" backwards!)

The branch opened its doors on September 15, 1919, a two-year institution. Though it was not long until Moore and Dickson succeeded in obtaining first three (1923) then four-(1924) year accreditation for the Branch from the regents, the 1919 Cubs began life on the lowest rung possible—as a freshman team.

To get the new school's athletic program started, they called upon one man, Frederick Warren Cozens. The original budget was so miniscule, Cozens was the entire athletic department, its director, and only coach trainer for every sport.

The football field, soon to be called Ernest Moore Field, had been used during the soon-to-be-ended world war as a parade ground for the recruits training on the campus of the normal school. The tramp tramp tramp created a surface as hard as adobe when dry, and it turned into sludge when it rained. What grass there was barely grew on the northern end zone.

Cozens, fondly called "Doc" or "Dad," was a young man, a graduate of Cal (1915) who had stayed on at Berkeley to coach freshman baseball and soccer. A quiet, intellectual man, his first season as a head football coach was an achievement in itself: He fielded a team.

The Branch still was basically a teachers college. Mostly women wanted to be teachers, as the seven-to-one female/male ratio at the school bore out. With the total enrollment at less than 1,000 at this time, Cozens' feat becomes more impressive.

The football itself in 1919 was much less acutely elliptical than at present—it was a fat blimp, difficult to handle, even more so to pass. The game was also different. There was no open substitution, which meant each player played his position on offense and defense, all game long if he could make it. If a player left the field for any reason (exhaustion or injury), he could not return for the rest of that half. Protective gear was not mandatory, and many individuals thought it manly to go without even a helmet. The players always called the plays, and a coach caught coaching from the sidelines or sending in plays would be regarded as a cheat and the game could be forfeited; in fact, if a substitute was sent in, he could not talk to his teammates until one play was run, for fear he was bringing in a play or some key information.

On the opening day of school, Cozens put out a call for players, and the first general gathering of prospects was held just one day after the school opened, Tuesday, September 16. The *Los Angeles Times* covered this event, and an article entitled "Football Life Shown at U. of C. Branch" described

12

the occasion:

"And now the southern branch of the University of California lets out a yip to let the world know that it is up and doing in the world of football....It is said that the men are heavy, averaging a fair beef."

Somehow the nearly 100 fairly beefy men who reportedly showed up for this muster dwindled by the time the first game rolled around. In fact, Cozens never had as many as 22 from that point forward—which meant he could never conduct a scrimmage. Cozens did the best he could, getting his team ready for the first opponent, Manual Arts High School.

Most frosh teams played high schools during this period, because it was cheap for both schools to do so, and because there were not that many teams to play against, high school or otherwise. Football was just returning as the nation's favorite fall sport, having been supplanted by Rugby when football was virtually outlawed, because of unchecked brutality, at the outset of the century. (In 1919, Stanford fielded its first football team since 1906.)

The Southern Branch Cubs sallied forth to meet the Artisans of Manual Arts High on the night of October 3, 1919. The Cubs lost, 74-0.

Again, the *LA Times* was there: "The best that can be said for Coach Cozens' team is that the men fought hard, but it was like a lightweight pugilist against a heavyweight. Not that the high school lads outweighed their opponents. It was probably the other way around...." Fullback Burnett Haralson was cited as the best player for the Branch.

The next team to face the Cubs came from Hollywood High, a contest viewed by both as just a practice game. The Cubs did improve, losing only by 19-6. The first points ever scored were by left half Wayne "Red" Banning, who intercepted a pass with only three minutes left in the game and ran it back 65 yards for a touchdown.

The team traveled two days later to Bakersfield, played the high school there, and lost, 27-12. At least the dance in the gym that night, in the visitors' honor, assuaged the pain.

Finally, in a game heralded as "The First Official Game of the Season," the Cubs did to the Occidental (Oxy) Frosh what they could not do to these high school teams—they beat them. It also marked the first game played at home, with 250 people venturing out after a heavy rain onto the just-dry bleachers to watch the Cubs battle the Tigers.

For three mud-ridden, fumble-rife quarters nothing was produced by either squad; then, early in the fourth quarter, the Cubs fell behind via a safety, 2-0. But the crowd was finally rewarded, as right half Abe Jacobsen recovered an Oxy fumble and ran 60 yards for the go-ahead points. Banning then kicked the conversion to make the final score a 7-2 victory for the Cubs.

Although they also won the next game six days later against Los Angeles Junior College, 7-0, injuries began to take their toll, and rematches against these two schools and a game with a team from the USS *Idaho* brought defeats.

That Cozens had at least put a team on the field and recruited games to play was no small accomplishment, and his efforts brought immediate reward. The Branch was invited in December to join the Southern California Intercollegiate Athletic Conference (Southern Conference), filling the void created when the University of Southern California bolted to become an independent. The Trojans later joined the newly formed Pacific Coast Conference (PCC) in 1922. In truth, the Southern Conference was not sorry to see Southern Cal go, as there had been annual complaints over the years about the Trojans' duplicitous standards regarding athletic eligibility.

That first team was a frosh team and, therefore, strictly speaking, should not be included in the annals of varsity play. But the players represent the proud pioneers (an oft-used term respecting the class of 1921) who made that first effort to form a football team. The essence of that team—and of UCLA teams to come—was summed up by center/right guard/fullback Raymond "Red" Meigs, who often told his teammates, "When the game gets rough, boys, I'm going home!" It was never too rough for Red, and he played every game, all season long. From the beginning, that's been the Bruin spirit.

Cozens' first season as head football coach was his only season. At the end of the spring he also turned the reins of the athletic department over to Gibson Dunlap. One of his last acts was to see to his successor on the sidelines and, in a letter to Dr.

Moore Cozens asked, "That Mr. Harry Trotter be appointed as part time coach of athletics at a salary of $1100 per year. Mr. Trotter has been very successful with his athletic teams around Los Angeles and is the right type of man to direct athletic teams in college. He has a splendid athletic record himself and is well liked by all his men."

Harry "Duke" Trotter, in the three years he coached, faced as great a burden as Cozens. For two years he was forced to field an all-sophomore squad, which in turn played Southern Conference games against four-year institutions. His overall record of 2-13-1 is somewhat understandable. Trotter took it all in stride, because he recognized his limitations and did not let them bother him. Not much did.

At least attempts had been made to improve Moore Field. Cozens made a written request to Dr. Moore in the spring of 1920, "Mr. Robb has given me an estimate of fifty dollars (maximum) on labor for the job. There would also be the cost of sawdust, lime, straw or whatever seems best to put on after the field is plowed and harrowed....Is it possible to find the money? The Department of Physical Education for Men cannot stand that amount as you well know...." An even greater amount must have materialized, because not only was the field further enhanced by a fence erected around it (which prevented freeloaders from avoiding the 11 cents being charged per game) but $1,000 allegedly was spent to outfit the team.

Returnees were all there were, so for the second year in a row there were not enough players to constitute two teams. Full scrimmages were impossible, substitutions when necessary became difficult, and injuries added to Trotter's misery. The team went 0-5 for 1920.

The 1920 season set two precedents for the record. First, the only points scored by the Cubs all year were against Redlands, all coming in the fourth quarter after the Bulldogs posted a 28-0 advantage. Right end Eddie Rossell received three passes, all good for touchdowns, but still the game ended with the Cubs short by 28-21; to Rossell goes the honor of being the first to score a point for the school as a varsity player.

Second, Whittier, which would become an unbeatable "jinx" in these early years, handed the Cubs the worst scoring defeat in their history, 103-0. This was the last game of the

S. B. C. U.'s First V

Left to right (back row): Coach Trotter, Williamson, Walters, Sargent, Collins, Binney, Wyatt, Huff, Carter, Nadeau, Bann-

sity Football Team

ing, Coach Cozens. Kneeling: Tubbo, Olson, Montgomery, Abrams, Haralson (Capt.), Lipman, Einzig, James, Rossell.

season, certainly catching the Cubs at their lowest point.

Conditions hardly changed for Trotter for the 1921 season, as again his record shows an 0-5 result. The reported 60 men who turned out to play fell to 40 by the first game and diminished from there. Injuries, playing miscues, and more injuries decimated the team. Also, Moore Field had by this time become as soft as cement.

Freshmen were allowed to play on varsity teams for the next two years, and into the limelight stepped Loran Peak. His foot was his early claim to fame, his punting ability and agility kept the Cubs from getting into worse trouble than they did. After missing the 1922 season (falling a unit short for eligibility), Peak would return and earn his spot in UCLA history as its first star player.

California up at Berkeley also began to make its presence felt at the Branch. Head Bear coach Andy Smith, whose "Wonder Teams" were creating such a national sensation, had developed his talent through his self-named "Smith System." It emphasized a high level of player conditioning with a style of play best described as "punt, punt, punt...and wait for the breaks." Smith personally installed his system at the Branch this year, with a set purpose in mind.

Up until the following year, when the Branch received

The multi-talented Loran Peak lofts a pass during the 1921 season.

three-year accreditation, the school had honestly pictured itself as a semi-integral part of the mother university at Berkeley, even though treated by Cal as a pariah. Cub students eagerly rooted for Cal whenever the Bears traveled south to meet the Trojans. The aim of many Branch students was to transfer after the first two years to the Berkeley campus, a goal shared by many football players.

When the Branch became a four-year institution, it began to work to keep its students (and its players) for the entire stretch. It was then too late for Smith to effectively realize he had actually had *two* frosh teams from which to draw his varsity talent, which would have essentially made the Branch Cubs the first collegiate farm club in history. Even so, Cal still managed to attract a few class players from the Branch during this period, most notably Gordon White, but its condescending attitude proved quite detrimental.

Trotter's third year opened with high hopes, as two successful practice games against local high school squads seemed to indicate that the Smith System was turning the trick. With the first real game against San Diego State College a victory, and even the conference opener against Redlands good for a win, the first conference win ever, the Cubs were earning some respect. But once again the lack of depth took its toll, and they failed to win another game, finishing 2-3-1. The only bright thought was that they were not losing by much.

Trotter resigned in order to coach track exclusively, and in 1923 24-year-old James "Jimmy" Cline replaced him. Cline was of the stocky mold that did not talk much—he was more the demonstrative type. He would get down with the boys and show 'em how to do it. He was a good all-sports coach and led the boxing squad to a conference championship. But after two wins to open his college football head coaching career, Cline was to never win another game during his two-year reign at the Branch, finishing at 2-10-3.

In explanation for this poor showing, freshmen were again no longer eligible for varsity play, leaving Cline with only sophomores on the squad. Furthermore, the Smith System backfired, as its heavy conditioning program was not suited to the Cubs, who lacked the hand-picked qualities found in the players at Cal, and they became even more injury-prone as a

Look 'Em Over Girls!

Top row, left to right: Ed. Kosberg, Charley Walters, "Laddie" Knudson, "Bus" Jennings, "Chuck" Barnett, Vic Obej, "Jeff" Brown, Horace Bresee, "Moose" White, Coach Cozens. Second Row: "Timmy" Timmons, "Scotty" Sanford, Bill Brenner, "Jack" Frost, "Bullets" Ruddy, Art Jones, "Cece" Hollingsworth, "Friday" Thursby, Ralph Plummer, "Army" Handy. Third row: "Capt." Bell, Jack Shaw, "Raw" Diehl, "Spike" Hess, Walt Westcott, "Cap" Haralson, E. Bussell, "Zuckie" Zuckerman, "Haywire" Sergel.

The 1922 team. Top row, far right, is UCLA's first football coach, Fred Cozens.

20

result.

A milestone was passed, for when the school acquired its four-year status in 1924, it was generally conceded that the totem "Cubs" was inappropriate. The more fierce totem of "Grizzlies" was then approved, in keeping with the Golden Bear heritage from Cal.

Life was paced differently in those days for Branch teams. In 1924 the Grizzlies traveled to play San Diego State. The train arrived on game day at 1:00 p.m., the players had their lunch at one-forty-five, and ran onto the field to start play at two-thirty! Their intense pregame preparation paid off in a tie, 13-13.

The players under Cline remember the losses with a shrug and a grin. The good men who did not go running up to Berkeley or elsewhere stayed mostly because they had to, either through family obligations or financial inability. So Cline kept Loran Peak, who averaged around 48 yards a punt, and Cece Hollingsworth, who stepped in as right guard as a freshman in 1922 and rarely missed a game in four years. Hollingsworth would remain with the school for many years, as an assistant coach and scout.

The Grizzlies in 1924. First row, far left, is coach Jimmy Cline. Holding the ball is Cecil Hollingsworth, long associated with UCLA football in years to come as a coach and recruiter.

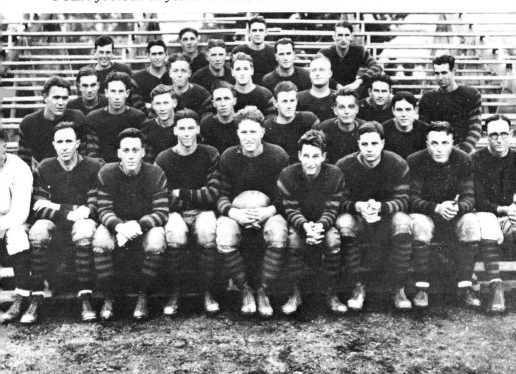

Action against Occidental in 1924, when "The Branch" was a member of the local Southern Conference.

The students did enjoy getting out to watch their team, though never expecting any sort of victory celebration when it was over. They wore their rooters' caps and white shirts (men only in the cheering section) and turned out in their pajamas for the annual Pajamarino and bonfire the night before the Pomona game. Come. hell or high score, they were loyal students, and the Grizzlies were their team.

By 1925 plans were underway to move the campus to a more spacious location. If the school was to achieve its destiny of greatness as conceived by Dr. Moore and others, its athletic program—and head football coach and team—should begin to reflect this higher level of excellence. Quietly, the school began to search for the man who would lead branch football into competitive distinction—to the "big time."

CHAPTER 2

1925-1931

William Henry Spaulding. The players called him Bill, Bunker Bill. Not Coach or Sir. Just Bill. There was no "reason" behind it, no contrivance by Spaulding to "get closer to the boys" by allowing them to so call him. It was just...natural. But there was no question as to who was in charge, who was the boss. Bill was.

Spaulding was born May 4, 1880, in Melrose, Wisconsin, and played football for Black River Falls High School. He went to Wabash College, Indiana (Class of 1906), played all four years there, and was a fullback n the 1905 team that beat Notre Dame in South Bend, the last such loss the Irish suffered at home until 1928. Upon graduating, he began coaching immediately as the head man at Western State Teachers College, Kalamazoo, Michigan, and stayed there 15 years, producing three undefeated seasons along the way.

In 1922 he became head coach at Minnesota, gaining national attention in 1924 as "The Man Who Stopped Red Grange," successfully crafting a defense to stop the "unstoppable" Illinois star. However, Spaulding also ran afoul of "The 'M' Club," a powerful, fanatical alumni organization which never forgave the school (or Spaulding) for replacing Henry L. "Doc" Williams, famous for "The Minnesota Shift," and one of the members' longtime cronies. In such an environment Spaulding could do no right, and he began to look for work elsewhere.

Knute Rockne, the first coach offered the Branch position, instead recommended Spaulding for the job, and Dr. Moore succeeded in luring Spaulding away from the prestigious Big

23

Bunker Bill Spaulding.

Ten. His challenge: develop Grizzly football into a topnotch program capable of playing the best.

Spaulding became head coach in 1925. He inherited a team that had gone 0-5-3 the previous year. But he also inherited some talent in kicking ace Loran Peak, strong lineman Cece Hollingsworth, and enterprising quarterback Scribner Birlenbach. Spaulding turned his first Grizzly team into instant winners.

San Diego State College was the first to fall, though it battled the Grizzlies evenly for almost three quarters. But finally Peak bulled the ball over, left half Jack Frost booted the conversion, and the team had a 7-0 victory—its first in almost two years. La Verne proved too small an opponent and also lost, 16-3. Then came Pomona. The branch had never defeated Pomona, and the Sagehens had stuck it to the Grizzlies the year before, 50-0, on their way to another conference championship. Pomona fell, 26-0. Pomona would never beat them again.

Whittier, however, was another matter. There were times in the past when the Branch should have defeated lesser Poet teams, but the breaks just seemed to go Whittier's way, and the word "jinx" was readily applied to explain the Branch's failures. This year, catching the Grizzlies lethargic during the opening moments of play, the Quakers (as they were also called) quickly rushed to score, then fell back to play hard defense the rest of the game, winning 7-0. The breaking of the jinx would have to wait another year.

The Grizzlies snapped right back and defeated the Oxy Tigers in what was a major conference upset, 9-0. This victory, for the first time in school history, put the Branch into prime contention for the conference championship.

The magic of Spaulding's Big Ten reputation achieved what had previously been thought a pipe dream—major schools began to consider scheduling the branch as an opponent. The first two schools to do so were St. Mary's, at that time a perennial powerhouse under the tutelage of Edward P. "Slip"

Spaulding, (white shirt, second row) with his first team in 1925.

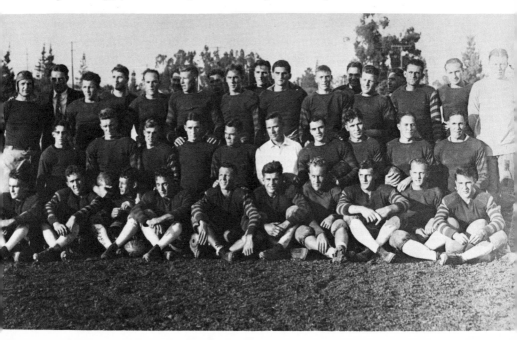

Madigan, and Stanford, coached by Glenn S. "Pop" Warner. Both schools were banking on the Spaulding name while also expecting a "breather" against an obviously much weaker team.

For the first major road trip in their history, the Grizzlies traveled to play St. Mary's Gaels in the Memorial Stadium on the UC campus in Berkeley. For the first 16 minutes of the game the Oakland team ran freely through the Branch forces, and it was quickly 28-0, Gaels. Then Cece Hollingsworth intercepted a pass to spot the next Gael drive, and like a handful of sand thrown into finely meshing gears, the St. Mary's scoring machine ground to a halt. Time and again the Branch defense checked St. Mary's offense. Though neither team managed a score for the rest of the afternoon, this Grizzly performance sent shock waves throughout the Bay area. Stanford was put on the alert that its game in two weeks against the Branch might be substantially more than a cakewalk.

The Grizzlies returned home and thoroughly beat Redlands, 23-0. With high hopes and dreams of a thundering upset in their hearts, the Grizzlies returned north and, in Palo Alto, met the Indians. Fearful of suffering the same embarrassment that befell St. Mary's, Stanford was not about to let this little team from the south even get close to scoring. The Indians crushed the outmatched Grizzlies, 82-0.

One game remained, a conference game that was to decide the championship, and if the Grizzlies won they would be number one. With two minutes left to go in the game, it was a 10-10 tie. Grizzly left half Grayson Turney, whose kicking talents helped put him into second place in the conference for points scored, attempted a game-winning field goal from the 38. It was long enough...high enough...it hit the right crossbar...the 6,000 fans held their collective breath...and the ball bounced back onto the field, the tie preserved. Once beaten (by the Branch) Oxy took the top honors, the Grizzlies taking second.

Spaulding had produced a major turnaround. The players began to raise their expectations and discovered they were winners. He got them bumping their heads against the clouds, and they came to believe that was where they belonged.

The next year the Grizzlies also finished second in the conference. The fortunes of the team of 1926 rose and fell, like an awakening giant unsure of what to do with itself. Still, top performances by quarterback Bert LaBrucherie and fullback Joe Fleming were turned in, the latter setting two records this year, still on the books: Most points scored in a game (Oxy, 26 - 3TD, 2FG, 2PAT) and most points in a season (108).

After three season-opening victories, another repeat of the Whittier jinx ensued. The teams were reported to be evenly matched physically, but with a slight edge given the Grizzlies in that, sooner or later, the losing streak *must* end. But a Poet 80-yard kickoff return for a touchdown after just scoring a field goal (scored-upon teams had the option of either receiving or kicking off) put the Grizzlies in a hole they could not climb out of, losing 16-6. The schools would meet but one more time. The Cubs never beat the Poets, and neither did the Grizzlies.

But before another game was played, the Grizzlies were no more. The University of Montana, upset over repeated newspaper wires stories confusing their Grizzly-named team with that of California's Southern Branch, filed a formal pro-

Center Charles Hastings with fullback Joe Fleming, who holds the single-game and single-season scoring records at UCLA.

test directly to the students on the Vermont campus. Once again, limiting itself to the bear motif, the school selected a new name that was all its own. On October 22, 1926, a team was reborn: The Bruins.

With much hoopla, instant fanfare, new songs and cheers, the University of California Southern Branch Bruins played their first game against old rival Pomona, the team tabbed to win the Southern Conference Championship (it did). It was also the first Branch game played in the Coliseum. Thanks in part to an 85-yard kickoff return for a touchdown by LaBrucherie, the Bruins won their first game, 27-7.

The team entered the last conference game with a chance to take the championship if it beat or tied Cal Tech when combin-

Tackle George Bishop, fullback Jim Armstrong, center Hastings and end Bob Henderson, members of the first Bruin team, 1926.

ed with a Pomona loss. Pomona lost, but so did the Bruins, and the Branch settled for second place again.

For the last game of the season, the Spaulding name again drew a major football team, the Iowa State Cyclones. Aided by a rainstorm that made the Coliseum turf slippery and playing beyond expectations, the Bruins kept the score down to only 20-0, though the Cyclones moved easily through the Branch defensive line.

The Bruins were quickly and not-so-quietly outgrowing the Southern Conference. With the basketball, track, and baseball teams continual winners during this stage, it seemed only the football squad had held the school back. But thanks to Bill Spaulding, this was no longer the case.

Three things happened almost simultaneously at the branch that would positively affect the Bruins' image on the West Coast: While the Westwood site had been selected as the possible future home of the rapidly expanding school, it was only after the passage of a bond issue in November of 1926 that it became a financed certainty—and the move was definitely on. Not long after, the administration pushed through the regents a bid to change the school's name from Southern Branch to something more indicative of its complete and separate status from Berkeley. Thus on February 1, 1927, the school officially became "The University of California at Los Angeles"—UCLA. Finally the athletic department was asked to join the Pacific Coast Conference, commencing in January 1928.

In only two years, Bunker Bill Spaulding had driven the school into the "Big Time."

But there was still a lame duck season left for the Bruins in the Southern Conference. Befitting the new status of UCLA, the Bruins showed there was good reason why they were leaving for bigger pastures.

After easy victories over Santa Barbara and Fresno State colleges, the Bruins encountered Whittier, in what would be the last contest ever between the two schools. The Bruin win was convincing, 24-6, and the jinx was over forever.

The season carried down to the last two conference games, against Pomona and Cal Tech. UCLA could only muster a 7-7 tie against the Sagehens, leaving both schools tied for first.

29

CALIFORNIA

Bruin Special

DAILY ◉ BRUIN

Bruin Special

Student Publication at the University of California :: Southern Branch, Los Angeles, California

VOLUME IV   FRIDAY, OCTOBER 22, 1926   NUMBE

'BRUIN' NEW TOTEM

The Stray Cat

SIGN FOR
A
PRECINCT

The

BONDS

Must

Be

Passed

SIGN FOR
A
PRECINCT

International Lunch Club Formed At 'Y'

Advertisers Today

Spaulding's Bruins In Crucial Game Of Year Against Claremonters

Victory Needed To Hold Prestige Made In Past Games; Fast Battle Is Anticipated By Dopesters

By Morris Kaplan

For Tomorrow

Watch For Passes

Depends on Pomona

Rally Song

Present Speeches And Stunts at A.S.U.C. Rally For Tomorrow's Game

Rally Committee Arranges Program To Arouse Support And Enthusiasm For Meet With Pomona At Coliseum

Art Students Offer Skits At Reception

Supper Meeting Is Planned By Y.M.

FIVE REPRESENT BRANCH FOR '27 RHODES HONORS

State Committee Will Select Men In December

ALUMNI AT WORK ON PROPOSITION

Jordan Heads List Of Activities In Present Campaign

R. O. T. C.

FORMAL OPENING OF NEW CAMPUS OCCURS MONDAY

Director Moore Welcomes State Celebrities At Investure

STUDENTS MUST FULFIL PLEDGES

Precincts Will Be Assigned To All Card Signers

DANCE PEPS UP COLISEUM GAME

Junior Class Sponsors Hop As Final Rally Tonight

Amendment Ten Stickers Will Be Given Out Today

Death Knell Of Grizzly Is Sounded; 'Bruin' N Official Athletic T

Action Follows Offer Of Executive Cor Of California At Berkeley Through McCarthy

Committee On Totem Issues Final Bulletin

University F

EDUCATION COMMITTEE

Though the Bruins entered the final game against the Engineers as decided underdogs, UCLA won 13-0. As Pomona also won its finale, the conference championship ended in a tie, both schools ending 4-0-1.

Spaulding drew another major team to the Coliseum for the last game of the season, the Drake Bulldogs out of Iowa. UCLA played them hard and tight, and it was not until the second half that Drake was able to break the scoreless deadlock, continuing on to a 25-6 victory.

An alum in the stands, watching UCLA finally defeat Whittier, was overheard to remark to his companion, "When I used to go here, we were licked by everybody. What has happened?" He received a one word answer: "Spaulding." To that answer should have been added, "Plus, we grew up."

It was a combination of several factors that brought about UCLA's incredible rise through the Southern Conference: A constantly increasing student enrollment, four-year accreditation, a rich pool of talent to draw from, the University of California name, and, of course, that man named Bill.

Athletically, the Bruins were always at a disadvantage: Playing sophomore teams against fully endowed institutions; dissolving an old image, the Cubs, to establish a new one, the Grizzlies, then having to turn around and do it one more time with the Bruins, all within the space of eight years; practicing and playing on hardened Moore Field. But all this time UCLA was moving, out of Vermont, into Westwood, out of the Southern Conference, into the Pacific Coast Conference, out of the shadow of Berkeley, into its own right. The school was constantly growing, expanding, fighting for more academic departments and degrees. One transition after another, overlapping, bumping into each other, team name, school name, campus location, student population, all at such a maddening pace unheard of in the annals of major university development. No other school before or since grew at the pace UCLA was virtually forced to undergo, becoming the only Top-10 academic university founded in the twentieth century.

The football team was just another facet. It had to keep up, just like everything else, with the fantastic growth of UCLA. It did.

But like the pure adolescent the Bruins were, they found

themselves seriously caught between two developmental stages during the 1928-1931 seasons. These teams were essentially too strong to compete in the Southern Conference but not strong enough to compete with the established schools in the PCC. The Bruins were in limbo. No other team anywhere was caught in the same amazing circumstance; there was no peer to schedule a game with. It was win big over teams left from the Southern Conference days, lose big to the established PCC teams, over and over again.

In 1928 UCLA outscored pre-PCC opponents still on the schedule 152-7. Against their new PCC foes, the Bruins were outscored, 129-12. There was no happy medium in 1929 either, UCLA outscoring pre-PCC teams 107-6, then getting walloped by almost all of the PCC gang, 184-0. Except for one.

It was the last game of the season, one last chance to win its first conference game. More importantly, it was a last chance to honor the grand move to Westwood, which had taken place that September. And it was UCLA's first meeting with...Montana.

The Bruins surprised the favored Grizzlies with two touchdowns, quarterback Eddy Solomon passing to end Richard Mulhaupt for one, sub quarterback Cliff Simpson striking to tackle Carl Brown for the second. On this Thanksgiving Day 14-0 victory, the Bruin football faithful performed the most spectacular "serpentine" in the school's history, the Coliseum fans lifted Spaulding high on their shoulders, and coiled and snaked their way around the field into the joyous night.

In 1930 and 1931, *some* improvement started to become evident. The only "old" teams left on the schedule were Pomona and Cal Tech, no longer a problem. In 1930 Southern Cal played a second runaway game in a row against UCLA, then dropped the series because both margins of victory were too great, 76-0 and 52-0. But in virtually every other case over this two-year period, the Bruins were at least putting up respectable fights and came as close as 7-0 and 13-6 against Oregon.

The Bruins were able to chalk up their second conference victory, against Idaho, in 1930, again the last game of the season. The only major difference between this and the Montana contest of 1929 was that the Bruins *expected* to win. Scoring seven points first, UCLA allowed the Vandals to convert a fumble recovery within the 20 into a score to get as close as one point, but in the third quarter the Bruins pulled away to earn the 20-6 victory.

The composition of the 1931 team was such that Spaulding recognized it as a young team that, if worked hard, would develop into quality, if not completely in 1931 then in seasons to come. At times the players would come together and sparkle, but more often the look was less than lustrous. But to a man there was one team scheduled, one jewel in the crown of the PCC hierarchy, that the Bruins most wanted to beat: Stanford.

After not scoring a point in their first three games that season, the Bruins ganged up on Pomona, 46-0, to get ready for the Indians up in Palo Alto. This rivalry, which would become the oldest continuing series for UCLA, began to develop a heart-stopping quality that has been its hallmark to this day: Every game seems to be taken down to the final seconds, and it is usually the last team with its hands on the ball that wins. It took a Stanford score in the last nine seconds in this one, a 25-yard touchdown pass to break a tie, to give the Reds the 12-6 victory.

One week later thunder struck. Into Los Angeles came the mighty St. Mary's Gaels, the number-one team in the nation, already having defeated the only other challenger for such accolades, Southern Cal, 13-7. Coming off an embarrassing defeat to the private Olympic Club of San Francisco the week earlier, the Gaels were keyed up to squash the lowly Bruins.

Bruin right half Bobby Decker scores against St. Mary's, sparking UCLA's 1931 upset victory over the Gaels, 12-0.

They did not. UCLA's quarterback Lenny Bergdahl hit left half Bobby Decker for six in the first five minutes of the game, then passed for another to right end Wally Wellendorf from the Gael 35, and the "Men From Moraga" never recovered. It was a cold, rain-threatened Armistice Day that brought the Bruins nationwide notice with the shocking score UCLA 12, St. Mary's O, toasted as "The team that beat the team that beat the Trojans!"

Though the very next week brought the Bruins back to earth against Oregon, losing, 13-6, they finished the season with another intersectional battle, highly regarded Florida. Once again the Bruins drew from some deep well of inspiration, throwing off first-half doldrums to defeat the visiting Gators, 13-0. Once again, UCLA's name was thrust into the national limelight. There was something going on out there in Los Angeles...thanks to Bill Spaulding.

In one of his rare moments of deception, Spaulding had used the power of the press to aid the Bruins' cause against the Gators. As any back could possibly receive the long snap from center in the single-wing formation used by the team, all week Bill made mention that he just could not make up his mind which of his backs would do the passing, fullback Norm Duncan or quarterbacks Ed "Spec" Hassler or Johnny Fletcher. But all along he planned on using junior halfback Joe Keeble, the only left-hander and the least likely suspect. It was a Keeble-to-Mulhaupt pass that first put the Bruins on the board, Bill figuring the Gators would not be looking for it—thanks to the papers!

The football presence UCLA was to become had just passed through its roughest period of growth. Bill Spaulding patiently fielded his teams, and, depending on the opponent, his heart either dropped or it soared. But as the school kept getting larger and larger, more talent naturally started to come his way.

That was a good thing. Bunker Bill Spaulding was not a recruiter. He believed in himself, his program, his boys. He did not feel it necessary to go out and sell, to push himself on some youngster if the boy was simply shopping. (Spaulding's assistants, however, did go out and sell the program, especially frosh coach Fred Oster and A.J. "Sturzy" Sturznegger.)

The advances made by these first Spaulding teams were

34

hard fought. The blue chippers, the All-Americas, were not to be found. Spaulding had a kind and gentle forcefulness that drew out of each of his players the best that each could give. Sometimes it was not enough to beat the other team, but it was given just the same. Spaulding was a teacher, and through football he extracted the best that athletics has to offer in the formation of character, creating from his players total human beings capable of living life with honor through healthy competiton. Character is what Bunker Bill expected, and that's what he got.

That's why his players loved him so much.

CHAPTER 3

1932-1938

Single platoon football meant 11 men were expected to play as much of the entire game as possible, playing on both offense and defense. The lineman who blocked a way clear for a teammate to carry the ball on offense was the same lineman who tried to shed a block to get to the enemy ballcarrier on defense. Each player had the one position.

Though simple in approach, this system had its complexities. A player trained offensively and defensively, but sometimes his talents leaned one way or another, and so a coach tried to compensate. He would play one player because of his defensive talents, hoping to offset him with an offensive complement, striving for a balanced team. Once in a while, he was lucky enough to land a player who was excellent "both ways," one who gave just what was needed at his position offensively and defensively.

Bill Spaulding had just such a player in Mike Frankovich, who just happened to be a quarterback.

As a sophomore, Frankovich stepped in to lead a team strong in experienced talent, most notable bullish senior center and captain Homer Oliver, fullback Joe Keeble, and tackle Houghton "Fat" Norfleet. This was also the first talent-rich crop of sophomore players in UCLA history, sporting right half Ransom "Pants" Livesay, guards Verdi Boyer and Clayton Yearick, and ends Sinclair Lott and Bob McChesney. All would make their mark, partly because Spaulding worked best with small teams, really getting to know his players, and this one numbered only 48 men (who averaged only five-foot-eleven!).

The catalyst was certainly Frankovich, who got his chance

Mike Frankovich, the quarterback who brought the Bruins national attention in 1932.

to start on the first string right from the beginning, because senior quarterback Lenny Bergdahl's severe elbow injury during preseason practice knocked him out for virtually the entire season.

That UCLA landed the services of Frankovich was a minor miracle. Throughout his high school days, the star quarterback from Belmont High in Los Angeles had only considered going to one school—Southern California. Lost and forgotten in the registration shuffle on the Trojan campus, an unhappy Frankovich vented his spleen to Bruin coaches Fred Oster and Cliff Simpson, who convinced Mike he should sit down and meet with Bill Spaulding. After that meeting, a deeply impressed Mike Frankovich came to play in Westwood.

The football fortunes at UCLA showed improvement from the first game that 1932 season, against a light Cal Agricultural (now Davis) team. Frankovich received the opening kickoff and ran it back 35 yards to midfield. He immediately marched the team down the field, passing to end Bill Maxwell for 30 yards, then passing to Maxwell again for the quick touchdown. The Bruins won easily, 26-0. So impressive were the performances of the sophomores Livesay and left half Walter Clark against the

Aggies, Spaulding started them with Frankovich and Keeble the next game, against Idaho. Though they all played admirably, it was the stalwart Keeble who tallied the six points needed to beat the Vandals, 6-0. For the day, Keeble carried 37 times.

With a conference victory under their belts, the Bruins amused themselves with the notion that, for the first time ever in the PCC, they were in first place! The next hurdle was tough Oregon, the first away game of the season. Though given the best chance in years to beat the Webfoots, the expected rain for the game did not enhance the Bruins' outlook.

The long train ride up to Portland was a new experience for many of the players—and they made the most of it. Frankovich entertained the diners in the club car with his array of magic tricks, and picked up some free meals for his efforts. Tackle Thomas "Slats" Rafferty and center Bill Merrill rode most of the way in the baggage car with the door open, picking up pebbles at each stop and throwing them at every sign they passed. The Bruins prided themselves in their ability to piece together clashing and outrageous pajama ensembles every night. And, of course, there was a never-ending poker game to while away the long hours.

Frankovich and Livesay, quartered together, ran through their imaginations what might transpire in the game ahead. In the process, they worked out an emergency play, a last resort deep pass, just in case their gridiron hopes grew desperate. The play was pure fantasy, but it amused them to make it up.

The weather was worse than expected, it was torrential. Late in the second quarter, the Ducks ran a reverse that was good for 45 yards and a touchdown. Other than that, it was a sloppy, messy, frustrating contest, one punt exchange after another, all game long. As time was running out in the fourth quarter, the Bruins found themselves on their own 33 with a little more than six minutes left in the game, still down, 7-0.

Frankovich got off a beautiful pass to reserve back Joe "Pappa" Berry, who raced to the eight-yard line, a 51-yard gain. Two plays later, Berry shoved his way those final eight yards and scored a touchdown. But Livesay missed the PAT by inches, and the Bruins were still behind, 7-6.

Oregon elected to kickoff, assuming correctly that its defense could hold its opponents, and the Bruins could not move the ball past the 44. The punt was blocked, and the ball went to Oregon with less than a minute to play. On third and long, the Webfoots passed, the ball was intercepted by Frankovich, and he was downed on the UCLA seven with 15 seconds remaining in the game.

Bruin history was about to be made.

While heading for the huddle, Frankovich turned to Livesay and said, "This is it," calling the play they had made up on the train. The plan was for Livesay to steam out of the backfield, driving deep into the secondary, then cut directly in front of Oregon's deep man, at whom Frankovich was going to aim the pass, figuring the Duck would just stand there in shock as the ball headed right for him.

Frankovich took the snap, faded back into the end zone, spotted that deep man through the pouring rain, and let fly. Hit immediately, he went down, and did not see what happened.

What he would have seen was that fantasy play perfectly executed. The Webfoot's total concentration on the approaching football was so keen it allowed Livesay to approach undetected from the side, streaking right in front of his opponent just as the ball arrived, then cutting upfield towards paydirt under a full head of steam. McChesney made two key blocks that kept the way clear, and Livesay scored.

UCLA beat Oregon for the first time ever, 12-7. All it took was a game-ending 93-yard scoring pass play, still the longest in Bruin history.

When the train arrived at the Glendale station, the team received the greatest reception ever known at the school. A rally back on campus topped that, with Spaulding and the team thanking everyone personally. But the victory, though savored for the moment, was quickly set aside, because a more immediate concern loomed in two weeks: Stanford.

The interim game against Cal Tech was not deemed severe enough for Spaulding to oversee the troops personally, so he used that weekend to scout Stanford in its game against Southern Cal in Palo Alto. Freshman coach Fred Oster, in his one and only turn as "head coach for a day," guided UCLA to a 51-0 romp over the Engineers.

Pop Warner, long the coach at Stanford, was stung by the Trojans, 13-0. The rumblings on the Farm spoke of alumni unrest over Stanford's weakening status. The Bruin game in Los Angeles figured to bring some spark back, for the Indians were decided favorites, their razzle-dazzle offense capable of scoring at a moment's notice.

Though at the start the double and triple reverses executed by Stanford confused the Bruins, the Indians could score but once in the first quarter for six points (PAT blocked), set up by a Bruin fumble on the 17. For the rest of the half it was a punting contest, both teams unable to generate an effective offense. But on the last play of the half, a Stanford punt was blocked by guard Verdi Boyer—with his *face*, knocking him out cold. The ball was recovered in the end zone by McChesney, and the half ended, 6-6.

In the second half the punting contest was renewed, both defenses stiffening whenever the opponent dared to near the goal. Then, early in the fourth quarter, with Stanford punting from its 38, end Del McGue, guard Ed Haslam, and Boyer teamed to block the kick, and the ball was recovered by the Bruins on the Stanford nine. The injured Joe Keeble, kept out of the lineup all game, was inserted, and the Coliseum stands joyously cheered their approval, picking up the spirits of the entire team. Keeble plunged at the line; Clark plunged; Keeble plunged; then on fourth down, Clark wrestled his way into the end zone.

UCLA beat Stanford for the first time ever, 13-6. The Bruins had come of age.

(The back-to-back losses to Southern Cal and UCLA cost Warner his job. Ironically, 1932 was the year the Warner-recruited frosh team, losers to the Trobabes, made their now-famous promise to themselves never to lose to the Trojans again. The Vow Boys made good.)

The Indian game was the Bruins' peak. The next week St. Mary's came to the Coliseum, bent on avenging the stinging loss from the previous year, and did, 14-7. After UCLA ganged up on weak Montana the next week, 32-0, host Washington State defeated UCLA, 3-0. The Cougars had taken advantage when, with the ball near midfield and the Bruins accepting the fate of a 0-0 tie, Spaulding had sent the first string to the showers as there were but 20 seconds left on the clock. Washington State succeeded in kicking a 47-yard field goal, the longest in the nation that year.

To further wipe out the Bruins' earlier strong conference showing, the Washington Huskies traveled to Los Angeles and heavily beat UCLA, 19-0. A postseason treat against Florida in Gainesville ended with the Gators upsetting the Bruins, 12-2.

The enormous gains made this season reaffirmed UCLA's ever-increasing ability to play big-time football, joining the ranks of those schools that, on any given Saturday, could beat any other school. The Bruins posted a 6-4 record, the first winning season since joining the PCC in 1928, and its 4-2 conference log put it in third place. Though the next two years would not be as remarkable, the Bruins had at least achieved the middle ground. It was certainly better than the bottom.

UCLA opened the 1933 season with a "double-header," the Bruins playing back-to-back games with Los Angeles Junior College and San Diego State on the Westwood campus one Saturday afternoon. At 34-0 and 13-0 respectively, these easy victories were essentially practice games for the Bruins, a warm-up for their conference opener in Palo Alto with Stanford.

Under new head coach Claude "Tiny" Thornhill, the Indians were in control for most of the game, though the only score came from a Stanford field goal late in the second quarter. At 3-0, it was a game marked by hard line play and deep punting.

After two easy victories over Utah (22-0, which featured a Bruin-record 27-yard drop-kick field goal by Frankovich) and Loyola (20-7), and a tough loss to Oregon (7-0), the Bruins faced the one team they had been waiting to play since their inception. The University of California at Los Angeles Bruins finally met the University of California Golden Bears at the coliseum. UCLA threatened three times in the first half to score, going so far as a Frankovich drop-kick field goal attempt from the 12 as time ran out that just barely went wide, but that was it. This first interuniversity meeting resulted in a 0-0 tie.

As the *Daily Bruin* honored it, "...both campuses must deal with each other in everything on an even basis. Because they profess identical policies and purposes, a keen rivalry can grow up to see which adheres to them the more excellently. The 0-0 score was a happy coincidence to start off a formal relationship that must always remain without handicap."

41

Three games later, the Bruins ended the 1933 season with a heady victory over Washington State, 7-0, via an intercepted pass run back for a touchdown by Mike Frankovich. It was a defensive battle, with each team successfully punting out of danger time and again. Team members playing their last games for the blue and gold included guard Fred Haslam, Del McGue, "Joltin'" Joe Keeble, and captain and All-Coast center Lee Coats, finishing out their careers with a 6-4-1 season.

The 1934 season opened with another "double-header," Pomona and San Diego State, racking up 14-0 and 20-0 victories for the Bruins over both. As in 1933, these games were Spaulding's quick way of assessing the stamina of unproven talent in game situations. If a rookie looked good in game number one against weak Pomona, he was further tested against slightly harder San Diego State, along with the first string. As these games were played in Westwood, they were the only times the students were privileged to enjoy what students on virtually every other campus in the nation regard as commonplace—seeing their classmates play football on the campus itself.

Though plans had been drawn up for a campus stadium, the depression gripping the nation made its construction impossible. The Bruins would continue to use the Coliseum, next to Southern Cal's campus, to play their home games for almost the next five decades.

Losing their conference opener at Oregon, 26-3, the Bruins hosted diminishing Montana. Junior left half Chuck Cheshire, all five-foot-ten inches and 169 pounds of him, teamed with senior Frankovich for a scoring feat that has stood the test of Bruin time. Early in the first quarter, the Bruins had taken over the ball on their own seven-yard line. Instead of automatically punting out of trouble, Frankovich told Cheshire he was giving him the ball. Cheshire did not *want* the ball. Frankovich told him he was going to get it anyway, and the decision of the quarterback was final. This resulted in the longest run from scrimmage for a touchdown in Bruin history, 93 yards! The Bruins went on to win 19-0, and Cheshire would go on to set all the UCLA rushing records for his time.

Next the Bruins played Cal for the first time at Berkeley. As in the titanic struggle the year before, the Bruins played the Bears even. The only margin of difference came with eight minutes to play in the game when a field goal won it for Cal, 3-0. Though it was generally conceded that the Bears had much greater depth and experience, the Bruins refused to fold.

Though the Bruins did post a 7-3 overall record for the year, it was not one of greatness. The losses against Oregon, Cal, and Stanford (27-0) meant another losing conference record. Some top players were graduating, most notably Verdi Boyer, "Pants" Livesay, and Mike Frankovich.

It would be wrong to simply dismiss this three-year stretch under Frankovich by suggesting that the promise of his 1932 season was not fulfilled. Spaulding was not a passing coach, and Frankovich's sophomore successes in that department were more from his own initiative than by coaching design. Frankovich himself saw his role as that of a defensive standout and enjoyed stopping drives as much as starting them.

The Frankovich years were marked by a definite sense of team pride, of togetherness, and of respect for Spaulding's judgment. The players enjoyed the game for its own rewards, making them winners no matter what the final point total. Most have been winners since.

Though Frankovich received no national or even coastal honors, *Sports Illustrated* magazine honored him 25 years later on its Silver Anniversary All-American roster. Time has a funny way of straightening things out.

A total of 32 players comprised the UCLA Bruins for 1935. These few players pulled together like no team had in school history. When the riotous season ended, they found themselves in a three-way tie for the championship of the Pacific Coast Conference.

Though the depth was shallow, Spaulding was comforted with quality. Senior Chuck Cheshire was still in the backfield, as was the supertalented and mysterious fullback junior Ted Key. Senior quarterback Bill Murphy, who had understudied Frankovich for two years, was an intelligent signal caller. The booming backfield toe of sophomore William Robert "Billy Bob" Williams was an added plus. Captain and end Bob McChesney brought his experience, along with junior right guard George Dickerson. Finally, the keystone at center was solid junior Sherman Chavoor.

The Bruins rambled to an easy 39-0 opening victory over

Utah State and then traveled to Oregon State where they beat the Beavers, 20-7, both victories attributable to the stellar work of Chuck Cheshire.

Against Stanford it was Ted Key who made the difference. Cheshire set up a touchdown with a tackle-breaking 28-yard run to set the Bruins up at the seven late in the first quarter, then Key punched it over and with his conversion put the Bruins ahead, 7-6. That score would hold until the final gun sounded. UCLA managed to thwart every Stanford scoring effort, as Key, Chavoor, and Murphy each intercepted a pass (the Indians went 4-17 in that department) and twice turned back "The Vow Boys" from within the 15. By unseating the conference champions, the dark horse that was UCLA suddenly looked like a comer.

Against Oregon the next week, there was no doubt the Bruins were Rose Bowl candidates as they thoroughly demolished the Webfoots, 33-6. The following game would be the test, the only remaining conference team on the schedule that had a chance of stopping them: California.

That week the "Ted Key Affair" came to light. Ted Key apparently was not Ted Key.

The mystery opened when a picture of Key appeared in his alleged hometown in Texas, where a teacher who taught Ted Key realized that this man at UCLA calling himself Ted Key was really Key's brother Clois. The teacher confidentially notified UCLA's dean of men, Earl J. Miller. Based upon this information, Miller appeared at the UCLA locker room just prior to the Cal game and suspended Key from the team and the school until a proper investigation could be conducted.

Key's absence cannot be cited as the sole excuse for the loss the Bruins then incurred to the Bears, 14-0. Nevertheless, Key served to instill a unifying aura of security for many of the players, who all deeply cared for the man and certainly respected his talents on the playing field. The Bruins would also lose their next game, against Rose Bowl-bound SMU, but would rally to win their remaining four games and finish the season with a strong 8-2 record, good enough for the conference co-championship. (Stanford made the trip to Pasadena, defeating SMU, 7-0.)

But Key's story should be told, for it is the story of a man

44

who wanted more than anything to be highly educated, who fell in love with UCLA, but who was too poor to afford the tuitionless school, regardless of the fact that he already had a college degree. That he almost got away with it should be credited solely to his earnest (albeit misdirected) desire for that education, not to any duplicity or lack of a proper academic verification process on the institution's part.

Clois Francis Key had already played two years of football while a junior and senior at the Texas School of Mines (later Texas A&M), from which he graduated in 1931, having already attended a prep school and a junior college. On a visit to Los Angeles to see the 1932 Olympics, he decided that UCLA was the best school he had ever encountered and determined to get a "real" education there. He enrolled at a local prep school under an assumed name, then managed to get those grades tacked onto the transcripts of one R.F. "Bob" Key (the same first initials as his brother), who had met him in Mexico and did not care if Clois used his name and scholastic background. Furthermore, Clois once had picked up some pin money by playing on a semiprofessional team in San Pedro under still *another* assumed name.

It was obvious that UCLA's Ted Key did not care who he was. Neither did his Bruin teammates. All they knew was that Ted was a quiet, shy man who gave his all for the team on the field but never spoke of his life or his past and avoided being photographed at all costs. Though they might have suspected there was some "secret" lurking somewhere, they all agreed that, if he did not want to talk about it, that was his business.

After his public exposure, Key virtually disappeared. Though some believed that Key could have seriously damaged UCLA's reputation by flagrantly tricking the school—and to some degree he did embarrass UCLA—the fact remains that he acted alone (though his family knew and was supportive). There was no way UCLA or any school that processes thousands of applications a year might have caught him. No action was taken against him nor were there any PCC sanctions imposed on UCLA over the Ted Key affair. He was dismissed, and that was the end of it.

The achievement of the conference co-championship meant that in eight years Spaulding had led the Bruins to the top. He had done so with a team small in number but big in heart. The 1935 team also just happened to be very good, good enough to be invited to the Sugar Bowl. Unfortunately, this invitation came before the last game of the season, against St. Mary's, and the administration asked the selection committee for a delay until after that game was played before confirming acceptance. The Sugar Bowl people could not wait until December 14 and instead selected Texas Christian to face LSU. The Bruins beat the Gaels but stayed home New Year's Day, their first bowl appearance still to come.

The Bruins ran hot and cold the next three seasons. In 1936 a massive turnout for the team meant that Spaulding started out with too many players, and he never worked comfortably with an overlarge squad. Also, as no one player shone out as a "great," Spaulding had a difficult time creating a set lineup. Billy Bob Williams was a junior returnee at fullback, as was small but dependable halfback junior Don Ferguson, and he had the stalwart Sherman Chavoor at center for a third year. Though some players would prove their worthiness as the season wore on, junior center Lee Frankovich (Mike's brother),

Chuck Cheshire (33) in action against Oregon State in UCLA's 20-7 victory in 1935, Sam Stawisky (35) the advance man.

junior fullback Walt Schell, sophomore halfbacks Izzy Cantor and Hal Hirshon, and sophomore tackle C.M. "Slats" Wyrick most notable among them, Spaulding found it rough getting the team to click at all times. His son, junior Bill, Jr., made a name for himself at halfback as the season began, but a subsequent injury affected his performance throughout his career.

The team opened with a double-header double victory over Occidental and Pomona, 21-0 and 26-0, respectively. This would be the last meeting between UCLA and its abandoned Southern Conference opponents, and the last time the Bruins would play an official game on their own campus. The Bruins' conference-opening victory over Montana at 30-0 was almost too easy, leaving Spaulding unsure as to how his team would fare against odds-on conference favorite Washington the next week. Washington beat UCLA, 14-0, the Huskies winding up in the Rose Bowl for 1937.

The Bruins marked their first notch in the win column against Bear brother Berkeley, with a resounding 17-0 victory in Strawberry Canyon. Halfback Hal Hirshon threw two scoring strikes to student body president and right end Bob Schroeder. Bob Williams added two PATs and a field goal, and in one afternoon the Bruins not only scored the first offensively earned points against the Bears (all others had been scored while on defense) but matched all the points they had ever scored against Cal in those previous three meetings.

Though tacking on another victory against Oregon State, 22-13, Bruin bowl hopes were crashed to earth under an opportunistic Stanford team and a thorough 19-6 beating. Starting senior tackle George Dickerson was knocked out of the game, as were three other linemen and two starters, and the increasing injury rate began to take its toll. UCLA squeaked by Oregon, 7-0, then lost dismally to Washington State, 32-7.

For the final game, an old series was about to be reopened in UCLA history, begun too early in the estimation of many, but now all felt it was time to start anew. Negotiations had been underway since the middle of the previous season, when UCLA was making its way to the top. Instead of opening their seasons against each other as in 1929 and 1930, this game was to close out the scheduled year in most seasons. It was destined to become the definitive Big Game on the West Coast. Time and again it would be the Rose Bowl decider. Most importantly, it was for the city championship of Los Angeles.

UCLA versus Southern California.

After Chavoor recovered a Trojan fumble on the Southern Cal 40 early in the second quarter, senior halfback "Iron Man" Fred Funk, Billy Bob Williams, and sophomore classmates end Robert Nash and backs Schell and Izzy Cantor moved the team down the field. Williams scored over left guard from the two and so became the first Bruin to ever tally against Troy, then kicked the PAT himself to make it UCLA 7, Southern Cal 0. The Trojans scored their seven in the third quarter on their first possession, and that was it for the day, with the final score a 7-7 tie. As the final gun sounded, there was a near riot for the ball, both sides scrapping for the right to keep the pigskin. The officials prevailed, and the ball was declared neutral, to wait until one team came away with a victory. The now-flattened ball would represent a perpetual trophy.

After this 6-3-1 season, the Bruins could not maintain in 1937 the success they had achieved in 1936, falling prey to ifs and gambles and juggled lineups. But a couple of spectacular sophomores made their debut in the Blue and Gold, end Woodrow Wilson Woolwine "Woody" Strode and halfback Kenneth "Kenny" Washington, the man venerable Bruin trainer Elvin C. "Ducky" Drake (UCLA 1927) considers one of the greatest all-around players in UCLA history and who became UCLA's first true All-America.

This Bruin team was one of mystery. It had the ammunition in Washington and Strode, and backs junior Hal Hirshon and Walt Schell had returned, and they fired at will...during practice. But on the playing field it seemed they could not put it together.

An easy opening win against Oregon was followed by a loss to Stanford, a tie with Oregon State, and straight losses to Washington State, California, Washington, and Southern Methodist. A second victory was then notched in an intersectional against Missouri, giving them a 2-5-1 record with one game remaining.

During this season, Spaulding, for the first time in his career at UCLA, began to receive heavy criticism, from some ex-players and school officials. He had been the head coach

UCLA and Southern Cal resumed football relations in 1936, making this game the traditional conference season-ender for both schools.

since 1925 and was now in his thirteenth year. He had brought the program a long way in an incredibly short period of time. He just faced some unpredictable problems on his team this year.

Senior star halfback Don Ferguson found his duties as student body president and his chores as a prelegal student prevented him from doing justice to his football obligations, and he resigned from the team. Though Washington had increasingly showed he was the key player on the team, Spaulding waited until his players asked him midway through the season to designate Washington as the signal caller before he did so. A general indecisiveness on Spaulding's part probably hurt him more than any field generalship he tried this year. On top of all this, it was one of the more injury-plagued teams he had ever encountered. Though his players publicly rallied around him, there was no denying that something had changed.

The high competition Spaulding brought to UCLA became a two-edged sword. Though it elevated the school's status, winning came to be all-important, expected unto itself rather than as an educational objective. It was not his program or his players any more, it was *the* program and *the* players, concepts he was not about to subject himself to. He was caught in the same web that had marked his last days at Minnesota, and outside interference was not a part of Bill Spaulding's world. He never cared to be scrutinized as a coach.

There were still bright spots left for Spaulding and his Bruins. Southern Cal head coach Howard Jones and Spaulding went a long way back, when the former was at Iowa and Spaulding helmed the Gophers in the early twenties. In Los Angeles the two men developed a warm and gracious friendship cemented on the golf course—where Spaulding referred to the Trojan head man as his "favorite pigeon," much to Jones' chagrin, Spaulding's personal way of balancing out the heavy edge Jones had over his friend on the gridiron. Their friendship is one of the happy sidelights to the early history of this cherished intercity rivalry.

And the warmest moment for them occurred in the 1937 meeting. Troy had built up a 19-0 lead going into the fourth quarter. Washington, Hirshon, and Schell's passing had been generally ineffective all day. Then, like lightning, Kenny Washington stole the show.

Midway through the quarter, he threw a pass from the Trojan 44, which was received by Hirshon on the 10, and he barreled into the end zone, the PAT good. The Trojans elected to kickoff, Schell received it and moved the ball up to the 27.

On the very next play, Washington caught the snap from center, wheeled to his right to avoid the rush, planted, and threw. Kenny Washington threw that pass *62 yards* in the air, verified by Fox-Movietone News. Hirshon again received the ball and took it in for another touchdown. It stands as one of the longest passes in collegiate history. Though the Bruins got their hands on the ball one more time and even had a touchdown questionably called back, the game thus ended at 19-13 in favor of the Trojans.

After the game, Spaulding went over to the Southern Cal locker room to congratulate Jones on his victory but found the door closed. After knocking a couple of times with no response, Spaulding is reported to have said, "You can tell Howard it's all right to come out now. Kenny's stopped passing!"

Before the 1938 season began, Spaulding announced that it would be his last as head coach, that he was going to concentrate on being the full athletic director.

He unveiled another crop of sophomores who seemed to be special, half Charlie Fenenbock, fullback Bill Overlin, and young Joe L. Brown, entertainer Joe E.'s son. With Washington and Strode, Hirshon, end Don McPherson, center Johnny Ryland, and tackle "Slats" Wyrick back, there were high hopes that Spaulding's swan song would be bright and clear. It wasn't, but it was good.

UCLA finished 4-3-1 in the conference, including a vengeful 13-0 victory against Washington, who under coach Jimmy Phelan had not allowed the Bruins a point in the four games they had played since he took over in 1932, and a 6-0 win over Stanford, featuring another all-out Indian pass barrage at game's end. For this latter game the Bruins were coached by Edwin "Babe" Horrell in lieu of Spaulding, who was attending the funeral of his mother. Though Spaulding's successor had not been named, Horrell's victory over nothing less than Stanford was duly noted.

Spaulding's last two conference games were against Southern Cal and Oregon State. His Bruins, the front line hobbled by heavy injuries, incurred a solid 42-7 loss at the hands of the Trojans and managed to just come from behind to tie a

Fullback Bus Sutherland scores against Stanford in 1938, a 6-0 UCLA victory.

scrappy pack of Beavers, 6-6.

The Bruins accepted their first "bowl" invitation to play Hawaii in the Pineapple Bowl in Honolulu. A retirement lark for both Spaulding and the graduating seniors, the Bruins defeated a prebowl aggregation of Honolulu locals just after Christmas, 46-0, and beat the Roarin' Rainbows on January second (the first being a Sunday), 32-7.

Spaulding's 14-year accomplishment was monumental. He took a school whose football team was on the lowest rung of a secondary conference and upon his retirement had brought it in to the highest levels of major college competition. Steady, warm, and thoughtful Bill Spaulding strived to instill spirit and build character in every one of his players.

This early spirit centered around the word respect. The Bruins learned to respect themselves as team players, winners regardless of a single game's outcome. By 1932 there was not an opponent that did not respect the Bruins of UCLA as a tenacious, dangerous foe.

The incredible rise of the only major university born in the twentieth century speaks of remarkably fresh resources at work, and Bruin football had the mystery of youth and surprise at its disposal because of it. Traditionless in many respects, the Bruins were forced to compete without the satisfying warmth found in years of support and systematic replenishment from its graduates. In time these things would come.

The school was forced to play "catch-up" at breakneck speed and was never allowed the leisure to reflect on its accomplishments—it just kept moving, ever earning more respect. This augered an impressive athletic destiny, and Spaulding understood he could best serve it by a deepening administrative role. It was his decision, one that both he and the university were ready for him to make.

Upon his hiring in 1925, the school needed someone who would dedicate his heart in developing a healthy football program, one the players would be proud to build with him. UCLA needed a foundation. Spaulding became its Gibraltar.

But the players just called him Bill.

CHAPTER 4
1939-1944

The man who succeeded Bill Spaulding as head coach at UCLA was one of his longtime assistants, Edwin C. "Babe" Horrell. He was regarded by all as a true gentleman, dignified, sincere, the quintessential "nice guy."

Born in Jackson, Missouri, in 1902, his family moved to Pasadena three years later, and there Horrell and his three older brothers formed a virtual sports dynasty at Pasadena High School. (In fact, when Babe finally graduated in 1921, they named the athletic field "Horrell Field" in the collective brothers' honor.) His considerable talents at center on his prep football team earned Horrell a spot with Andy Smith's California Golden Bears. He played three years of varsity ball and became the centerpiece of a three-year undefeated period for Cal, was captain of the "Wonder Team" of 1923, and earned All-Coast and All-America honors.

Horrell graduated in business in 1925 and went into private business for himself back in Los Angeles. Spaulding's arrival in 1925 brought Horrell out to the Branch campus, and in 1926 he volunteered his services as a coach and finally was hired permanently as an assistant in 1931. Horrell was instrumental in the development of the All-Coast centers from UCLA Homer Oliver (1931), Lee Coats (1933), and Johnny Ryland (1938). (These players constituted three of the six All-Coast honors voted UCLA through the 1938 season.)

Horrell inherited a very, very good team. In his backfield were senior halfback Kenny Washington, possibly the greatest football athlete in UCLA history, and a flashy newcomer who would go on to blaze a trail in sports history for himself and his

"Babe" Horrell, All-America center at Cal, who coached UCLA to its first Rose Bowl.

race, junior halfback Jackie Robinson. The team also featured the indomitable pass catching of the long tall senior end Woody Strode, the bullish running of sophomore Leo Canter, and the able line work of sophomore Nate DeFrancisco.

The team came out of the blocks with back-to-back wins over Texas Christian, 6-2, and Washington, 14-7. A tie was achieved against Stanford, 14-14, as poor Bruin punting allowed the Indians, led by the all-time great Frankie Albert, to take a 14-7 lead, but Robinson intercepted a pass late in the game which set up the tying Bruin score. The team increased in estimation with wins over Montana (20-6), Oregon (16-6), and Cal (20-7). Then a second tie emerged, a 0-0 affair with Santa Clara, which UCLA almost pulled out with a last-second field goal attempt from the 15. This was followed by still another tie, 13-13 against Oregon State, which was achieved by the Bruins marching 82 yards with 70 seconds remaining to tie it up with a touchdown. Against Washington State, an 18-point second-half surge put the Cougars away, 24-7.

UCLA's opportunity to visit the Rose Bowl was riding on the outcome of the game against Southern Cal. This game has been recognized as one of the most exciting games in this series, and its ending had a residual effect on Horrell in the years that followed.

It was a closely fought game, UCLA getting over some fumbling jitters in the first half to settle down to play the kind of game Washington, Robinson, and Strode were capable of playing. The first half belonged to Troy, who virtually camped out in front of the Bruin goal yet could not score, the closest attempt silenced when a Trojan fumble was recovered in the end zone by Strode. The second half belonged to the Bruins, but they never scored either.

The last few minutes of play brought all 103,000 spectators to their feet. UCLA had taken the ball on the 18 and had marched it to the two, with first down and goal to go, six feet from glory, from the championship, from the Rose Bowl. UCLA had driven there via the slashing running of Washington. The players argued in the huddle what to do next. As no coaching was allowed from the sidelines, Horrell was not able to immediately tell his team what to do. Unfortunately, Horrell failed to send in a sub who would have been able to give instructions after the first down was played. Junior quarterback Ned Mathews, expecting guidance from the bench after each play but receiving none, called each play himself, running plays by Washington, Leo Canter, then Canter again.

Then, fourth down from the five, Mathews shunned the field goal attempt and instead called a pass play, Washington to junior end Bob McPherson. It was batted away in the end zone, preserving for all time the 0-0 tie.

The Bruins and the Trojans ended up co-champions of the Pacific Coast Conference, and the vote to determine the Rose Bowl representative went to also undefeated Southern Cal, on the strength that it had fewer ties (two) and was the defending Rose Bowl champ. (The rule selecting the school that had yet to visit or had not been there since the other school had was not yet in effect.)

From the stellar heights of UCLA's first undefeated season, Horrell's 1940 team made a complete reversal. Instead of 11 men playing as one, there was one man playing for 11—senior Jackie Robinson. Though he was a magnificent athlete, it was too much to ask from one man.

Robinson opened the season with an awe-inspiring 87-yard punt return for a touchdown against Southern Methodist. But his teammates began to wear down by the fourth quarter, and 70,000 fans, the Bruin faithful who had seen such great action the year before, saw the Mustangs go ahead to win via a field goal and post a 9-6 victory. One week later the Bruins virtually repeated this performance against Santa Clara, and the result was the same 9-6 score. Robinson failed to answer the bell in the second quarter the next week against Texas A&M, and the Bruins lost another, 7-0.

One week later the Bruins continued to sink, as Cal kicked a fourth quarter field goal to take a 9-7 nod. An uncomfortable note about this game was the fact that UCLA, with one minute remaining, had the ball first and goal from the five, and, in a bizarre repeat of the sequence of events against Southern Cal the year before, Horrell failed to send in the obvious fourth

Jackie Robinson, UCLA's all-everything athlete. Dodger Blue was in his future.

down field goal message that would have done the trick—the final line plunge coming up empty.

Oregon State took the Bruins 7-0, as did Stanford 20-14, as did the Oregon Ducks 18-0. The one and only breath of victory was drawn against Washington State, as the Bruins came from a 20-6 halftime deficit to win it, 34-26. Typically, it was all Jackie Robinson, who alone scored 22 of those points and ran 127 yards on 18 carries, six of which were no gain!

The Bruins took to their losing ways immediately thereafter, taking a heavy 41-0 loss on the chin from Washington, and closed out the season with a 28-12 loss to the Trojans. Only Montana fared worse than UCLA. Jackie Robinson was to have better luck—and make history by breaking the color line—on Dodger basepaths.

The UCLA season of 1941 was marked by the introduction of the T formation. Instead of having the ball hiked to a player standing in the backfield, the quarterback took the ball while standing directly behind the center. Also, the three remaining backs lined up side-by-side, forming a T in relation to the quarterback. It was eventually to be UCLA's formation for the forties.

It was not a smooth transition. Not willing to "live or die" by this one formation, Horrell juggled his backfields, one geared to the single wing, the other *kind* of to the T, with a wing back floating around, a formation Horrell dubbed the QT.

The difficult part was Horrell's background as solely a single-wing coach (and ex-player). He basically did not allow for the adjustment in the blocking assignments between the two, different by design and philosophy, the single wing relying on strength, the T on finesse. The Bruin players had difficulty in getting their assignments straight and their bodies to adjust on cue. Bernie Masterson, brought in from the Chicago Bears where his T had been so effective in the pro ranks, did what he could to install it by the beginning of the season.

As the first string struggled through the QT, the second and third-string players, the men who were working exclusively in the "real" T, would step in now and then as a unit to show what UCLA had the potential of doing.

The year 1941 also introduced to UCLA fans a few players who would contribute to the future success of the Bruin program, sophomores quarterback Ernie Case, halfback Al Solari, fullback Ken Snelling, and center Jim Dougherty. Plus, there was one player who would go on to nothing short of a brilliant professional career, though his college days were not the smoothest—quarterback Bob Waterfield.

A bit of skullduggery transpired after the season opener against Washington State (a 7-6 Bruin victory). The gift to the pep squad from the UCLA Alumni Association in 1939, a large railroad bell to ring out every point, was stolen by some enterprising pranksters from Southern Cal. The Trojans did not give it back until October 1942, with the proviso that UCLA agree to make it the perpetual trophy for The Big Game. (Although the Bruins did require the Trojans to pay for half the bell's value, this agreement is something like granting a kidnapper visitation rights as a part of the ransom payment.)

The Bruins took a disappointing 4-5 season record into the game with Southern Cal, taking only three conference wins along the way. The Trojan game then became the entire season for UCLA.

Battling to a 0-0 standstill until late in the third quarter, Waterfield etched a 60-yard touchdown drive, putting the Bruins on top 7-0. But just as the Bruins exhaled after their exertion in the blazing heat of the afternoon, the Trojans inhaled and started a return march of their own from the 27. They scored their touchdown and kicked the tying PAT just as the gun sounded to end the quarter—and the scoring for the day, the final score a 7-7 tie.

This tie truly indicated the even terms under which these two teams competed—UCLA had 250 total yards, Southern Cal 246. That slight edge in yardage reflects the slight edge the Bruins had over their most heated rivals in the final PCC standings: UCLA seventh, Southern Cal eighth.

It was a game that, under different circumstances, would have been talked about and mulled over all through the coming months. But it was quickly forgotten. It had been played on December 6, 1941. The next morning would bring the shock of Pearl Harbor and World War II.

The Bruins still had one more game scheduled in this 1941 season, an engagement with Florida down in Jacksonville. It was almost cancelled, but both schools decided to honor the contract. It was one of the more memorable and colorful excursions in UCLA history.

It was a *long* trip. The train was constantly being side-tracked in order to make way for the trains mustering a nation to war. Because many of the stopovers involved hours of delay, some players would go off on their own to sightsee and shop. With no timetable for reckoning their sojourns, the train would sometimes leave before the detrained players got back. Doing just that left Waterfield and several others behind across the border from El Paso. It also happened to a part of the team while in Dallas. Expecting to arrive in Florida four days before the game, the entire team made it, in parcels, the night before.

That night, the local "greeters" presented the players with the opportunity to place, well, wagers on themselves. Believing they would beat the Gators, they bet. Every cent they had.

The Bruins had to win by three. The Bruins were losing 20-6 at the half. In the locker room at halftime, Horrell, unaware of the bet, admonished the team, asked that they consider the honor of the school, then left them alone to dwell on it. It was then that Leo Cantor stood up and put things into perspective: He told his teammates to forget the school, their mommas, their girlfriends. He reminded them that, should they lose, their stopover in New Orleans on the return trip might as well be Glendale, because they'd all be *broke!*

It was a radically different Bruin team that faced the Gators in the second half. Cantor led the way, Ken Snelling's foot scored and scored again, and Waterfield led the Bruins back until it was 27-20 in their favor. Florida came back to tie, but late in the fourth quarter Snelling kicked the game-winning field goal and the Bruins won, 30-27.

New Orleans proved slightly better than Glendale!

The Bruins finally hit it big in 1942. Waterfield was in charge of the T, the bugs had been worked out from the transition from the single wing, and all seemed shipshape. Teaming with junior Waterfield to make this a memorable squad were seniors captain and right tackle Charlie Fears, left guard All-Coast Jack Lescoulie (no, not the announcer), ends Herb Wiener and Milt "Snuffy" Smith, left tackle Jack Finlay, and juniors fullback Ken Snelling, halfbacks Al Solari and Ev Riddle, and right guard Al Sparlis.

Things did not start well. The Bruins lost the opener against Texas Christian, 7-6, a game in which the Bruins showed little offensive punch. Then, against St. Mary's Pre-Flight, one of the many service teams the Bruins would face the next four years, the Navy trainees outmuscled the Bruins, 18-7, with arch-nemesis ex-Stanford quarterback Frankie Albert keeping his personal undefeated record against UCLA clean.

Then the onslaught began. First to fall was Oregon State, who literally did not know what hit them, losing, 30-7. Cal was no problem, 21-0. Santa Clara fell, 14-6.

Stanford presented the first major obstacle, and it was not an easy game. The Indians scored first and were on their way to scoring again. The Bruin defense went into a long huddle. When they broke it was as if the players had undergone a transformation. Stanford was not to score again that day, as UCLA went on to a 20-7 victory.

It turned out the players huddled for one simple reason: They were embarrassed at playing so poorly. They bet a dollar a man on who would make the next tackle! Halfback Ev Riddle shoved guard Al Sparlis out of the way to make that tackle and win the $10, and the momentum of that tackle sparked the team through to victory.

The Bruins suffered a sloppy, rainy loss to Oregon in Eugene, 14-7, and their Rose Bowl hopes wavered. Their fortunes reversed against Washington the week later, but it was not without a struggle and some luck. UCLA scored a touchdown the first time with the ball, easily marching the ball downfield in quick, efficient order. It was *too* easy, the players stopped taking the game seriously, and the team's concentration instantly disappeared. The squad never mentally got back into the game. The Huskies went ahead, 10-7, and were beginning to march for what would be the clincher in the fourth quarter when a quick eye saved the day.

Bruin guard Morrie Harrison detected that when the center hiked the ball to set up a fullback sweep from Washington's single-wing formation, which requires the hiker to "lead" the back with the ball as the play begins, this Husky center had a tendency to drag the ball along the ground before shooting it back. Harrison saw the earmarks of this play as Washington lined up, got in tight in front of the center, and as the play

60

began he was able to get a piece of the ball as it was hiked. It landed behind the unfortunate Husky back, and the Bruins' end Milt "Snuffy" Smith fell on it. Waterfield led the team to a score and the Bruins won, 14-10.

There was now only one roadblock: Southern Cal.

The Bruins opened the scoring by getting the ball on the Trojan 35 via an intercepted pass snagged by Waterfield. Expected to pass and pass, Waterfield found rushing the ball to be the most effective at this point and simply ran the ball up the middle and on down the field. Because of a penalty, the Bruins found themselves first and goal from the 14. Though tempted to pass his way out of this predicament, the temptation quickly passed and Waterfield did not. Three running plays later, all up the middle, UCLA scored.

The Bruins took to the air for their next score, Waterfield now able to mix up the Trojan secondary by passing when they least expected. Up now by 14-0, the Bruins kept it that way throughout the afternoon, and two desperation passes late in the game gave Southern Cal its only score. At UCLA 14, Southern Cal 7, it brought many Bruin firsts: first win over Troy, first sole possession of the conference championship, and the first turn to try its fortunes in the Rose Bowl.

The game was against Georgia. The Bulldogs had the Heisman Trophy winner that year in their backfield, Frank Sinkwich. But though the award-winning halfback was the season-long star for the Bulldogs, the star of the day in Pasadena was teammate Charley Trippi, who served as a valuable release valve whenever the Bruins keyed too heavily against Sinkwich.

UCLA staged one of the more impressive defensive performances against the high-scoring Bulldogs, as time and again Georgia would drive close to the Bruin goal but never score. The UCLA zone defense was giving up the middle of the field in chunks from the 30 to the 30 but would "scrunch up" near the end zone and shutoff the 'Dogs. This lasted long into the afternoon, and it was still 0-0 in the fourth quarter when the game broke for Georgia.

A Bulldog tackle, Willard "Red" Boyd, was able to block a Waterfield punt, which resulted in a safety and a 2-0 Georgia lead. UCLA desperately went to the air in its next possession and was intercepted deep in its own territory. Sinkwich scored the game's lone touchdown, the PAT making it a 9-0 final.

Once again, having enjoyed a top season, Bruin football immediately fell on hard times. Though the escalating war effort certainly could be cited as a factor, other schools were operating under the same hardships. UCLA even had a large portion of navy recruits housed on campus and eligible to play, as did Southern Cal across town. The Trojans went to the Rose Bowl during this period three straight years. The Bruins simply dissolved.

The 1943 season was simply disastrous. Because of the war, the PCC was divided north/south, and UCLA played the Trojans and the Bears twice each. The Bruins lost all four. The only Bruin win all year was against an old nemesis, the St.

All-America end Burr Baldwin catches a pass in the 1943 Rose Bowl, a 9-0 loss to Georgia.

Mary's Gaels. With college all-stars and some pros sprinkled on the service teams they played, the Bruins virtually gave up the ghost.

The 1944 season started strong, but Uncle Sam periodically plucked the best players from the team, and the Bruins ended badly. A 13-13 tie with Troy began the season, the tie achieved by two Bruin touchdowns in the last three minutes of the game. The final points were the result of an 80-yard punt return by halfback Johnny Roesch, reaching the end zone after the game-ending gun had sounded; down by one, Bob Waterfield (who had returned to the campus after a year in the army) kicked the PAT, which hit the crossbar, hung there for a second, then fell over to the other side to earn the tie.

The Bruins were to have some spotty success from there, but the midseason loss of Roesch to the war effort had a great negative impact. UCLA split the games with Cal, lost the season final to a still-mighty (and draft-free) Trojan eleven, and ended with a disappointing 4-5-1 record.

This two-year Bruin collapse became a sore point for many players and many more alums. Though some players had been called up to serve their country, the argument was that it was not as if an entire team had disappeared overnight. Tension and unrest began to permeate and affect the team, and the players began to react negatively to the careful coaching style of Babe Horrell.

Player dissatisfaction with Horrell went public in the middle of the 1944 season, as Waterfield, center Ron Paul, and others presented Horrell with a list of grievances. The alums began increasing their pressure on the school, as they could not understand how Horrell failed to develop any All-Americans since UCLA's first, Kenny Washington in 1939, citing the amazing talents of Waterfield going unrewarded. They also had never forgotten (or forgiven) the 1939 tie with Southern Cal that they felt had shortchanged UCLA a Rose Bowl visit. Internally and externally, all confidence in Horrell was evaporating.

When Horrell understood that his contract was not going to be renewed, he tendered his resignation on January 5, 1945.

Nothing can take away the happy moments, the memories found in great victory or close-fought defeats under Horrell. The Babe was one of the kindest, most thoughtful and sincere

Al Solari brought down in the Rose Bowl. Also seen are Captain and tackle Charlie Fears (10), quarterback Bob Waterfield (7), end Burr Baldwin (38), half Al Izmirian (33), and tackle Jack Finlay (17).

individuals to ever grace the college football sidelines. He was a very able assistant coach. And though his head coaching career at UCLA was not an overwhelming success, his loyalty to the Bruin football program in the years that followed never wavered, a true reflection of the class that Babe Horrell embodied.

CHAPTER 5

1945-1948

UCLA's new head coach for 1945 was Bert LaBrucherie, who played right half for Spaulding back in the late twenties, making him the first Bruin grad to be hired as head man. Born in 1905 and raised all his life in Los Angeles, after graduating from UCLA he went directly into prep head coaching at Los Angeles High, first with the "B" team, then heading the varsity for 10 years. There he compiled a 67-10-2 record, three undefeated seasons, and seven titles. He was the best at that level and still is revered for those accomplishments.

Preceding this first season at UCLA, LaBrucherie commented, "Collegiate coaching is virtually the same as high school. The boys know more and thus give you an opportunity to do a lot of things you would never try in high school. Fundamentally, however, there is virtually no difference." At UCLA in the midforties, however, postwar football players were not simple and logical high school graduates.

Many players, some with prior college experience, went to UCLA when released from the military and, naturally, went out for football. Combined with these war-scarred men were kids not long out of high school. It created an odd mix. Such experience differences, physically, emotionally, and philosophically, made for a team personality that did not fit into LaBrucherie's more halcyon high school methods.

That first season, 1945, was not an overwhelming success. The north/south division of the Pacific Coast Conference was still in effect (although the Bruins did play Oregon), with two service teams filling out the nine-game bill. It did bring UCLA a second All-America, guard Al Sparlis, a war vet who returned to UCLA after playing on the varsity teams of 1942 and 1943.

The home opener was against Southern Cal. Though UCLA scored first, it became apparent that the Bruins had no passing attack and the Trojans adjusted to win the game, 13-6. The Bruins bounced back with a tight upset against San Diego Navy, 20-14, then mauled Pacific, 50-0. Against the team that was tabbed to give Southern Cal its toughest struggle on the way to the Rose Bowl, UCLA outmuscled Cal, 13-0, on the strength of the great right half, sophomore Cal Rossi.

Although the war was officially over in August, there was still that period of transition, of getting men demobilized, that took several months. In a sublime case of meeting the wrong team at the wrong time, UCLA met St. Mary's Pre-Flight on the very week none other than Frankie Albert returned, the great All-American quarterback from Stanford, who had last met the

Bert LaBrucherie, first to play and serve as head coach at UCLA.

Bruins in 1942. Albert had never lost to UCLA, while at Stanford or with the Pre-Flight. That is still the case, as in his first game back in the States he led the Airdevils to a 13-6 victory.

For the Oregon game, Rossi ran for 160 yards from scrimmage, five less than the entire Duck effort, as the Bruins downed the Webfoots 12-0. After this game, with preseason commitments to the then-war effort still being honored, UCLA lost the services of Rossi, when the Bruin star left to make good his navy commission.

Then, in shades of 1931, the Bruins met renewed powerhouse St. Mary's. The Gaels had forged an undefeated season, including a 26-0 trouncing of Southern Cal just two weeks before. The Gaels were number five in the nation and 14-point favorites. It was a brutal affair, with several players from both squads requiring medical attention afterwards. This great game was capped when Bruin quarterback junior Ernie Case scooted a pass to right half freshman Gene "Skip" Rowland, good for 16 yards, and a touchdown, lifting UCLA to a 13-7 victory with just 48 seconds remaining.

The return engagement with Cal was one of the muddiest fiascos ever in the Bruin/Bear rivalry. The home Bears scored the only points midway through the third quarter, after both teams had volleyed with the pigskin after a blocked UCLA punt. A total mud bath by this time, almost neither team could distinguish its own players once each play began, and the game was marked by constant midplay exchanges of the ball via mistaken-player laterals and the like. Cal took it, 6-0. Southern Cal ended the Bruins season with a 26-15 loss.

LaBrucherie's initial season ended 5-4. There had been some players who had not fought to earn their positions or even to keep them, just guys playing because they showed up. Some were very good, some were just bodies filling out the roster. That LaBrucherie was able to take such a disparate bunch of players and make them as effective as they were is much to his credit, this first year out.

And then there was 1946.

This season stands as a landmark in UCLA history. The Bruins went undefeated and untied and were recognized as one of the great teams in the nation that year. It was that first game in 1947, however, that broke the spell.

Right half Cal Rossi rounds a California corner in the first of the two games played between the Bruins and the Bears in 1945, won by UCLA 13-0.

Where did this team come from? Los Angeles was usually the jumping-off point for many a serviceman headed for the Pacific conflict, and college-age boys from parts north, east, and south took a look around the California southland and decided that at war's end that L.A. was the golden place to be. As previously alluded to, a number of these emigrants-to-be happened to play football, and as UCLA was the only academic university in the area that was additionally state-supported (i.e. economically), they gravitated to Westwood. In droves. And the confluence peaked in 1946.

The first game of the season was against one of the teams tagged to finish near the PCC top, Oregon State. The Bruins were pegged to beat the Beavers by seven, but ended up beating them by 50-7. Something was up in this major victory.

Up and running out of the T was a great set of backfield men, including quarterbacks senior Ernie Case and junior Bennie Reiges; junior backs Cal Rossi, Jerry Shipkey, and Jack

Myers; sophomore backs Skip Rowland and Art Steffen; and a host of others. (In this first game against the Beavers, 17 backs in all saw action.) They were also up and passing, as the great All-American end senior Burr Baldwin and the redoubtable junior end Tom Fears (Bruin Charley's brother) teamed with junior end Phil Tinsley and senior Roy Kurrasch to create an awesome receiving corps.

The next game was a pick 'em against Washington. UCLA won, 39-13. The Huskies led 7-0 at one point in the first quarter, but LaBrucherie's Bruins stifled the Washington team from there on out, able to successfully juggle two bona-fide backfields, one geared for power (Reiges, Steffen, Shipkey, Myers), the other for speed (Case, Rossi, Rowland), though it was usually the rabbit squad that did most of the damage. Both backfields reaped the benefits of a solid line to work from, thanks to junior centers Bob Keefer and Don Paul; guards sophomore Bill Clements, juniors Bob Russell, and Mike Dimitro and senior Jack Watts; and tackles Tom Asher, Herb Boom, and the great Don Malmberg, seniors all.

The Bruins faced another Rose Bowl contender in Stanford. The Indians fell, 26-6. For this game, the only Bruin concern was the loss of Rowland, so in his place the team inserted a talented back who had been out all season because of a knee injury, junior Al Hoisch. Also, one of the more interesting plays used in this game was a "triple pass" (forward pass-lateral-lateral), Case to Baldwin to Fears to Clements. In fact, the game was loaded with laterals, which continually brought the Coliseum crowd of 90,000 to its feet time and again. Fears, unfortunately, incurred a knee injury.

So Fears did not travel with the team to play Cal. And the Bears put up a heavy-handed, ugly defensive front that left Rossi out for the season with a broken ankle, Case requiring smelling salts at one point, and the rabbit squad helpless. It was the power squad that made the difference, as UCLA muscled out a clean 13-6 victory.

With this victory the Bruins were being hailed as "The Army of the West," the West Point Cadets at that time also putting one of the most powerful teams in college football history on the field each week. It was the dawning of a new age, the initials UCLA being introduced into the leading football

Fullback Jerry Shipkey's 73-yard run against Cal in 1946.

circles of the East and South, for little was known about this college on the Coast. This college had grown to 20,000 students, had one of the most beautiful campuses in America, and now was suddenly fielding a great football team.

UCLA climbed the rankings to number three, after beating Santa Clara, 33-7. Next, Oregon stood in the way, but the undefeated (once tied) Ducks fell, 14-0. The Bruins then eased through a 61-7 win over hapless Montana.

This set up the clincher with the Trojans. As seems to be their perennial lot, the Bruins and the Trojans met to decide the conference championship and the Rose Bowl berth. It was a game which can best be described as bizarre, which in a way is only natural.

First of all, it rained, a deluge. In response, LaBrucherie opted for one of the more ancient game plans, "Punt, punt, punt, and wait for the breaks." To a team used to solid, open-style play, this was a shock to its sensibilities. The Bruins actually punted four times on first down, four on second, and eight on third!

The game underway, the Bruins were able to capitalize on the first break early in the first quarter, blocking a Trojan punt attempt from the 16, the ball landing in the arms of Bruin tackle Don Malmberg, and he cakewalked into the end zone for a 6-0 lead. The Trojans scored their points via a Bruin penalty turnover on the UCLA 48 and marched it in from there. Their missed PAT left the score 6-6 at halftime.

In the locker room, some of the players begged LaBrucherie to let them pass or at least run with the ball a little. LaBrucherie refused, telling them, "I'll take the rap."

Then, late in the third quarter, the Trojans fumbled a Bruin punt on the five, thanks to a trememdous Al Hoisch tackle, and three plays later Case snuck the ball over from the one for the winning margin, the successful PAT icing it at 13-6 (a tie would have sent UCLA to Pasadena as well).

And that is how the Bruins made it to their second Rose Bowl. "The Game Plan is Right When You Win" philosophy left some Bruin players and many Bruin fans uncomfortable. It may not have been pretty, but it did the job, and that was enough to convince Bert LaBrucherie he had made the right decision.

There was one more game on the regular season schedule, against Nebraska. In the stands that day at the Coliseum was Ray Eliot, coach of the Illinois team that was to face UCLA in the Rose Bowl. The game he saw was dreadful, UCLA winning it, 18-0, but playing as if its shoelaces were tied together. He was warned the next game would be different.

But first comes the unusual story of how the Fighting Illini became UCLA's Rose Bowl opponents, and what the Bruins did to affect their performance.

UCLA wanted to play Army. After all, being called "The Army of the West" was in a way demeaning; how much better to have Army called "The UCLA of the East!" And the Bruins

The 1946 Bruins, "The Army of the West," UCLA's second Rose Bowl team.

did not keep it a secret, letting it be known loud and clear that they wanted to play Army in the Rose Bowl.

However, the PCC and the Big Nine (soon to become the Big 10) had that year entered into an exclusivity pact with the Rose Bowl, and no other conference or team could participate, so Western Conference Champion Illinois was already set as UCLA's opponent for January 1, 1947.

The Fighting Illini, as could be expected, did not quite hanker to the idea of being considered a weak sister to these proceedings. In fact, everywhere they went after they arrived in Los Angeles they were reminded that they were undeserving, that UCLA was monumental, that the Illini might as well just fold up their jerseys and go home quietly.

Thus are opponents fired up. As a final note, Illinois just happened to be a very good and very big team. Western Conference Champions usually are.

Though the game started out relatively normally, it was eventually all Illinois. The Illini marched 60 yards after the opening kickoff to score, the PAT missing. Then UCLA, on its first possession, impressively marched 55 yards to score well, the successful PAT putting it ahead, 7-6. The strong UCLA defense was now supposed to shore up as it had all season so that the offense could really begin dominating. Neither of these two "automatics" happened. Instead, Illinois could not be stopped, scoring 39 more points before the Bruins knew what hit them.

At least there was one bright moment for UCLA in this debacle. It occurred as the half was about to end. Illinois had just scored and kicked off. The ball was received three yards into the end zone and brought out by Al Hoisch, who ran the length of the field and scored a second touchdown for UCLA. It was a New Year's Day feat that never has been broken or equaled, a 103-yard kickoff return for a touchdown in the Rose Bowl, and it belongs to UCLA.

But the final score was Illinois 45, UCLA 14. The Bruins finished at number four in the nation, still the highest final spot attained so far.

With the vision of forging UCLA's first completely undefeated and untied season far behind him as the 1947 season began, LaBrucherie started anew. Many of the starters that had reached such heights the year before had returned. But, though not as radically as Horrell's team fell after the 1943 visit to Pasadena, LaBrucherie witnessed a disheartening turnaround of Bruin fortunes this next year, which later escalated in 1948. The deterioration of the Bruins was the result of increasingly poor relations between the players and the coaching staff. There was still that steady influx of war veterans perpetuating a lack of respect for the authority of the coaching staff, and there was actually very little the head coach could do about it. It spread like a cancer from season to season, the returning lettermen insinuating this attitude into those new to the varsity.

The team seemed to either win or lose on its own unalienable talents, for internally its morale was in a state of turmoil and decline. It is therefore understandable that no matter what tinkering or external adjustments LaBrucherie attempted, the team responded with increasingly lackluster performances spelled by occasional bursts of brilliance these next two years.

The Bruins gained some "revenge" against the Big Nine in the season opener against Iowa, 22-7, but then traveled to Chicago and were defeated by underdog Northwestern, 27-26. When LaBrucherie returned to Westwood, he decided his backfield needed to be shaken up.

This change in personnel succeeded in chalking up victories over Oregon (24-7) and Stanford (39-6), and even though these scores lean heavily in UCLA's favor, the Bruins' work was marked by sloppy play and lucky breaks in both games. Then Southern Methodist came to town and defeated the Bruins, 7-0, the Mustangs capitalizing on the talents of tailback Doak Walker, who would go on to win the Heisman Trophy the following year.

When LaBrucherie went back to the practice field on Monday, his backfield was almost entirley struck down with stomach flu. This did not help matters, coming the week before the game that might presage the Bruins' Rose Bowl prospects, as UCLA was still undefeated in league play. The game was against Cal.

UCLA lost, 6-0, LaBrucherie fitfully trying to adjust his backfield during the game. If a player made a mistake, he was pulled and benched until *his* replacement made a mistake, an unpleasant experience for all.

73

The Bruins "got healthy" by beating Oregon State, 27-7, and continued against Washington, 34-7. The Bruins headed into the contest against Southern Cal with the Rose Bowl on the line after all, the victors receiving the honor of getting eaten alive by a mighty Michigan team, then number one in the nation and destined to stay there.

The Trojans scored in the second quarter, making it 6-0, and that was it for the day. But the game was not without a great UCLA rally—and controversy.

The Bruins drove deep and hard as the game was nearing a close, combining a sparkling array of line plunges and clutch passes to ends Phil Tinsley and Tom Fears. The final play of this drive was at the Southern Cal five, fourth down, three for a first, five for a tie. The play called for Tinsley to route his way into the end zone in a pattern the Trojans had never seen, saved for just this sort of moment. The play underway, two Trojans grossly held Tinsley, who never even made it across the line of scrimmage. After being handed the ball by junior quarterback Carl Benton, junior halfback Ernie Johnson had to circle around looking for another receiver, found senior end Bill Hoyt open, but just as Johnson let the ball fly Hoyt slipped, the ball was intercepted, and the game was over. The holding on Tinsley, unfortunatley, was missed by the officials.

This and other allegedly missed infractions became the subject of a heated public argument between representatives from both institutions. As nothing is strictly provable in regards to an official's intent to aid a team by calling or ignoring infractions, the issue was moot, and the controversy eventually quieted down...for the time being.

The 1948 season was one of almost total frustration. It started out with a high-scoring win against Washington State, 48-26, then the Bruins drew a total blank against Rose Bowl-bound Northwestern, 19-0. After a 28-12 respite against Idaho, it was all downhill from there.

The Bruins incurred three injurious losses to Washington, Stanford, and Oregon State. The team by this time was playing as if it had been handed its helmets and cleats for the first time each week just minutes before the kickoff. In the Oregon State game, the Bruins amassed just one first down in the first half, and that was via a fumble that was kicked forward before a

UCLA's Tom Fears, future pro player and coach, one of two Bruins in the Pro Football Hall of Fame.

Bruin fell on it.

Time was running out for Bert LaBrucherie. The rift between his coaching staff and the players was growing wider and wider each week, and after the loss to the Beavers it blew up in public. His firing after the 1947 season of longtime favorite line coach Ray Richards upset many players and even bothered some within the department itself. "Dutch" Fehring, Richards' replacement, was much more the disciplinarian, which also acted to create resentment.

The Bruins' next game was against Nebraska, who also was suffering through a dismal season. It continued for the Cornhuskers, as UCLA thoroughly beat them, 27-15, amidst a lot of fighting and player ejections there in Lincoln.

The Bruins played their hearts out against eventual conference champion Cal but lacked that added plus of able manpower to make good and lost another, 28-13. Then came misery. The Bruins were no match for Oregon State and quarterback Norm Van Brocklin; the Oregon Ducks also strongly defeated UCLA, and Southern Cal finished the job, 20-13.

The Bruins fell to 3-7, from first to last in two years. In a show of good faith, after the Trojan loss the students and band surrounded the UCLA locker room and shouted to LaBrucherie, "We'll see you next year."

They did not. LaBrucherie resigned December 14, 1948, and his entire staff followed suit.

There was, without a doubt, a large number of players who believed in Bert LaBrucherie, who loved him, who recognized the innate goodness that was housed in his heart. For some, he was their inspiration, and in a few cases these players were carryovers from his rewarding high school coaching days. Those happy years are the ones he is most often remembered for, as well as those quieter years he subsequently head coached football and track at Cal Tech. He was, and deservedly so, well loved and respected.

The UCLA job may have just been wrong for him at the time. (Perhaps no one, short of Patton, could have handled those vets.) But let it be remembered that, until a coach comes along who will forge an undefeated season that includes a Rose Bowl victory, his 10 wins in 1946 are the most in any single season in Bruin history and formed the longest win streak at UCLA as well.

He ultimately deserves credit for the best.

CHAPTER 6

1949-1953

Legends spring from true stories that through the years take on a veneer of nostalgia, of Camelots and nobility, of champions and conquests. In a modern sense, at UCLA the years 1949 through 1957 have taken on this inexplicable quality that comes with legends, and this period even is referred to as "The Golden Age of Bruin Football." Henry Russell "Red" Sanders was its Merlin, appearing seemingly out of nowhere to work his alchemy on a tarnished Bruin image, transforming it virtually overnight into the model football program on the West Coast.

He did not push Bruin football into national prominence; he skyrocketed it. Along the way he was named Los Angeles' "Outstanding Citizen of 1950" and National Coach of the Year in 1954. In 1955 he was voted one of the greatest college coaches who ever lived, including Notre Dame's Knute Rockne, Stanford's Pop Warner, Southern Cal's Howard Jones, and Michigan's Fielding Yost.

Sanders was one of the most quotable coaches who ever faced a battery of sportswriters and developed many lasting friendships among the best in the business, including Grantland Rice, Jim Murray, Fred Russell, Jack Murphy, and Red Smith. He was the first to say, "Winning isn't everything; it's the only thing," incorrectly attributed to others since. Another classic Sandersism was, "In football, blocking is the essence of offense, tackling is the essence of defense, and spirit is the quintessence of all." He *never* made excuses for losing and always credited the players and his staff for every win. For Red Sanders, there was no arguing with a final score, for it always

77

told the truth.

Sanders was born March 7, 1905, in Asheville, North Carolina, but his family moved to Nashville, Tennessee, in 1907 to stay. He picked up the nickname "Red" when his uncle noted that, with the red sweater he always wore, Sanders looked like "a red bull calf," and the endearment "Red Bull" eventually was shortened to just plain "Red."

Growing up in its shadow, he attended Vanderbilt University, never rising above reserve quarterback, but he played good baseball and combined athletics with his prelaw studies and active collegiate service. Though his gridiron exploits were limited, a keen awareness of how the game worked prompted his coach, Dan McGugin, to comment that Sanders had "one of the finest football brains I have ever seen" and helped Red decide to take

Henry Russell Sanders. They called him "Red."

the road leading to a coaching career.

After graduating from Vandy in 1927, Sanders played semi-pro baseball during the summer for three years while also coaching the Clemson backfield each fall. From there he went into head coaching prep football in Tennessee, going 55-4-2 during an eight-year stretch. As this was accomplished at two military academies, Sanders perfected his recruiting skills in keen competition with the many other academies that proliferated in that area, with a $100-per-recruited cadet bonus adding considerable incentive beyond improving his lot on the playing field!

Hired as an assistant at Florida and then LSU, Sanders was elevated to the head spot at his alma mater in 1940, that first year producing the only losing season in his entire career. (From the start Sanders recognized the value of securing top assistants, and the line coach on his first staff was the young Paul "Bear" Bryant.) Still, it was a marked improvement from seasons past at Vanderbilt, and his further success the following year earned him Southeastern Conference Coach of the Year honors. He spent three years' war service as a commander in the navy, and during that time he met and married his second wife, Ann Daniels of Lakeland, Florida. Returning to his job at Vandy, he continued to improve the Commodores' seasonal record, his 1948 squad climbing to the number-12 spot in the nation.

But Sanders felt he would never be able to shake the "local boy" image, open to unsolicited advice from all sides, and became receptive to the notion of moving on. Attending a coaches' convention in San Francisco, Sanders met with UCLA athletic director Wilbur Johns, who had been told to seek out Sanders by Grantland Rice, the dean of American sports reporters. Johns, hoping to replace quickly the departed Bert LaBrucherie, had no one specifically in mind, but upon Rice's recommendation he became determined to have no other than Red Sanders. The offer was made, and Sanders orally accepted.

When Sanders returned to Vanderbilt the school offered him a lifetime contract, but Sanders was not about to back out of his agreement with UCLA. His word was his bond, and he had shaken hands on it. That meant more than any ink on a page to Sanders.

Sanders arrived in Westwood in the spring of 1949, and the

change was instantaneous. He brought along his entire Vanderbilt staff but wisely retained frosh coach George Dickerson from the past regime. Sanders was organizationally brilliant, with the confidence to delegate complete authority to his assistants (and he made certain that their salaries reflected their indispensable value). That staff included Tommy Prothro, future head coach at Oregon State and UCLA, who continued on to a colorful professional head coaching and administrative career; Dickerson, former Bruin player and future head coach at UCLA; and Jim Myers, future head coach at Iowa State and Texas A&M and offensive coordinator for many years with the Dallas Cowboys. In 1950 Sanders added Bill Barnes, another future UCLA head coach.

Believing that top quality equipment is absolutely necessary for top quality play, Sanders replaced every pad and cleat with the best. He modernized the uniforms, changing the primary color from dark blue to powder blue for better visibility on the field and on film (dubbing the new color powder-*keg* blue!), and also designed the unique shoulder loops which made the uniforms *look* faster, now refered to nationwide as "The UCLA Stripe," and sported by LSU and the Minnesota Vikings. He later individualized the jerseys even more by using Clarendon rounded numbers.

Even the Bruins' new "serpentine" style of breaking the huddle added an extra air of showmanship to every game.

Sanders' most fundamental change was to switch the Bruins from the T formation to the "ancient" single wing. This, to some, was retrogression, like forcing jet pilots into Sopwith Camels. But Sanders was in control, it was the formation *he* had mastered, and he knew he could win with it. There was some concern that talent-laden players would forego UCLA for schools sporting the modern T derivatives. Sanders believed the formation would not be the reason a player should want to play for UCLA, but his coaching and teaching (and, of course, the superior education to be found in Westwood). It either dawned on a recruit that it was an honor to play for Sanders or it did not.

In practice, as during game time, every player was required to wear his helmet at all times. "That way," he explained, "a man forms the habit and when ordered into a game doesn't have to spend half a day looking for a hat to go with his head." Also, there was a platform above the practice field, used primarily for filming, from which Sanders surveyed his troops in action, megaphone in hand, barking out orders, plays, and criticisms. He had an incredible eye, with the nuances of individual movement for each position so internalized the smallest infraction did not pass unnoticed. It made for demanding, strict, exacting, and ultimately rewarding practices. For Sanders, games were not won or lost on Saturdays, but on Thursdays.

The players learned more than just football from Red Sanders. He made no excuses for his harsh verbal jabs at any shortcomings displayed by his Bruins in practice. "I'm sometimes very rough on a boy on the practice field or in my office," he admitted. "However, many have come to me years afterwards and expressed their thanks for some of my scathing comments as the greatest preparation for life they received in college."

Fundamentals were at the heart of Sanders' approach to the game. "If you block and tackle better than the other fellow, you win. Period." Every team was built from the ground up on this principle. He later listed his "Ten Commandments of Football," put them on a large board, and kept it displayed in the locker room in Westwood and carried it to every game, home or away, sometimes using it to stress individual points when necessary. They were:

1. The team that makes the fewest mistakes, wins.
2. Press the kicking game, for it is here the breaks are made.
3. Play for and make the breaks; when one comes your way, score.
4. If at first the game or break goes against you, don't slow down. Put on more steam.
5. Cover and pursue relentlessly—here is the winning edge.
6. Linemen: Protect your kicker and passer; rush their kicker and passer. Backs: Protect your kicker and passer.
7. Carry the fight to your opponent and keep it there all afternoon. Hit first and hit hard.
8. Be mentally alert at all times and leave nothing to chance.
9. Be determined to carry out your assignment.
10. Win the surest way.

Above all, he was realistic. "I can't speak for other coaches, but I know what it takes for me—some big, strong, phenomenal animals who can run fast. I can't put in what God left out; I am no miracle man."

That these instructions and conditions were absorbed by his teams at UCLA is reflected in their year-to-year records. Sanders never had a losing season at UCLA. He never lost more than three games in any season. His .773 winning percentage has never been topped at Westwood. Though some criticized his use of the "outdated" single wing, he simply said, "Winning is still stylish, isn't it? I don't know of anything more unfashionable than losing."

Sanders stressed total team play and team sacrifice. There was no room on a Sanders team for a star or a "showboater." The true reflection of a player's talents and value would be his contribution to a team victory, and any personal accolades, if deserved, would come of themselves. They did. Under Sanders there were nine All-Americans, two selected twice. The more these players helped their teams win, the easier it was for them to excel and to receive the necessary coverage for such recognition. It was the Sanders Way, and it worked.

Southerner Sanders was asked the inevitable question of the times regarding his attitude towards blacks. "I'm prejudiced in favor of any boy who can play football, and intolerant of any player who won't block and tackle." Case closed.

The team Sanders took over in 1949 was weak in morale and manpower. Considering it was changing over from a familiar T to the balanced-line single wing, preseason evaluations had the Bruins pegged to finish near the bottom of the Pacific Coast Conference. The coach knew better, and it was not long before the team knew better too. Bruin spirits were rekindled with senior players like halfbacks Ernie Johnson and Ray Nagel, tackle George Pastre, and center Leon McLaughlin finding instant success with Sanders, and talented juniors halfback Howard Hansen and end Bob Wilkinson represented a foundation of future promise.

It started with Oregon State, the only other single-wing team in the PCC. Tabbed as a fairly even game, the Beavers lost, 35-13. The next game was a visit to Iowa, and the Bruins unveiled a surprise pass attack, featuring end Wilkinson (dubbed "The Arrowhead Antelope"), and the Hawkeyes fell, 45-25.

A big test came the following week against Oregon. The Ducks had designs on the Rose Bowl, but the Bruins put an early kibosh on that, 35-27. Facing Stanford in Palo Alto, the Bruins were finally taken seriously as they beat the Indians, 14-7.

Santa Clara spoiled that unbeaten mark, stopping four Bruin scoring drives in the first half, the Broncos winning 14-0. Tragedy sent Sanders to Nashville upon the accidental death of his father, leaving his assistants to guide the team to a tough come-from-behind victory over Washington State, 27-20.

The largest hurdle was California, the best team on the West Coast. Behind the sturdy play of quarterback Bob Celeri, the Bears downed the Bruins, 35-21, and went on to face Ohio State in the Rose Bowl. The Bruins kept in the game by the undaunted play of Wilkinson, who scored two touchdowns on pass receptions (one a wrestling match with two Cal defenders)

End Bob Wilkinson, "The Arrowhead Antelope," in the debut of Sanders' 1949 team against Oregon State.

and sparked the third on a 30-yard end-around.

The next game, against Washington, the Bruins went wild, as the 47-26 victory indicates. Wilkinson had three touchdown receptions, setting a Bruin record for most in one game.

One thing the players learned about Sanders during every game was that he never broke concentration or character. He kept an even keel and calm demeanor at all times, his mind totally on the game. In time all players would assume a similarly absorbing interest in every game, toeing the sidelines, intent and ready to join the fray.

Finally, the time came for Sanders' introduction to The Big Game. The Trojans, led by Dean Schnieder and Frank Gifford (who, having just had an appendectomy, was only used to kick extra points), defeated the Bruins 21-7. It was also Sanders' introduction to Big Game oddities, as one Bruin was questionably ejected for fighting but his Trojan counterpart remained on the field; there was a dubious pass interference penalty which included an official shoving the "guilty" Bruin around, and more. It was one of the rare times the imperturbable Sanders lost his composure on the sidelines, a small indication of this game's impact on him. But Sanders never made mention of officiating, then or ever. As he one day flatly put it, "I never question or criticize officiating."

Red Sanders' first year record of 6-3 was, to many, astonishing. He had reevaluated his players and their obvious or latent talents and applied them where they would perform best. His desire was to build a strong running team whose defense would make easy scoring opportunities possible, something he expected would take a year or two to fully realize . In the meantime, in order to play competitively, he turned to a more risk-filled wide-open offense, and in stepped Bob Wilkinson. Though his role would be diminished the following year as the running attack began to materialize, (he would only catch two more touchdown passes the following year), his 10 in one season is still the Bruin record.

An impressive player position shift occurred before the 1950 season, as Sanders moved sophomore Donn Moomaw from end to linebacker and offensive tackle and center. Moomaw thought it was a demotion and a mistake. Moomaw became UCLA's first two-time All-America at linebacker.

Other outstanding players on this second chapter included seniors Wilkinson at end, tackles Breck Stroschein and Captain Bob Watson and guard Bruce MacLachlen, linemen whose contributions escalated Sanders' single-wing master plan.

The season opened with Oregon, and the Bruins breezed to an easy 28-0 victory with touchdowns in each quarter, Moomaw receiving instant recognition for his smothering pass defense. The next game against Washington State UCLA won in a runaway, 42-0, as five different Bruins scored rushing touchdowns, Sanders' style of play beginning to come together.

The Washington Huskies, one week after upsetting tough Minnesota, opened their conference schedule at home with a come-from-behind victory over UCLA, 21-20. It was a rough-and-tumble contest, the Bruins scoring first and easily and then getting another opportunity to score as the Huskies misfielded the ensuing kickoff. But when the Bruins fumbled the ball away at the one, the tide slowly began to shift, and a poor Blue pass defense enabled the Huskies to eventually come back, scoring the game-winning touchdown with two minutes to go. UCLA's return rally fell short at midfield, and as the gun sounded both sides exploded with flying fists, the benches emptied, and the harmless set-to helped release pent-up frustrations from both camps.

UCLA played the gracious host to Illinois, losing, 14-6, falling prey to similar defensive mistakes as in the Washington game. Then the Bruins snapped back against Stanford, as Wilkinson went pass crazy, Moomaw was MVP of the day, and sophomore left half Ted Narleski fooled the Indian defense time and again with key runs and fakes for passes in the 21-7 win.

Next the Bruins traveled to East Lafayette, Indiana, and thoroughly surprised a strong Purdue team, 20-6. The dormant defense returned, with complete performances from Moomaw, Stroschein, sophomore end Joe Sabol, Wilkinson, and juniors half Luther Keyes and full Cappy Smith. Purdue's 90 plays to UCLA's 55 makes this score even more impressive.

The Bruins had a letdown against Oregon State in the Coliseum, the 104 degree weather making things uncomfortable for both squads, but UCLA still managed to win, 20-13, thanks to "Ready Teddy" Narleski, who passed for 11 of 15 and established himself as UCLA's number-one back. Moomaw, defensive team leader, promised the Bruins would look much sharper against Cal the next week in Strawberry Canyon.

But on their way to their third consecutive appearance in the Rose Bowl, the Bears walloped the Bruins, 35-0, with Cal sophomore fullback ace Johnny "O" Olszewski ripping for 144 yards and two touchdowns. Yet it was what transpired before the game that set the future tone for this series.

Cal head coach Lynn "Pappy" Waldorf brusquely refused Sanders' request to allow the Bruins to wear their light-blue "home" jerseys, Red hoping to set up a friendly intra-university tradition. Waldorf's cold snub embarrassed Sanders, an embarrassment intensified by this defeat, the worst he's ever suffered and the worst for UCLA with Cal. Sanders also did not appreciate Waldorf's decision to continue playing his first string well into the fourth quarter, even though the game was well out of reach. This game and Waldorf's conduct were things Sanders would never forget.

The finale against Southern Cal was the Bruins' chance to bounce back after this stinging defeat. The team wanted to win, and the most eloquent example of this team commitment can be found in the courage of senior Howard Hansen's request to fulfill his starting assignment though his wife had died from a long illness two days before the game. Hansen believed she would have not only wanted him to play but would expect it of him. Sanders, reluctant at first that it might appear as a callous motivational gambit on his part, resolved to honor Hansen's desire to play. Red knew that no one worth taking seriously would ever imply he would stoop to that level of inspiration.

At 39-0 it was the worst defeat suffered by the Trojans in conference history, and only Michigan's 49-0 Rose Bowl win in 1947 and, later Notre Dame's 51-0 victory over the Trojans in 1966 surpass it overall. Troy had gained 427 yards against Washington the week before; UCLA held it to 30. Ted Narleski had a field day, solid walls of Bruin interference leading him to 138 yards and three touchdowns. Hansen picked up 61 yards on six carries and earned the game ball.

Senior end Bob Wilkinson had to leave his final game as a Bruin early in the first quarter because of a knee injury, but his two-year contribution as Sanders' star receiver earned him two All-Coast selections, and his records for most touchdown passes

Halfback "Ready" Teddy Narleski scores in UCLA's 39-0 victory over Southern Cal in 1950.

in a game (three), a season (10), and a career (12) are Bruins records that still stand. Stroscheim was also All-Coast, and Moomaw was selected All-America.

Lastly, with the day already his against Southern Cal, Sanders pulled Narleski early in the second half and began wholesale insertion of his second and third stringers. Sanders was a gentleman.

The Bruins of 1951 were Sanders' first army of varsity players who had never played under anybody else. Though the wing's sweeping system was a difficult one to learn, there were signs that UCLA was making strong progress. Still, this was the team with the "worst" record under Sanders, 5-3-1. A winning season, but not the top. Sanders wanted his Bruins to reach the top.

This team was hampered by a rash of injuries. That the Bruins were able to operate as effectively as they did was largely a case of too much Paul Cameron for opposing defenses to handle. Arriving in the backfield as a sophomore, Cameron's impact was immediate.

Cameron powered a fourth-quarter drive against season-opening Texas A&M that almost brought the Bruins a come-from-behind tie, but a man-in-motion penalty nullified a first and goal opportunity and the game ended with the Aggies on top, 21-14. The following week at Illinois, the Bruins held the Illini to a 7-7 tie at the half before the stronger Big-10 team pulled away to a sound 27-13 victory. Defensive star Donn Moomaw was felled with an injury, which precluded his performing up to his All-American expectations for the remainder of the season.

After a fast victory over Santa Clara, 44-17, the Bruins took it on the chin from Rose Bowl-bound Stanford, 21-7. Cameron, who had had a spectacular day against Santa Clara (starting for the first time) was absolutely flat against the Indians. And that accounts for the losses on the season.

After whumping Oregon, 41-0, UCLA took its first victory from California since 1946, 21-7. Sanders would carry the sting from the 1950 game with him for the rest of his life, and this game was pay-back number one. Cameron sparkled, senior back Luther Keyes ably contributed, and Moomaw simply devastated the competition. The injured Bear star back Johnny Olszewski did not play, but the Bruins looked so unstoppable he might not have been a factor. Sanders admitted that a flame had been lit under the team and advised one and all, "Stick with us. I think we just might win another game."

The next week, they did, defeating Oregon State, 7-0. Then came Sanders' one and only tie at UCLA, against Washington, in one of the most unbelievable cases of Husky good fortune in series history. Down 20-13, Washington was staging a desperate game-ending comeback but bogged down midfield. The Husky quarterback, Sam Mitchell, faded back to pass and let fly with a floater. The two defenders on the intended receiver successfully batted the ball away, but it stayed up in the air long enough to accidentally fall directly into the path of the streaking (and unwitting) Husky immortal back Hugh McElleny. It plopped into his surprised arms, and he continued on untouched for the touchdown, and the PAT tied it at 20-20.

The Bruins upset Southern Cal, 21-7, to close the books on 1951, as Paul Cameron had as good a day as Frank Gifford had bad. The Bruins hit harder, played harder, and simply outpowered the Trojans, who were limited to but 33 yards rushing for the day. When on defense, the Bruins presented their opponents with a strange V-wedge formation before each play, which they would maintain until the Trojans set themselves offensively in one of their predicted four formations, then the Uclans would shift into an appropriate defensive alignment. Southern Cal was flustered by it all day, and a fourth quarter courtesy touchdown was all that Troy could muster.

The Bruins finished second in the conference. It was not good enough for Sanders.

For 1952 UCLA was again snakebitten by injuries to key players but constantly overcame its difficulties to win. This year it was the turn of junior Paul Cameron, who twisted his right ankle in preseason practice and never regained complete form all season long. Still, it was a turning point for the Bruins in another way, for the players all felt they were part of a great team and played that way. Forging an 8-1 record, it was the

Left half Paul Cameron on his way to a score in UCLA's victory over Cal in 1951.

finest season for UCLA since LaBrucherie's 1946 squad and firmly established Sanders as one of the premier coaches on the West Coast.

Though starting off choppily in a victory over Oregon, 13-6, the Bruins started uncoiling with wins over Texas Christian (14-0), Washington (32-7), Rice (20-0), and Stanford (24-14).

Against the Indians, Paul Cameron, making up for his weak showing the year before, came out smoking in the first half, throwing for the three Bruin touchdowns before succumbing to his nagging injuries to sit out the second half. His replacement was a sophomore back who would go on to sweep his name into the memory banks of many Bruin fans and foes—Primo Villanueva.

It was after this game that another great "Sandersism" was born, Red describing the Stanford rooting section after

Donn Moomaw, All-America Bruin linebacker, future pastor to President Reagan.

Cameron had scored the game-winning touchdown. "They were so quiet," he said, "it was as if a world convention of undertakers had just been informed somebody had really discovered the secret of eternal life!"

The next week UCLA traveled to Wisconsin and upset the favored Badgers, 20-7, holding the great Alan Ameche to his fewest yards ever in his career, thanks in part to junior right end Myron Berliner. This set up a return to Strawberry Canyon and the feared California Golden Bears.

Head coach Lynn Waldorf in his years at Cal had never lost in the Coliseum, nor to UCLA, until the previous year's loss to the Bruins. The potent Cal offense, again led by senior fullback Johnny "O" Olszewski, was going to bump up against All-America senior linebacker Donn Moomaw and the young but rock-ribbed Bruin defense of sophomore guards Terry Debay and Sam Boghosian; sophomore tackles Jack Ellena, Johnny Peterson, and Jim Salsbury; and junior tackle Chuck Doud, with Berliner holding down his end.

Red Sanders had an additional surprise for Waldorf, who had rebuffed Sanders' request to allow his Bruins to wear their "home" light-blue jerseys in 1950, in hopes of establishing a pleasant intra-university tradition. For the 1952 game Sanders had his Bruins in their travel whites all right, only they sported a special numbering system employed for that game only. The guards were all issued jerseys that read G1, G2, G3, on down through every player, the tackles T1, T2, T3, T4, etc., and the four backfield starters were L1, R1, F1, and Q1!

As for the game, Braven Dyer of the *Los Angeles Times* described the Bears after this game with just one word: "Demolished." Waldorf sadly admitted, "UCLA was just too good," and the Bruins were, 28-7.

An easy bench-clearing 57-0 victory over Oregon State followed, then the match-up of the two titans dawned, the undefeated Bruins and the undefeated Trojans. Once again, the winner would be in the Rose Bowl.

In what has been recognized as one of the finest games ever played between the two institutions, Southern Cal managed to come from behind to beat UCLA by a 14-12 margin. Unique in Bruin annals is the fact that UCLA scored once in every way possible (at the time), via a touchdown, extra points, safety, and field goal. It took a fourth-quarter interception of a Cameron pass by Trojan Charlie Ane to set up the Trojans' clincher over the Bruins. Troy went on to Pasadena for the PCC's first Rose Bowl victory over a Big-10 team, beating Wisconsin, 7-0.

All UCLA had done this past season was almost go undefeated into the Rose Bowl, establishing itself as not only a team for the future with solid sophomore and junior linemen, but as the team that had set the standard for the next three years to see how far above it the Bruins would be able to climb.

A major rule change in college football preceded the 1953 season, as the rulesmakers decided to return the game to the single platoon system (abandoned during the war), bringing back the need to have players who could play "both ways." (Along with this rule came the elimination of unlimited substitution, now requiring a player to remain out of a game for an entire quarter should he leave play.) The majority of coaches reacted negatively, claiming this would place an unfair burden on their players, that fewer boys could participate, and that it would increase the likelihood of injuries. Sanders demurred.

Early in 1953, he commented to Dan Hafner in the *Los Angeles Examiner*, "I don't think it's a question of what's best for any one coach or team, but what's best for football as a whole." To Vincent X. Flaherty of the *Examiner* he later added, "Actually, the two-platoon system prevented too many good players from playing the game. There will be less injuries next fall, because the boys will have to be in better condition if they want to make the team. Now, without the platoon system, the fellow who isn't in condition will be exposed. He won't make the grade."

The single platoon did not affect the Bruins, as a healthy Paul Cameron returned for his senior year to team with juniors Primo Villanueva and Terry Debay, senior Bill Stits, and sophomore Bob Davenport and forge a backfield unit so powerful that, if not taking control of each game at the outset, it was simply a matter of time before an opponent gave way. Other key Bruins included sophomore guard Hardiman Cureton, senior end Myron Berliner, senior tackles Larry Britten and Chuck Doud, junior guard Jim Salsbury, and junior end Bob Heydenfeldt.

Rolling to a 41-0 everbody-plays victory over Oregon State

92

to open the season, the Bruins conquered Kansas, 19-0; Oregon, 12-0; and Wisconsin, 13-0. Stanford became the season's only flaw, and it was the result of one of the few sideline coaching errors ever committed by Sanders. With the Bruins leading, 20-7, midway through the third quarter, he pulled Cameron and company, leaving the game to the reserves. By the time the first string could return, 15 game-minutes later, it was too late. The Indians had staged a two-touchdown rally to take a 21-20 lead, lifting them so sky-high no late-game Bruin heroics could bring them back to earth.

If anything good can come from a loss, it is the determination of a great team not to let it happen again. The Bruins summarily dismissed Washington State, 44-7; Cal, 20-7; and Washington, 22-6. A victory over Southern Cal would put the Bruins in the Rose Bowl—if Stanford lost or tied with Cal that same day.

Cal achieved that tie with Stanford. The Bruins controlled their own destiny.

It was not easy. The Bruins unleashed some of the most powerful blocks they could muster. The Trojans took them all. The Trojans returned the favor. The Bruins would not budge. The difference between the two teams was slight. The Bruin defense was opportunistic, as Paul Cameron's booming punts and quick-kicks pinned the Trojans time and again deep in their own territory, and whenever Troy mishandled the ball, UCLA recovered. Two of those recoveries led to touchdowns. The offensive edge of the Bruins could not be denied all afternoon, finally outrushing their crosstown foes 250 yards to 71. The Bruins won, 13-0. UCLA was in the Rose Bowl.

Sanders got the word in the postgame locker room that many in the stands thought this game was, in a word, dull. His immediate response was to the point. "I'll assure you nobody on the field thought it was dull," later adding, "I don't know how it affected anyone else, but the way things turned out, those of us at UCLA thought it was interesting!"

So into Pasadena the Bruins rolled, there to face Coach Clarence "Biggie" Munn and Michigan State College, also 8-1 for the season. The Spartans were comprised of many of the players from the National Championship team of 1952 and were favored by six-and-a-half points. UCLA was considered to be the team of power, while Michigan State relied on speed, though each team packed the same average weight, 188 pounds per man. The Spartans were ranked third in the nation to the Bruins' fifth. It looked like it was going to be a great game. It was.

UCLA completely dominated the first half and before long had built a 14-0 lead, Paul Cameron passing to end Bill Stits for a 12-yard touch-down in the first quarter, Paul Cameron barging his way over from the two for the second. But an ominous twist in the Bruins' fortunes occurred just as the half was about to close. A Cameron punt deep in Bruin territory was blocked. It is rare when a blocked punt is not just simply pounced on, rarer still when it comes down into the arms of the man who blocked it, and rarest when that man is able to carry it un-molested into the end zone for a touchdown. Spartan end Ellis Duckett made just this play. It was the emotional lift that Michigan State desperately needed, entering the locker room down by just a touchdown, 14-7.

The Bruins had stymied the Spartans that first half, holding the Michigan State attack to only 56 yards in 32 plays. An unheralded Spartan, right half Billy Wells, injured during the season, had been used sparingly in the first half. In a very short time, he would explode.

Sanders' halftime announcement, "Men, you owe me a touchdown. That is the first kick that has ever been blocked against a team of mine," was honored by the team, but it was not enough. As effective as the Bruins were in that first half, the momentum completely shifted when the contest was resumed.

Michigan State took the second-half kickoff and smartly marched 78 yards in 14 plays to stuff the ball into the end zone and tie the game at 14 all. Deadlocked for a time, the two teams seemed to have achieved parity, and just when it looked as if UCLA might be coming back after preventing the Spartans from advancing on a big third-down play midfield, a roughing penalty against the Bruins gave their opponent's drive new life, and the Spartans and Wells shoved their way down the field for the go-ahead score, 21-14.

Cameron was not through. He led his team on a return scoring drive and threw a chilling 28-yard touchdown strike to sophomore end Rommie Loudd, though the receiver was blanketed by Spartan Earl Morrall. But for some still unexplainable reason, the snap from center for the PAT took an incredibly long time, kicker Johnny Hermann's kick went wide, and the Spartans held their thin one-point lead.

The game was iced for Michigan State when a UCLA punt was run back for a touchdown, a scattering and inspired 62-yard run by none other than Billy Wells, the only scoring punt return against UCLA all season. The final score reads: Michigan State 28, UCLA 20.

Red Sanders paid a visit to the victorious Spartan locker room, and was as magnanimous and memorable as always. He told reporters, "Michigan State easily was the best team we faced during the season. They have three things that mean football greatness—speed, agility, and the ability to recover." The Spartans also cited a deep motivational reason to outdo the Bruins—Munn told them this was to be his last game. After this victory, Biggie Munn retired from coaching, stepping up to the athletic director's chair, opening the door for his fine assistant,

Paul Cameron scores against Michigan State in the 1954 Rose Bowl, a 28-20 UCLA loss.

Left end Rommie Loudd pulls down a 28-yard Cameron pass for a fourth quarter Bruin touchdown in the Rose Bowl.

Hugh "Duffy" Daugherty.

Both the Bruins and Spartans then became automatically ineligible to return to the Rose Bowl the next year, a "no-repeat" agreement made by the two respective conferences to prevent one school from overly dominating the proceedings. Only in 1956 might the two meet again in the winter classic. They did.

But there was that interim year to play first. It was the year the Bruins played for glory and conquered the nation.

CHAPTER 7

1954-1957

Pride and responsibility. Ineligible as defending champions of the PCC, the Bruins of 1954 were determined that whoever was going to the Rose Bowl was not going to get there at the expense of UCLA.

A wealth of experienced players returned from the 8-2 team of 1953. At the top was senior left half Primo "The Calexico Kid" Villanueva, who with senior quarterback Terry Debay, junior "Pogo" Bob Davenport at fullback, and junior transfer Jim Decker at right half formed the first-string backfield that would sweep the opposition from its path.

The interior line was superb, consisting of captain senior center John Peterson, guards senior Sam Boghosian and junior Hardiman Cureton splitting time on the left side, senior Jim Salsbury and junior Jim Brown on the right, and seniors left tackle Jack Ellena and right tackle Joe Ray. The left ends senior Bob Heydenfeldt and junior Rommie Loudd and right ends senior Bob Long and junior Roger White provided exterior stability.

Sanders once said, "A well-prepared team develops confidence, and from confidence, spirit comes in quantity." This quantity was deep on this team, and exemplified what Sanders and others came to call "The Flaming Bruin Spirit."

UCLA's head coach continued to strive for the best-equipped team possible. He was the first on the West Coast to equip his team with the lighter plastic helmets. He provided his Bruins with combat nylon pants with double-stretch seats. He had the players' names stiched on the backs in UCLA's special Clarendon script.

Plus Sanders originated some innovations, such as shorter

Red Sanders' wife Ann often accompanied her husband on Bruin road games.

sleeves on the jerseys, lighter pads, and working his team out in heavy shoes during practice so they would run and "feel" faster with their lighter shoes during the games. This striving for excellence, for every advantage over an opponent, was a major contributor to the Bruins' overall belief in their being a pure reflection of the coach—the best.

He brought his imagination to the playing field as well. As documented by Vic Kelley, past sports information director at UCLA, "Sanders, who brought to the West Coast the balanced-line single wing...also originated the now-famous 4-4 defense, copied by college and pro mentors alike all over the nation; developed the 'squib kick' as substitution for the out-of-bounds punt; and exploited and popularized the now almost universally used spread punt formation."

Sanders himself briefly outlined the general properties and advantages of his favorite formation. "From the single wing, we can attack any point with deception and/or concentrated power. We've had high-scoring teams without once using a flanker, splitting the line, or having a man in motion. Every running play in our attack has a companion pass with both plays starting alike. Our system is paradoxical in that the offense is deceptive to opposing teams, yet the fans in the stands can follow the ball all the time."

The Bruins crushed their first two opponents, Naval Training Center of San Diego, 67-0, and Kansas, 32-7. Against NTCSD Sanders literally tried every combination in the book with his entire bench by as early as the middle of the second quarter. With Kansas, the Bruins scored almost too quickly the first two times they had the ball, losing that competitive spark against the Jayhawks, who essentially handcuffed UCLA during the middle periods. Finally, the Villanueva-led Blues struck for two touchdowns in the last four minutes to make it a late-blooming runaway. One of the few injuries incurred that year befell center Peterson.

UCLA met its first mountain in the form of Maryland. The visiting Terrapins were the defending national champions, and were returning 26 of the previous year's players. Jim Tatum, coach of the year in 1953, had faced Sanders twice when Red was at Vanderbilt and had achieved a split. Running from a sliding-T formation, Maryland hoped to outmuscle UCLA and thereby maintain their still number-one position.

As was expected, the game was rough and low scoring. Each side hammered into the other with determined force and heart. The Bruins scored first in the first quarter, set up by one of the two Maryland goofs the Bruins capitalized on, this a dropped punt-snap that UCLA recovered on the 11. Long Beach's Bob Davenport pogo'ed over the line from close range into the end zone to make it 6-0, the conversion wide.

Both teams were stymied for the rest of the half and well into the third quarter. At this point, the Terrible Terrapins put together a gambling 63-yard touchdown drive that culminated in a touchdown on the second play of the fourth quarter. The successful extra point gave Maryland a 7-6 advantage.

A second Maryland mistake, a shanked punt deep in its

territory, gave UCLA the ball on the 15. Villanueva's chilling third and six run around left side to the one set up another Davenport pogo over the top, putting the game into the record books at 12-7.

The national championship was now up for grabs.

In the following game, the Bruins barely survived a surprising comeback by Washington, 21-20. Up once by the full 21-point margin, UCLA allowed the Huskies to take advantage of Bruin fumblitis, missed tackles, bumblitis, and generally disintegrated play in the last 20 minutes of the game. It was only a missed PAT after the second Husky touchdown that preserved the Bruin win. These two tough games took their toll on the Bruins, as Decker, Debay, Boghosian, Ray, and junior right half John Hermann all briefly added their names to the injury list.

Right half Jim Decker on the move against number-one Maryland in 1954. This 12-7 Bruin victory opened the door for UCLA's National Championship drive.

All this makes the following game even more astounding. In some quarters on the West Coast, the less said about the 1954, 72-0 Bruin victory over Stanford the better. The Indians never stopped trying, relentlessly led by future pro great John Brodie, but all efforts came a cropper, as the Bruins snagged eight Cardinal passes that day. In comparison to Stanford's 203 yards gained passing, UCLA gained 210 yards through those interceptions alone. Furthermore, the Bruins' quarterly score increased at each juncture, 13, 14, 21, and 24.

Stanford coach Chuck Taylor, asked whether he felt UCLA had poured it on, responded, "On the contrary. They used everybody, but you can't stop a team when it gets rolling like that." Sanders came to the same conclusion but honestly added, "I don't believe in deliberately trying not to gain. That wouldn't be fair to either the players or the fans. You naturally rest and save your regulars in game like this, and that's what we did."

UCLA was now ranked third in the nation, directly behind Oklahoma and Wisconsin and just ahead of Ohio State. The Bruins gained two resounding victories in the next two weeks, 61-0 against Oregon State , and 27-6 over California. These two wins, coupled by weak showings by the other three teams in the top four, put UCLA into the number-one spot in both the AP and UPI polls, this in spite of the fact that Oklahoma and Ohio State also remained undefeated. But though the Bruins next breezed past Oregon, 41-0, and UPI still pegged UCLA as number one, a bye before the game with Southern Cal allowed the Buckeyes to sneak past the Bruins in the AP poll to the number-one slot. (In this poll, the Bruins outpointed the Bucks in first-place votes, but when all the votes were tabulated, the count became 2010 for Ohio State, 2003 for UCLA.

During all this squabbling, Southern Cal was quietly forging an impressive record of its own, suffering only one early season loss to Texas Christian, and the Trojans were also in the top 10. Prior to their meeting, Dick Hyland of the *Los Angeles Times* wrote, "The Bruins are a team, the Trojans are a collection of great stars." That would mean a world of difference between the two squads.

The Bruin line so dominated the Trojans there was no doubt in any observer's mind as to the eventual outcome, even

Left end Bob Heydenfelt makes a reception in UCLA's incredible 72-0 victory over Stanford in 1954.

though non-scoring Southern Cal kept the game as close as 7-0 into the third quarter. Like a heavyweight boxer with a second, a third, a fourth wind, the Bruins wore down their opponents until, in the fourth quarter, they hammered for 27 unanswered points.

Southern Cal finished with a net five yards rushing for the day. The great Trojan left half Jon Arnett was constantly swamped. Sanders virtually had two starting-caliber lines at his disposal, so that at every crucial turn he could insert rested and ready replacements to shut down any Trojan threat. In a picture-perfect Los Angeles day with the temperature reaching 110 degrees, the Bruins capped their first perfect season since 1946 with a resounding victory over Southern Cal, 34-0.

The coaches of America agreed that UCLA was the best team in the nation, and so the Bruins remained the number-one team in the UPI poll. The talented Trojans met the AP number-one team, Ohio State, in the Rose Bowl but were unable to do the crosstown campus any favors, going down in defeat to the Buckeyes, 20-7.

Though these polls split, everybody agreed that Red Sanders deserved to be named Coach of the Year, the award now named for his great friend who had passed away, Grantland Rice. Three Bruins received All-America honors: Jack Ellena (consensus), Jim Salsbury, and Bob Davenport. Three more, Villanueva, Boghosian, and Long, also made All-Coast. Plus the Bruins led the nation in most points scored (367) and fewest points given up (40), the latter still the UCLA record.

Red Sanders humbly had said, "I don't subscribe to the theory of the super coach. We all rise and fall, sink or swim in direct proportion to the number and kind of football players on

"The Classic Sweep." Right guard Jim Salsbury (64) and quarterback Terry Debay (40) lead the charge, followed by left guard Hardiman Cureton (60) and fullback Bob Davenport (27) with Villanueva packing the ball.

our teams." Over the locker room in Westwood, Sanders had hung a sign: "Through these portals pass the most spirited athletes in the world—the UCLA Bruins." These were the kinds of players Sanders sought, who would exhibit "The Flaming Bruin Spirit," and who came to Westwood in numbers. And it was only to them, the players, that he felt this highest honor his peers could grant any team was bestowed. As a designation formally recognized by the NCAA in 1936, UCLA became the first team on the West coast to receive it. The UCLA Bruins for 1954 were named the National Champions.

Half-kidding after the 1954 Southern Cal game, Sanders said, "Only bad thing about today is that just about our entire starting lineup was wiped out. We lose 9 of our 11 starters. Guess we'll have to start our rebuilding program, probably tomorrow!" Entering 1955, he knew there was a large degree of difference between the first and second-team lines but felt as a whole his Bruins would be more versatile than his 1954 champions. They would have to be.

As if to prove a point, senior John Hermann was moved from halfback to end, junior Don Shinnick was moved from linebacker to right guard, senior Rommie Loudd from left end

The National Champions.

to right end, and senior Jim Brown from right guard to left guard. Other Bruins returning were seniors Jim Decker at halfback, captain Hardiman Cureton and Gil Moreno at tackle, Steve Palmer at center, Bob Davenport at fullback, and junior Bob Bergdahl at quarterback. Finally, the Bruins sported the excellent junior left half Ronnie Knox, a transfer from Cal, who prompted Sanders to admit after his first game, "(He) stands to be the finest tailback I've ever had."

UCLA entered the season ranked number-one, but Sanders had his own way of dealing with polls, "...ordinarily, preseason ratings good or bad don't mean a thing. If your team has the stuff, and the coaching staff knows what it's doing, you're going to win, regardless of praise or abuse."

Sanders believed, correctly, that Bruin football was on solid ground, that he had established a season-to-season continuity that would annually produce winning teams. A dynasty was in the making. Sanders could even joke about it, "When I first came here, they would have been satisfied to win the city series. Now they are talking about championships every year!"

The Bruins opened with a sound 21-0 victory over Texas A&M, which showcased Knox's pinpoint passing technique. The Aggies came close to scoring at the very outset via a Bruin fumble deep in their territory, but it was quickly squelched as the regenerated Bruin front line arrested the Texans until an interception by center Palmer put it to rest. A famous Bruin squib-kick to the Aggie 11 began the turnaround, and shortly thereafter UCLA began to roll. (This victory tied the consecutive-win streak of 10 originally set in the 1946 season.)

For a return engagement from the previous year, the Bruins traveled east to visit Maryland. Sanders predicted a low-scoring game, with the reserve strength of the Terrapins probably to be a primary factor. Indeed, a lone Maryland touchdown as the second half began was all that was needed to knock UCLA from the top spot in the nation, which would finally go to Bud Wilkinson's mighty Oklahoma Sooners. This 7-0 loss was the first Bruin shutout since the 1950 Cal game.

The Bruins uncorked their offense in the weeks that followed. Washington State was the first victim, as the Bruins ran the Cougars ragged, 55-0. Next to fall was Oregon State, 38-0. But there was more to this last shutout than this score indicates.

Head coaching the Beavers in his rookie season was ex-Bruin assistant coach Tommy Prothro. If the childless Sanders family ever "adopted" a son, he was Prothro. Sanders had first coached him as a boy at Riverside Military Academy in 1936 and kept in close contact during Prothro's college years at Duke University.

Failing to land him as an assistant at Vanderbilt upon his graduation in 1941, Sanders literally plucked Prothro from a semi-pro pitcher's mound in 1946 and sold him on abandoning his potential baseball career to coach under him back at Vandy. That began a nine-year professional association that lasted until the Oregon State job opened up in February 1955.

The deepest personal affection continued to exist between Sanders and Prothro, yet as sideline opposites their roles as pure adversaries were total and complete. Though encounter number one went to the master, the game was left on the field and always would be.

The next game was against Stanford, and Sanders right or wrong decided that Stanford had pointed for the Bruins all season long to retaliate 1954's drubbing. UCLA came out running and scored 21 quick points in the first quarter. Then a combination of Bruin haplessness and Indian perseverence, along with a star performance by junior quarterback John Brodie, almost pulled the rug out from under UCLA, but at 21-13 it stayed the Bruins' day.

UCLA hosted Iowa, and the Hawkeyes, after keeping it close for the first half, could not contain the Bruins' senior back Sam "First Down" Brown, who wound his way through their defense for three touchdowns. Knox contributed by tossing for one touchdown and running for another, and the Bruins took it in a runaway, 33-13.

Against what Sanders had doped out as the weakest Cal team he had ever seen, the Bruins proved him right by shellacking the Bears, 47-0. A singular occurrence took place during this bench-clearing game.

Sanders made a special effort to show just how far the football fortunes at Cal had plummeted by calling a red-shirt player out of the stands to the sidelines, instructing him to go suit up, and then inserted him into the game. This was Sanders' subtle way of indicating that he had essentially run out of players to use against the Bears. Earning a midseason move from the scrubs to the varsity was accomplished (with great fanfare from Sanders) solely on the practice field, but the honor of being the only player in UCLA history to be so elevated during a game goes to fullback Ken Perry.

UCLA put together another shutout the following week against College of the Pacific, 34-0. In this game, Knox quick-kicked his team out of trouble from the 16, the ball eventually coming to rest on the three for an 82-yard credited kick.

Favored to beat the visiting Huskies by as much as 27 points, the Bruins were in for a rude awakening. Knox was knocked out of the game the first time he touched the ball, yet the Bruins scored quickly and easily to open the game at 7-0. Then Washington intercepted a pass and ran it back 61 yards for a touchdown, and a quick march to a score the next time they had the ball put them on top at the half, 14-7.

A field goal to open the second half extended the Husky margin to 17-7. It was at this point that Bob Davenport was reinserted for UCLA, and together with Sam Brown barreled down the field and into the end zone to make it 17-14, midway through the third quarter. The game became stalemated, each team failing to make any headway against the other on into the fourth quarter.

Then, with the game coming to a close and with his back to the wall, Husky quarterback Steve Roarke made the wise decision to accept a safety, making the score 17-16, in order to free-kick his team out of danger from the 20.

As the seconds ticked off in the last minute of play, the Bruins managed to move the ball to the Husky 19. Decker coolly booted the ball 35 yards through the uprights to achieve the heart-stopping victory, 19-17, automatically sending UCLA to the Rose Bowl. Knox's injury was a broken leg, but he was expected to recover in time for January 1.

One game remained. Trojan coach Jess Hill guessed that without Knox his team did not have to concentrate as heavily on the pass. The Bruins still had their two ways to run the ball, up the middle and wide, and that was one too many things for any Trojan to think about.

The tone for this game was unintentionally set when Trojan quarterback Jon Arnett returned an opening kickoff reception 97 yards for a touchdown, only to have it called back because his team failed to line up properly when the ball was kicked off for a second time after the first had gone out of bounds. Kickoff number three was deep into the Trojan end zone. There would be no more flukes to bother the Bruins.

Sam Brown broke the existing single-season rushing record held by Bruin immortal Kenny Washington with this game. Even so, it was a tight, tough contest, the supposedly battered Bruins holding their own against their more healthy opponents, as UCLA won, 17-7. It was the first time UCLA had defeated Southern Cal three consecutive times, something the graduating classes of 1956 from both schools have never forgotten.

The opponent on January 1, 1956, was Michigan State University, headed by Hugh "Duffy" Daugherty. (Big-10 Champion Ohio State was ineligible because of the no-repeat rule still in effect.) Both the Spartans and the Bruins were 8-1 and were ranked number two and number four respectively. Though the Bruins were pegged as six-point underdogs, in all areas of comparison, weight, team size, points scored, and points prevented, they were virtually a perfect match.

Spartan quarterback Earl Morrall's first pass of the game was intercepted by Bruin player of the game Jim Decker, setting up a Bruin touchdown with but three minutes elapsed, "Pogo" Davenport doing the honors from the two. Morrall brought his troops back to score one touchdown in the second

Sam "First Down" Brown on a halfback sweep, led by quarterback Bob Bergdahl (44) and Davenport in UCLA's 1955 victory over Southern Cal, making it three straight against the Trojans.

quarter, a 13-yard pass to left half Clarence Peaks, to send the teams tied, 7-7, into the halftime locker room.

Things remained even throughout the third quarter. But in the fourth, Peaks put the Spartans ahead by passing for a touchdown to left end John Lewis, 67 yards on the play. Ronnie Knox, playing for the first time since breaking his leg against Washington, stepped in to shock the Spartans and the fans by punching the ball down the field from the Bruin 45 in five plays, the tie initiating touchdown coming from a one-yard plunge by senior fullback Doug Peters.

With five minutes to play, the Spartans took the ensuing kickoff and Morrall, Peaks, and fullback Gerry Planutis rapidly marched the team down to the Bruin 22 before stalling. From this point the tie-breaking field goal was attempted, but the 30 yarder was wide, and it was UCLA's ball at that spot with but minutes remaining.

Then the game went bonkers.

Mass confusion set in among the Bruins, who huddled frantically, not knowing what to do. An unidentified player stepped away from the huddle, looking to the sidelines for...something. Instinctively, line coach Jim Myers cocked his arm as if to indicate "pass." Whammo! Fifteen-yard penalty, unsportsmanlike conduct, coaching from the sidelines, moving the ball back to the seven.

The ball was finally snapped, Knox faded back into the end zone, and a horde of Spartans came streaming in after him; desperately trying to avoid a game-losing safety, Knox let the ball fly, and it hit Bruin tackle Gil Moreno. Whammo! Ineligible receiver, and the Bruins found themselves second down with the ball on the one.

Though the word was sent in from the bench for Knox to throw the ball again and stall out the game, he took it upon his own to quick-kick the ball out, but not having kicked a ball since that Washington game he got off a poor kick. To add insult to injury, normally impeccable guard Hardiman Cureton charged down the field, assumed that the Spartan receiver was not the one to catch the ball, and blocked him. Whammo! Interference, and it was the Spartans' ball on the Bruin 25 with less than two minutes to play.

The madhouse continued. Two plays, two fumbles, two

Spartan recoveries, yet this actually crawled the ball up to the 19. They took too long to get off the next play. Whammo!Delay of the game, and the ball was moved back to the 24. Seven seconds remained on the clock. On a *hunch*, Daugherty called for Spartan end Dave Kaiser to attempt the 31-yard field goal. Not only was it his first try of the year, or in his career, it was the first successful field goal for Michigan State all season! And so the Spartans defeated the Bruins, 17-14.

Bruin All-Americas that year rose by four! Cureton (consensus), Davenport, Loudd, and Sam Brown. Though all this talent made this Rose Bowl one of the most exciting on record, it still left UCLA winless after four trips to the big one. It was also Sanders' second Rose Bowl loss in as many games.

Fate would see to it that he never would return.

Between the 1955 and 1956 seasons, one of the most incredible debacles in college football history began to unravel. In its wake, schools, teams, and lives would be adversely affected, some permanently. It came to be known as the PCC Scandal, and the primary victim would be UCLA.

It all came down to money. The Pacific Coast Conference's rules regulating aid to athletes, sarcastically called "The Purity Code" because when money and amateur athletics mix the ugly word "professional" crops up, were unbelievably

Left half Ronnie Knox looks for a receiver in the 1956 Rose Bowl against Michigan State, won by the Spartans 17-14.

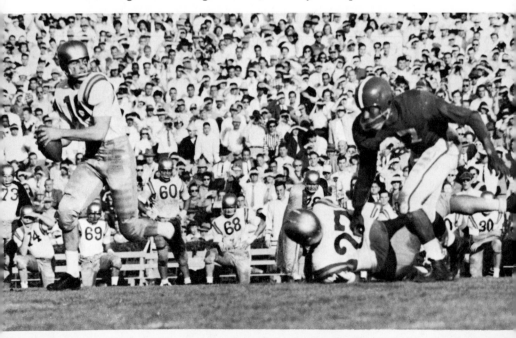

silly. A football player had to attend class, study, and practice football, plus work 50 hours a month on campus to earn $75. Any industrious student-athlete could hold another job, to supply whatever the difference was between the meager $75 allowed by the conference and the "actual" cost of his room, board, and incidentals.

Not only was this 50-hours-a-month job open to widespread abuse, the supplementary job off-campus was in most cases simply nonexistent, the money covertly provided by alums and booster groups. This cheating took place to varying degrees at *every* school, was tacitly accepted by the entire conference, and as long as everybody kept their mouths shut no one would get hurt.

This mystifying code was written by the dean of law at Oregon, Orlando J. Hollis, a dominant voice in the PCC for years. It was patently geared to neutralize the advantages that the four California schools and Washington would have over the northwest schools located in less densely populated areas (obviously making violations all the more likely). Placing a further burden on UCLA was the lack of on-campus dormitory housing, enjoyed throughout the Northwest, which meant that Bruin players had to take off-campus apartments at a much higher cost.

(Only the Southeastern Conference had the foresight as early as 1935 to establish full scholarships, providing tuition, room, board, and books. Conceived by Dr. John J. Tigert, president of the University of Florida, this realistic approach was in time adopted by every conference in the nation—except the PCC.)

Then Red Sanders came along. Not only did his brilliant success on the playing field rankle the Northwestern schools, but he refused to subject himself and his players to a system that required them to lie and cheat. He determined that $40 extra would be just about right, and that's what he provided his players, starting fullbacks and red-shirts alike, and he did not try to keep it a secret. Sanders refused to have his players treated as second-class students simply because they happened to be athletes who chose to play for UCLA.

It was only a matter of time before the hypocrisy of the conference-wide situation was exposed. When it was, Red

Sanders, the only totally honest person in relation to it, became the target of abuse, vilification, and job subversion. The nascent UCLA dynasty had to be destroyed.

John Cherberg, head coach at Washington, was fired in late January of 1956. In retaliation, he immediately blew the whistle on the slush fund that was providing illicit aid to the Husky players.

The can of worms had been opened.

For no apparent reason, (possibly linked to the scene in Seattle), on March first an ex-Bruin trying to make it on the Cal Bear team admitted that he and others had received that $40 per month in illegal aid while at UCLA.

In response to these "irregularities," the PCC eventually placed Washington on two years' probation, all athletic teams ineligible for any championships or postseason play. UCLA was summarily placed on three years' probation with similar restrictions. Both schools were heavily fined. Furthermore, the commission also decided to cause every remaining 1955 Bruin player, varsity and freshman alike, to be penalized additionally in their senior years, as detailed later.

Then it got dirty.

J. Miller Leavy, deputy district attorney for Los Angeles, revealed the existence of a slush fund operation at Southern Cal. Leavy further disclosed an operation at Cal administering fake job situations. And it was only May.

Stanford's athletic director Al Masters allowed there were some "minor" athletic code infractions on The Farm, but later, because of immunity granted for secret testimony rendered to the governor by several Indian players, Stanford completely avoided penalization. Masters then aligned himself with the Northwest Schools in meting out punishments to the "guilty."

Southern Cal's football team, on the other hand, was slapped with a two years' probation similar to Washington's, a penalty later increased by the NCAA to include all Trojan athletics. Cal was fined.

The conference punishment handed down to the seniors on both the 1956 Bruin *and* Trojan squads was eligibility to play only half the season, five games, to be played consecutively. It was blatantly vindictive, an outrage, completely irrational, and more than anything else spelled the eventual doom of the PCC.

The conference had become entrenched, implacable, and unrepresentative. Its dogged determination to insist that its manipulative, antiquated Purity Code was honorable and enforceable created an atmosphere of contempt and disillusionment among its most important members. A campaign by representatives and nonofficials for UCLA and Southern Cal, demanding the schools withdraw from the PCC, began in earnest.

Such was how the 1956 football season got underway.

Just more than 50 players turned up to begin fall practice. There were no scrimmages before the season began. The seniors had the depressing chore of deciding which five games they wanted to play. Their decision, made under the advisement of the coaching staff, was to spread themselves across the season, two playing the first five games, most playing the first five conference games, and the rest playing out the last five.

Conceptually this plan seemed to balance out the penalty's impact, but it resulted in some internal confusion and hurt feelings when a sophomore or junior felt his "earned" position had to be relinquished simply because a senior became available. As a final blow, Ronnie Knox abandoned the team to play pro ball in Canada.

With but two seniors on the squad, Sanders hoped to achieve a split in the first two games. Utah was first, and he showcased his new sophomores, notably end Dick Wallen, tackle Jim Dawson, guard Clint Whitfield, right half Don Duncan, and fullback Barry Billingham. The Bruins secured a 13-0 halftime lead and hung on to beat the Utes 13-7.

The following week UCLA traveled to mighty Michigan, and it was babes to the slaughter. The Wolverines had too much going for them, great players like fullbacks Jim Dickey and John Herrnstein, end Ron Kramer, and quarterback Jim Van Pelt. The 42-13 defeat speaks for itself.

The Bruins as a team bounced back from this harsh loss with fresh determination. As they faced their first conference game, many seniors rejoined the ranks. The opponent was Oregon. There was not a player on that team who did not recognize how much Oregon's Dean Hollis had worked to tear down his team and his coach. Captain Don Birren scrawled on the blackboard before the game, "NO VICTORY FOR DEAN

113

HOLLIS.''

Wallen recovered a Duck fumble early in the fourth quarter; Long then converted it into the game's only touchdown. The Bruins beat the Ducks, 6-0.

The Bruins had an easier time with Washington State, defeating the Cougars, 28-0.

Next came Cal, and credit for UCLA's success over the Bears goes to assistant coach Ray Nagel, a senior on Red's first Bruin team in 1949, who almost pinpointed the Bear passing attack, enabling Bruins Wallen and senior end Pete O'Garro to score a touchdown apiece on interceptions, with a third interception also nabbed by junior halfback Lou Elias.

The star Bear quarterback Joe Kapp, after Cal had spotted UCLA 14 points in the first five minutes, engineered two great drives to tie the game. But Wallen's tie-breaking interception score put the damper on the Cal spirits, and the lighter Bruins so outcharged the Bears on the front lines it was only a matter of time before the game was decided in Westwood's favor, 34-20. This game was the last for seniors quarterback Bob Bergdahl and left half Doug Bradley.

Oregon State, Corvalis, Tommy Prothro, running back Paul Lowe, and Beaver heart and desire all added up to UCLA's first conference defeat in 20 games. Having done a superb job a la Sanders in creating a winner out of seemingly nowhere, Prothro's single-wing team, led by the ever-threatening (and future pro great) Lowe, stabbed sharply through the Bruin line, winning, 21-7. The pupil had evened things up with the master and took his team to the Rose Bowl.

The most coveted game for the Bruins lay directly ahead. For the first time in almost two decades, it was not the game against Southern Cal. It was Stanford.

At one point during the early goings of the "scandal," it was learned that if UCLA fired Sanders and athletic director Wilbur Johns, leniency would be shown the school, including the reinstatement of the players' eligibility. This shocking extortion attempt was unceremoniously refused. It was a poorly kept secret that Stanford's Al Masters perpetrated this proposal, and his general efforts to erode the Bruin football program were legion. That Stanford "stayed clean" was perhaps the most galling aspect of all. Pointedly, this game marked the heartbreaking farewell of seniors guard Birren, right half Chuck Hollaway, tackle Preston Dills, and O'Garro.

Though there were attempts to disguise it, to subdue it, there was that gnawing emotion of revenge against the unscathed Indians. On the Monday before the game, addressing his team on the practice field, Sanders announced that the Bruins would defeat the favored Indians on Saturday. Sanders had never predicted a game before—the players knew a precedent had been broken. They set about their preparation for this game with deep determination. This game was for Red.

The crowd at the Coliseum was expected to top 75,000 and did. The Indians were tabbed by 14 points, as they sported the star players quarterback John Brodie and tackle Paul Wiggin. The Bruins jumped out ahead of the Indians, 14-0, in the first eight minutes, First, the great junior Bruin center Jim Matheny tackled Stanford fullback Lou Valli to cause a fumble, recovered by junior end Hal Smith on the Indian 20. Five plays later junior left half Ed Griffin scored for the Bruins, Duncan kicking the PAT. Minutes later Smith blocked a Brodie punt, picked off midair by O'Garro, which he ran back the 42 yards for the second Bruin touchdown. Senior quarterback Don Shinnick kicked what would turn out to be the deciding point.

Brodie was spelled by Jack Douglas, who drove the Indians to a second quarter touchdown. Brodie returned to lead Stanford to a touchdown in the third quarter, but Bruin Shinnick burst through the line to block what would have been the tying extra point.

Throughout the game and especially from that point on, the Bruin defense stunted, it swarmed to the Indian runners Valli and Gordy Young, it stifled Brodie, and it kept the game on ice. Final score, UCLA 14, Stanford 13.

Sanders admitted, ''That's the most deserved victory I've ever seen a bunch of players earn. I've never witnessed a greater team victory. All things considered, that was the finest win I have ever enjoyed.''

One magic word, more than anything else, brought about this great Bruin victory: ''Omaha!'' The Bruin coaching staff had studied the Stanford game films and detected Brodie's Achilles' heel. Whenever a run was called, Brodie stood behind

115

Red Sanders doing what he loved best—teaching.

the center with his feet parallel, but when it was to be a pass Brodie unconsciously moved either his right or his left foot slightly back. That was the cue. The instant Brodie stuck that foot back, the Bruin linebackers began to shout "Omaha!," up stepped an eight-man front, and the defense would swarm straight for number 12, and so harrassed the brilliant John Brodie all game long.

The Bruins defeated Washington the following week, 13-9, coming from a 9-0 first half deficit to take it via Shinnick and Smith touchdowns. A game with Kansas followed, in which Bruin sophomore left half Kirk Wilson set a PCC single-game punting record by averaging 58 yards a punt, and the underdog Bruins put a 13-0 victory over the Jayhawks.

In the game between the local insurgents, UCLA was unable to surmount a late 10-0 Southern Cal lead and lost, 10-7. That three-point margin came from the first successful Trojan field goal ever kicked against UCLA, by Ells Kissinger.

The Bruins finished with a 6-3 record and a tie for second place in the conference. Sanders was extremely proud of this team, seeing it reach far beyond its normal potential in spite of the circumstances that might have had a devastating effect on its morale. Sanders said of his Bruins, "If I was going to coach a football team that was my last team of all, this would be the team. It had been the greatest season for any team I have been associated with."

Obviously, to the Northwest presidents and faculty representatives, restricting UCLA's seniors to only half a season was not enough to keep the Bruins down. Therefore, crueler penalties must be devised. (The conference coaches were not a party to these procedings, and their joint recommendations for leniency were flatly ignored.)

For 1957, it was decided not to allow the Bruins or Trojans to field *any* seniors. All appeals were denied. There would be no reconsideration. It was the most merciless act possible, based solely on spite, and still is unforgiven. The fact that so many players' prospects for furthering their sports careers were at stake was ignored. Center Jim Matheny was one such player whose brilliance at UCLA pointed to a pro career, but whose inability to play his entire senior year caused irreversible damage to his chances.

The opening game had Florida penciled in, but an outbreak of influenza on the Gators forced a cancellation. Replaced with the Air Force Academy, the Bruins made off with an easy 47-0 victory. The next week the Bruins hosted Big-10 Illinois, and the hosts put on another game-winning performance, beating the Illini, 16-6.

For the first time since 1948, Oregon beat UCLA. It was, as so often was the case at Oregon's Multnamoh Stadium, a sloshy mudbath. The Ducks scooted around the Bruins with relative ease, as they earned a 21-0 victory. Oregon would go on to represent the PCC in the Rose Bowl, as conference co-champion Oregon State was ineligible (no repeat rule).

Against Washington, it was Dick Wallen's turn to shine, as

117

he made one of the most spectacular pass receptions (repeating a similar feat against Illinois two weeks earlier), a one-hander of a ball thrown 'way over his head. UCLA outeverythinged the Huskies, 19-0.

Into town came Tommy Protho's strong Oregon State team. The Uclans remembered the loss from 1956 and the talkative Beavers who needled their opponents gloatingly at the time. The Bruins punctured the nationally number-seven ranked Beavers, 26-7, Kirk Wilson peeling off long punts, one a 71-yard quick-kick, and Wallen enjoyed another fine day.

More than anyone else, Tommy Prothro respected the remarkable coaching job Sanders was performing this year. To have his championship-caliber Beavers defeated by the seniorless Bruins was almost miraculous, deepening the pride each shared in the other's accomplishments. The master had gone up 2-1 over the pupil. There would never be another rematch.

The Bruins had been at a fevered pitch against Oregon State and were ready for a letdown. It came against Stanford, who under the quarterbacking of Jack Douglas defeated UCLA in Palo Alto, 20-6.

UCLA squeaked by the much more powerful Cal Bears, 16-14, and put in a similar performance in a 19-13 victory over Washington State. With the College of the Pacific, the Bruins were faced with a decidedly lesser opponent, which brought on a case of listlessness. The choppy 21-0 win struck down Kirk Wilson, who missed the last game.

For Southern Cal, Sanders once again predicted to the team during practice that it would win. The Bruins had amazingly no trouble picking apart the Trojans for a 20-9 victory. Sophomore Don Long almost single-handedly defeated Troy, throwing for two touchdowns, running the third in himself, intercepting an errant Trojan pass when things were still tight, and even scoring a safety.

The Bruins finished 7-2, and tied for the conference co-championship with Oregon and Oregon State. There was even a consensus All-America selection, end Dick Wallen. Once again, Sanders was courted by another school, Texas A&M trying to replace the departed Bear Bryant. Sanders decided to stay. He felt he had a job to finish in Westwood and also owed his allegiance to the many fine administrators and faculty members who stood behind him during his ordeal.

Sanders' fight against the PCC was dynamically effective in bringing about its self-destruction. As the most quoted coach in the West, his opportunities to speak out against the injustices rendered by the conference presidents were plentiful and rich. "If they want good, decent Americans they should be emphasizing football, not subjecting it to continual petty attacks."

Alums and the general public rallied to his cause. Finally, the Board of Regents of the University of California, representing both UCLA and Cal, followed immediately by the Board of Trustees for the University of Southern California, gave notice of their withdrawal from the Pacific Coast Conference on December 13, 1957, effective July 1, 1959.

It was over. Sanders deserved the final word. "It was the only thing to do."

The Bruins for 1958 were beginning to get their minds back on football, preparing to assemble for the beginning of fall practice, when they received a shock more profound than any penalty might be. The emotional and personal toll from fighting the Purity Code, from piecing together two winning teams in spite of the penalties, plus a personal life-style one might characterize as demanding, had taken their toll on their coach.

On August 14, 1958, Henry Russell "Red" Sanders died of a heart attack in Hollywood.

Dick Hyland of the *Los Angeles Times* wrote about his friend: "He was the greatest coach, teacher and leader of men I have ever known....Red Sanders had the ability to give and the ability to permit others to give. Those things are basic to genius."

Author and screenwriter Paul I. Wellman gave the eulogy at the funeral and put into words what these last two years of Red's coaching career meant:

"When he was stripped of his best by what I shall always regard as an act malicious and unjust, he gathered about him the boys he had left and with them went on to teach all men what real coaching was, what real inspiration was, what real leadership was, what undying determination was."

Sportswriter Al Wolf often used a phrase in these last years in reference to Sanders. To him, Red was "The Wizard of

Westwood." Though John Wooden would coach Bruin basketball to never-to-be-equaled 10 National Championships and was also more permanently so dubbed, Sanders was the first. His last two seasons stand as evidence.

Sanders once outlined his formula for coaching success to Fred Russell as: "Material, 80%; luck in injuries and weather, 10; coaching and strategy, 9; master-minding and magic, 1." Red took more advantage of (and reveled in) that last one that meets the eye.

Red Sanders instilled in his players "The Flaming Bruin Spirit." His 66-19-1 record at UCLA shows how brightly that spirit burned. In December 1956 he proudly said, "We've created a kind of a football heaven at UCLA, and anybody that's not in heaven is not happy."

That's all there is to it.

CHAPTER 8
1958-1963

Red Sanders gave one of his assistant coaches, who was on the verge of accepting a head coaching spot, some sage advice: "Never follow the coach who led them out of the woods." The man hired to replace Sanders himself, however, had no choice. George Dickerson was that man. His story as head coach is a short one, ended midseason his first year by a breakdown brought on by physical and nervous exhaustion.

Fall practice was approaching when Sanders died. Normal preparatory work naturally halted immediately. Athletic director Wilbur Johns was forced to come up with a new head coach without delay, and there was no time to seek an outsider.

The assistant coaches found themselves uncomfortably jockeying against one another for the job. George Dickerson, who by 1956 had become the senior assistant on Sanders' staff, emerged the "winner."

Dickerson was the second alumnus to rise to the head coaching position, Bert LaBrucherie being the first. Born July 27, 1913, in Galion, Ohio, the family moved to Los Angeles in 1922. He attended Fairfax High, then played at UCLA under Bill Spaulding, was captain of the 1936 team, and graduated in 1937. After five years of coaching prep ball in northern California, he enlisted in the navy, served four years through World War II, and was discharged in 1946 with the rank of lieutenant.

By now married to Bruin coed Betty Axline (1936), Dickerson joined LaBrucherie's staff as freshman coach and was the only assistant Sanders retained when he came West in 1949. Joining the varsity staff in 1950, Dickerson moved up to the senior aide spot when Jim Myers took the head job at Iowa

George Dickerson, head coach for a brief period in 1958, the second Bruin player to later serve as head coach at UCLA.

State in 1956. Two years later, he was head coach.

The team assembled for play in 1958 was highly complex. Sanders' death was singularly traumatic, as was the subsequent uncertainty of who the next head coach would be. Then came the adjustment between the players and an ex-assistant who becomes head—they cannot be as familiar with one another anymore. There was also the anxiety of whether the PCC would grant the seniors any playing time.

When the seniors were allowed five games to be played consecutively (as in 1956), there was again that problem of how their eligibility should be distributed, break the players up through the season, play just the first five conference games, or the first or last five games period. (Plus UCLA, Cal, and Southern Cal had officially withdrawn from the PCC, so this was their "lame duck" season.)

Any *one* of these conditions can disturb a team's morale and performance. But the problems were not over.

Dickerson briefly manifested the strain from the shock of Sanders' death compounded by his having to then essentially fill his legendary shoes. Fed up with a certain Cal recruiter's continually blatant tampering with several quality players fully committed to UCLA, he collared a sportswriter, flew up to Berkeley, and stormed unannounced into Cal head coach Pete Eliott's office to demand that it stop. (As a result UCLA did not lose a single player to California.)

This episode, as he intended for emphasis, was splashed in the newspapers. To the more restrictive minds above him, Dickerson, admittedly a red-blooded kind of guy, had involved himself in a matter that should have been left to the higher representatives from the respective athletic departments. He was quietly censured.

Stretched to the breaking point, he was hospitalized the night before practice opened. Assistant Bill Barnes was unofficially appointed head coach for the short time Dickerson would be away.

The decision for the penalized seniors to play only the first five games was made. It was felt that staggering the players throughout the season as was done in 1956 was detrimental to team morale, causing friction between the players who felt they had secured their starting assignments and the seniors who upon their reinstatement in some cases automatically got their jobs back. This way the seniors expeditiously played out their skein, giving the players stepping into the void more time to prepare for their positions. Technically the team opened at full strength from the 8-2 team the year before, with a few key junior college transfers added for support.

The problems were not over.

Dickerson returned and was at the helm for the opener against Pittsburgh. Favored by as much as seven points, the Bruins lost at home 27-6. The only highlight was the introduction of sophomore transfer Bill Kilmer, who scored the lone UCLA touchdown on a reception from senior left half Don

Long.

The team recovered its composure the following week, traveling to Champaign-Urbana, and defeated tough Illinois, 18-14. This game featured a 98-yard interception-runback for a touchdown by halfback senior Phil Parslow to set a new Bruin record, and the first (unsuccessful) attempts to capitalize on the new two-point conversion option. But a trip to Oregon State brought another defeat, 14-0.

The problems were not over.

Arduous travel, unexplainable losses, and intense pressure began to hammer at Dickerson. He was caught in the throes of mental exhaustion and stifled emotional anguish. The veneer of strength, the show of fortitude, merely disguised the true condition, the manic-depressive episode he was enduring.

The day before the Florida game, a grim Bill Barnes announced to the team that Dickerson again was hospitalized but soon would be back. Barnes again would be the acting head coach.

The Bruins lost to the Gators, 21-14. Making their last appearance before their hometown fans were Long and Wallen, the former passing for 14 of 16 on the night, the latter catching 10, two for touchdowns.

That Monday the team learned that Dickerson was gone for the year. In reality he was never to return to coaching at UCLA.

He was treated at UCLA Medical Center and since recovery has had a very successful business career. He has maintained a continued interest in UCLA athletic and academic programs. George Dickerson remains, as always, proud to be a Bruin.

There was no time for Bill Barnes to prepare himself for his new role. It was thrust upon him; he was forced to cope with all that his predecessor had plus the added burden that faced any assistant who rises to the head spot within any program. But there was no time for all that. There was a game to play that Saturday, an important one against Washington. Worrying about team psychology would have to wait. There was a game to play.

Barnes, looking for something to snap the team out of its doldrums, remembered that Sanders had tinkered with a formation for use against Washington in 1956 (but did not), briefly trying it out during the spring. It was a spread formation he had called the "W" formation for the occasion. Barnes resurrected it and sprang it on the Huskies in Seattle weather approaching typhoon level and completely surprised the opponent. The Bruins tabbed a 20-0 victory, making it seven straight over Washington.

But this also marked the early end to the Bruin careers of Dick Wallen, elected consensus All-America while a junior; Don Long; center Dick Butler; tackle Jim Dawson; back Steve Gertsman; and guard Clint Whitfield. This contrived attrition, plus injuries incurred by Kilmer and other players, with more on the way, was going to make for a long season.

A string of losses followed, against Stanford, Washington State, and Cal. The lone remaining victory came against Oregon, once the victor over Southern Cal by 25-0, as the Bruins beat the Ducks, 7-3, untainted senior fullback Kirk Wilson lofting two passes to senior halfback Phil Parslow to set up junior fullback Ray Smith's come-from-behind game-winning touchdown in the fourth quarter. A 15-15 tie with Southern Cal finished out the year, giving this final broken season a 3-6-1 total.

Barnes' introduction to the general public as head coach of the Bruins, abrupt as it was, offered small opportunity for anyone to get to learn about the man in advance.

They would have found in William Fletcher Barnes a trait of sincere concern for his players' welfare and a deep-rooted understanding of single-wing football. Born in Missouri in 1918, his family moved to Memphis, Tennessee, when he was a boy. There he grew up. He played at the University of Tennessee under the eminent General Bob Neyland, the great tactician of the single wing.

As a blocking back, Barnes played on the Volunteer team that faced Oklahoma in the 1939 Orange Bowl game. Though a hamstring injury prevented him from playing, he was on the sidelines when the Vols made their first appearance in the Rose Bowl in 1940.

Barnes then coached one year as a freshman assistant under Neyland while finishing his work toward his B.S. degree in education, granted in 1941. He entered the army during

125

Coach Bill Barnes, who guided the Bruins from midway through the 1958 season to 1964.

World War II in 1942, and in four years rose to major, earning Silver and Bronze Stars and the Legion of Merit. Discharged in 1946, he assisted at Arkansas for four years before being tapped by Sanders to become part of his staff at UCLA in 1950. Barnes' permanent installation as head coach became effective as of the 1959 season.

His new job came at a turning point in the UCLA sports program. On July 1, 1959, UCLA entered into its new life as a member of the Athletic Association of Western Universities, officially severing relations with Oregon, Oregon State, and Washington State. In order to preserve continuity with their past relationship to the Rose Bowl, the major powers from the old PCC that formed the AAWU, UCLA, Cal, Southern Cal,

Washington, and later Stanford, established their exclusivity with the "Granddaddy of Them All." The AAWU then also became to be known as "The Big Five."

Looking into the future, the university sought a national athletic consciousness, intent on building the kind of reputation major independents had enjoyed for years. Many exciting cross-country home-and-away series were initiated with like-minded schools, Syracuse, Air Force Academy, and as begun in 1958 especially Pittsburgh.

This 1959 step meant UCLA finally was free from restrictions, penalties, emotional shocks, and enmity toward its fellow conference opponents. With Cal (last year of no repeat) and Southern Cal (lingering NCAA penalties) ineligible, UCLA had optimistic designs on reaching the Rose Bowl.

The all-around excellence of junior half Bill Kilmer triggered the Bruin attack. The team included senior and captain fullback Ray Smith; juniors half Gene Gaines, center Harry Baldwin, and end Marv Luster; sophomore half Bobby Smith; and seniors half Skip Smith, end Trusse Norris, and quarterback Bart Phillips. Also on this team was junior end Earl Smith, making it four Smiths on one squad, none related.

After opening with a 0-0 tie against Rose Bowl-bound Purdue and a last-minute loss to Pittsburgh, 25-21, UCLA picked up its first victory in the AAWU over Cal, 19-12. It took five exchanges of the lead before a third score put it away for Westwood, Ray Smith's 49-yard scoring rush sandwiched between two short Kilmer bursts for touchdowns.

Air Force shocked the Bruins with a 20-7 victory, and then Washington, who would meet Purdue January 1, flattened UCLA 23-7. The Bruins reversed themselves by overwhelming Stanford, 55-13, the third most points ever scored by UCLA against the Tribe.

In a game pitting future pro opponents Kilmer and Roman Gabriel, UCLA defeated a hardy North Carolina State team, 21-12. Star Bruin back Skip Smith enjoyed a 71-yard touchdown romp to open the second quarter, scoring what would be the winning points.

By the time The Big Game arrived, UCLA had managed to pull up to a 3-3-1 record. Southern Cal was 8-0 and ranked number two in the nation. The Trojans were favored by 10.

Playing only the second half, Billy Kilmer stole the show.

Though he did not score, Kilmer's clutch running and passing, including a 46-yard pass that was intercepted but returned to the Bruins on the spot via pass interference to set up the game's only touchdown, kept the Trojans floored. A Bruin come-back effort plus an inspired defense snuffed out Southern Cal's National Championship hopes, 10-3.

After an uninspirational win over Utah, UCLA still had one more undefeated team to face, hosting the number-one ranked Syracuse Orangemen in the final game of the season. But the New Yorkers took note of what befell the Trojans and were not about to be caught lightheaded, downing the Bruins, 36-8.

Though the loss to Washington kept them from the Rose Bowl, UCLA's victories over the other three conference members put it into a tie for the Big-Five Championship. Bill Barnes was off on the right foot.

Bruins returning to make 1960 a year of promise were seniors right end Earl Smith and fullback Skip Smith, left halfs junior Bob Smith and sophomore Rob Smith, maintaining four unrelated Smiths on the roster. Also on this squad were captain and senior center Harry Baldwin; seniors left end Marv Luster, left guard Jack Metcalf, left half Billy Kilmer, and right half Gene Gaines; juniors right tackle Marshall Shirk, guard Tom Paton, left tackles Steve Bauwens and Foster Andersen, and quarterback Bob Stevens. Sophomores making their presence felt were left half Ezell Singleton, fullback Mitch Dimkich, right tackle Phil Oram, quarterback Joe Zeno, and right half Kermit Alexander.

College football began to modernize in 1960. Illegal coaching from the sidelines had been ignored for years. A step toward ending this hypocrisy was taken when a "one-man free substitution" rule was added, allowing a coach to shuttle one player in and out between plays as he saw fit.

Barnes intelligently took advantage of this rule right from the start, juggling Kilmer and Singleton in the season opener against the favored Pitt Panthers. With 33 seconds left, a two-point conversion try was good for an 8-7 Bruin victory.

Though an eventual 7-2-1 overall record was a great improvement from the previous season, the Bruins finished third in a five-team conference, suffering key losses to Washington and Southern Cal. Even so, the season was not without many stirring moments, most provided by UCLA's All-America from Azusa, Bill Kilmer.

Kilmer threw for three touchdowns and ran for one more in a second consecutive tie with Purdue, 27-27. The loss to Washington, 10-8 was followed by a big win over Stanford, 26-8.

In a second match-up with Roman Gabriel-led North Carolina State, though both Kilmer and Gabriel had an off-night, the Bruins beat the Wolfpack, 7-0.

Kilmer played only 19 minutes against Cal but helped bring about all four Bruins scores, as UCLA pulled even in the series record with Berkeley, 15-15-1, with this 28-0 victory. After a 22-0 breeze over the Air Force Academy, the Bruins faced hard-luck Southern Cal, but new coach John McKay made his Big Game debut an upsetting success, the Bruins losing to an injury-laden but gutty Trojan team, 17-6.

After another easy go (though played in a snowstorm) over Utah, 16-9, the Bruins regained national face by beating Cotton Bowl-bound Duke on national television. Kilmer's performance put him on top of the national total offensive list, the Bruins beating the Blue Devils, 27-6.

Barnes so far had gone bowlless in his first two years. The memorable 1961 season would change that. The resurgence of junior right half Kermit Alexander, plagued with injuries the previous year, would be the primary catalyst. Other juniors to see action included left tackle Tony Fiorentino, right end Tom Gutman, and fullback Mitch Dimkich.

Yet there was no question this was a senior-stocked team, the last recruits from the Sanders years. They included left end Don Vena; left tackle Foster Andersen; left guard Frank Macari; center, captain, and All-America Ron Hull; right guard Tom Paton; right tackle Marshall Shirk; right end Chuck Hicks; quarterback Bob Stevens; left half Bobby Smith; and fullback Almos Thompson.

The Bruins entered the season ranked number eight in the nation. Three opening away games punched the air out of that balloon.

The first was against the Air Force Academy, the Bruins

Billy Kilmer, electrifying the Coliseum in the 1960 17-6 loss to Southern Cal.

presenting a most formidable front line that so dominated the weaker Falcons it was no contest at 19-6. The next game was in Ann Arbor. In what looked on paper to be an even match was anything but, as the Wolverines took advantage of a slew of Bruin miscues, Michigan winning, 29-6.

The following week found the Bruins in Columbus facing Ohio State. In this first meeting between the two schools, Woody Hayes' Buckeyes struggled with the Bruins but still managed a 13-3 victory, thanks to outstanding performances by future pro stars left half Paul Warfield and right end Matt Snell.

The home opener found the twice-stung Bruins ready for easier handiwork with Vanderbilt. A porous Bruin secondary allowed the Commodores to score three touchdowns through the air, but the grueling Bruin ground game earned four touchdowns and a 28-21 UCLA victory. The last opponent before league play, Pittsburgh, tried the aerial route but found an awakened secondary that repulsed the Panther challenge and won it for UCLA, 20-6.

Big Five opponent Stanford fell, 20-0. The jolt of this game was Kermit Alexander's reception of a missed field goal try, taken on the 13-yard line with three seconds to go in the first half, which he blithely ran back for Bruin touchdown number two.

Cal was the next victim, an easy 35-15 victory. It was not a pretty game, as the frustrated Bears and the hot-tempered Bruins mixed it up throughout the game, and two near-riots erupted in the waning moments of the game. University of California president Clark Kerr later demanded and received apologies from both teams.

"Alexander the Great" had a field day in a Bruin breather against Texas Christian, as he teamed with tosser Bobby Smith to unveil a formidable passing attack for the first time that season. The 28-7 victory suddenly seemed to put a lot of pieces together, front-line work, a potent rushing backfield, a tested defensive secondary, and apparently a way to score through the air.

Then Washington happened. After the visiting Huskies ran back the opening kickoff 90 yards for a touchdown, UCLA got

Halfback Kermit Alexander "The Great," assisted by fullback Mitch Dimkitch's leveling block, during his remarkable performance against Stanford in UCLA's 20-0 victory in 1961.

pass happy and the Huskies took advantage of it with three interceptions, also recovering two fumbles. The Bruins fell, 17-13, though a dropped pass in the end zone in the last minute of play almost pulled it out.

The Bruins had fallen to second place behind once-tied Southern Cal. This Big Game was the first time since 1952 both teams would play for the right to the Rose Bowl. But Alexander had suffered a shoulder pointer during the Husky game severe enough to prevent him from playing.

It was apparent that his services were essential if UCLA was to prevail over Southern Cal. Though it was a great physical sacrifice for him to practice that week and play in the game, he felt there could be no way to pass up a chance to help beat the Trojans. "Since I live here, if I don't take every opportunity to beat them, then I've got to live with that for the next year." And the pain? "After the first couple of blows, I just didn't care about it any more," Alexander recalled. "But...as long as I was out there, somebody was going to pay for my discomfort!"

It rained, and as Paul Zimmerman in the *Los Angeles Times* described it, UCLA's offensive output became "4 yards and a shower of mud." But the hard-and-fast Bruin line proved a stubborn wall, and though the Trojans were up 7-3 at halftime, the Bruin line was beginning to take its toll. Southern Cal never got closer than the Bruin 23, except when Trojan junior fullback Pete Beathard scored on a 52-yard quick-kick return that did not involve charging into the Bruin defensive front.

Then well into the third quarter, Bruin sophomore left end Mel Profit partially deflected a Beathard pass into the hands of senior tackle Joe Bauwens, who ran it back to the Trojan 33. The Bruins finally made the winning score from the six, Bobby Smith doing the honors on a left sweep. Later, a Trojan field goal attempt that hit the crossbar and bounced back kept it from a heartbreaking tie. It was close, 10-7, but it was enough. UCLA was in the Rose Bowl.

The agreement between the Big-10 and the Rose Bowl, first signed in 1947, had ended with the game in 1961. Though offered the spot, Big-10 Champion Ohio State declined. There was some talk of inviting Alabama, but UCLA's black players threatened a complete boycott as a protest to the racial situation in the South at the time. Alexander, who was to become a top leader in the Los Angeles black community, was most adamant on this point. The offer was not tendered.

UCLA's heritage of racial equality stretches back to its very inception. In 1919 a Bruin end Frank Williamson was black, and the varsity of 1920 also included black Jeff Brown. Of the major football schools in Los Angeles, UCLA was alone in embracing blacks until the mid-fifties. The richness of this tradition of total equality can be found on the rosters of Bruins through the thirties, names like Rahbar, Aguiar, Zarubica, Chavoor; the Wai and Zaby brothers; and great black stars like Kenny Washington, Woody Strode, and Jackie Robinson. As always, the only colors that truly concern a Bruin are Blue and Gold.

Finally, another Top 10 team accepted the Rose Bowl bid, Minnesota. The Golden Gophers were 6-1 in conference play to the Buckeye's 6-0 and were favored over the Bruins by eight.

In what was charitably called a dull game, after UCLA showed great promise in marching to an early 3-0 lead, the Bruins crumbled in front of Minnesota's quintessential "three-yards-and-a-cloud-of-dust" offense. Sportscaster Mel Allen, covering the game for television, recalled, "Crowd reaction was so slight we were worried viewers would think their sound had gone out." UCLA lost for the fifth straight time in the Rose Bowl, 21-3.

Barnes then made a major offensive decision between seasons. He had been tinkering with the inherited single wing from the moment he took over, trying out spreads, opening it up, always moving away from its pure form. Additionally, he and his staff believed that they were losing too many key recruits who were more inclined toward the T formation. Lastly, from a spectator standpoint, it was felt that UCLA's style of play needed jazzing up. Barnes capitulated and agreed to switch his offense to the T.

And so history repeated itself at UCLA for virtually the exact same reasons as in the early 1940s, as a coach basically unfamiliar with the workings of the T formation attempted to install it at the major college level. Like Babe Horrell 20 years before him, Barnes had a rough time making it work. Unlike the Babe, Barnes' program immediately came down around his

Left half Bobby Smith kicks the lone points scored by UCLA against Minnesota in the Bruins' 21-3 loss in the 1962 Rose Bowl.

ears, as the next three years the Bruins went 4-6, 2-8, and 4-6. Even the best intentions must result in winning seasons if a coach expects to survive.

The senior-laden team from 1961 meant that 1962 would be a rebuilding year. Still, there were a number of fine senior returnees, tackles Joe Bauwens and Phil Oram, halfbacks Rob Smith, Carmen Di Poalo, All-America Kermit Alexander, fullbacks Mitch Dimkich and Joe Zeno, and quarterback Ezell Singleton. Juniors Mel Profit and Dave Gibbs at end, guard John LoCurto, and sophomores quarterback Larry Zeno (Joe's brother), and tackle Kent Francisco, were prime additions.

That first "T" season started out impressively, as the Bruins shocked an incredibly talented and number-one ranked Ohio State team in the Coliseum. The Buckeyes fumbled on the second play of the game over to UCLA, and Alexander immediately rushed 45 yards for a touchdown. As the PAT was missed, a Buckeye score in the second quarter with the extra point made it a 7-6 Ohio State halftime lead.

Though the Midwesterns controlled the game throughout, they were unable to score again, UCLA keeping them at bay several times within the 10 and once holding them four straight times after the Bucks had it first and goal from the six. Then late in the fourth quarter the Bruins staged a remarkable surging drive that went 70 yards before stalling on the seven, at which point Larry Zeno kicked the field goal that beat Ohio State, 9-7.

After 35-7 over Colorado State, an 8-6 loss to Pitt and a 17-6 loss to Stanford, another remarkable performance was engineered by Alexander, as the faltering 2-2 Bruins engaged Cal, quarterbacked by the talented sophomore Craig Morton. The Bear leader proved he was as good as everyone had heard, throwing for 18 of 32 passes, 236 yards, and a touchdown. But Alexander simply blew away the Bears, setting a UCLA record by scoring four touchdowns in one game, three by rushing, bringing on a 26-16 victory.

But losses to the Air Force Academy, Washington, and Southern Cal; a defeat of Utah; and a loss to Syracuse on national television put the season to rest.

The AAWU became the Big-Six with the inclusion of Washington State in 1963. But there was a change of command within the UCLA athletic department that year as well, one that

Buckeye quarterback John Mummey in the arms of Bruin right end Mel Profit in the Bruins' stunning 9-7 upset of Ohio State in 1962.

UCLA's dynamic Athletic Director J.D. Morgan, who was to create on the Westwood campus "The Athens of Athletics."

would have not only a profound effect on Bruin football but the entire athletic program.

In 1963 UCLA replaced retiring athletic director Wilbur Johns with Bruin alumnus J.D. Morgan (his initials were his name). After coaching the tennis team for 12 years and to six national championships (and continuing as coach for several more years), Morgan stepped into the top sports administrator's role at UCLA.

If there was one thing the domineering Morgan loved to do, it was win. He brought the same competitive fire he had as a player and coach into the athletic director's chair and planned to create the nation's greatest collegiate sports environment. His plan included football. Barnes needed to win big, but did not.

Barnes, as he had with the single wing, toyed with his T formation, at times trying a semi-pro T set involving a split end plus a flanker back, and also experimented with his personnel formats. Nothing seemed to work for long.

Only three season-long senior starters graced this team, guards John Walker and Walt Dathe and end Mel Profit. Barnes tried various combinations out at quarterback (juniors Larry Zeno, Mike Haffner, and John White) and started three sophomores, end Kurt Altenberg, half Byron Nelson, and fullback Jim Colletto.

As if on cue, virtually all of UCLA's opponents enjoyed super seasons. Losses to Pittsburgh, 20-0, and Penn State, 17-14, were temporarily stalled by a surprise 10-9 victory over Stanford. Then the losses continued, 29-7 to Syracuse, and in the first meeting in either school's history, UCLA bowed to Notre Dame in South Bend, 27-12.

The Bruins lost to Rose Bowl-bound Illinois, 18-12; Cal 25-0; and to the Air Force Academy, 48-21. Then a Barnes midgame switch created a major upset against Big-Six Champion Washington. He started the game with the drop-back style of junior quarterback Steve Sindell, then for the second half unleashed Zeno's rollout game. The Huskies were completely floored, losing, 14-0.

Speculation had begun prior to the Washington tilt as to how long Barnes was going to remain as coach, and Barnes himself admitted he had become the victim of "the silent treatment," where no one would tell him (or knew) where he stood in the department. As Southern Cal was due, many wondered whether, win or lose, Barnes would keep his job. It was all set for November 23, 1963.

History intervened, of course, as President John Kennedy was murdered the day before, and all collegiate sports throughout the nation were canceled that weekend. After both squads endured an extra, awkward week of practice, Southern Cal defeated UCLA, 26-6.

The following day, J.D. Morgan announced Barnes would be back for the 1964 season, stating, "Billy took a young team that looked played-out in midseason, then performed an excellent job of bringing it back. We faced by far the toughest schedule in the history of the school."

The 1964 season had Bruins hopes on a higher plane. Senior Larry Zeno had a firm hand on the quarterback position, with seniors Steve Sindell and Mike Haffner able back-ups. Junior Kurt Altenberg was set at end, and senior tackles Mitch Johnson and captain Kent Francisco, center Prentice O'Leary, and guard Dick Peterson added their experience to an otherwise junior-led squad.

Enough time had passed from the injustices caused by the PCC scandal to allow for the regrouping of its most athletically competitive members. Therefore the AAWU increased its fold by two, adding Oregon and Oregon State. The awkward-sounding AAWU would soon give way to the more catchy Pac-Eight appelation.

An odd quirk in the rules this year led to an unusual situation if the coach saw fit to take advantage of it. A coach was required to select at the outset of the season between two playing formats, a single-platoon first team of 11 men with only wholesale substitution allowed by an entire second string, or two platoons on offense and defense. (Individual substitutions were allowed through injury only.)

By using the latter, a sharp coach saw that he could go beyond the legal time-out limits set for each half whenever a need to punt arose. By purposefully drawing a delay of game penalty the defensive platoon could be exchanged for its offensive counterpart.

Barnes employed this clever procedure in the nationally televised defeat of favored Pittsburgh, 17-12, as the single-platoon Panthers faced the Bruin defensive squad on every UCLA punting situation. The rule was erased by 1965.

The Bruins continued to drum up high expectations with upsets over Penn State, 21-14, and Stanford, 27-20. Then, in some of the cruelest scheduling ever foisted on an ascending team, the Bruins were brought to earth with four successive road games, the first three losses to Syracuse, 39-0; Notre Dame, 24-0; and Illinois, 26-7. Suddenly the Bruins were 3-3 and in a small state of shock.

Playing up in Strawberry Canyon, UCLA once again thwarted Cal's Craig Morton, staging two comebacks in the last seven-and-a-half minutes to sting the Bears, 25-21. Then the bottom fell out, with losses to the Air Force Academy, 24-15, and Washington, 22-20.

UCLA was still capable of making the Rose Bowl if the right set of circumstances teamed with a victory over Southern Cal. The Bruins lost, 34-14. Tommy Prothro's Oregon State Beavers would visit the Rose Bowl instead.

UCLA ended up 4-6, and three losing seasons in a row do not make for healthy coach-employer relations, no matter how personally well liked he may be, and Bill Barnes was a truly likable guy. But Morgan offered him no hope. Barnes tendered his resignation when he learned his contract was not going to be renewed, and his entire staff followed suit.

CHAPTER 9

1964-1970

James Thompson "Tommy" Prothro. The last direct connection to Red Sanders to coach at UCLA. The man with the ever-present briefcase on the sidelines. Tall, imposing, with a deep resonant voice that penetrated into his players and demanded results. Aloof, confident, consistent.

Prothro was not the players' "friend." He did not seek their approval as a person. They just knew he was the best damn coach they would ever play for, and if they did not take full advantage of it that was their mistake. They knew if they played the game the way Prothro asked them to, the way Prothro expected them to, they would win a lot of games.

They won a lot of games.

Born in 1920 in Memphis, Tennessee, Prothro was a tremendous athlete all his life and played football, basketball, track, and baseball while in high school and at Riverside Military Academy, where he was coached by Sanders. His college days were spent at Duke University in North Carolina, where in 1942 he played in the only transplanted Rose Bowl game, played in Durham, North Carolina, when the Blue Devils lost to the Oregon State Beavers, 20-16. He graduated in June of that year.

After his war service as a naval officer, he coached under Sanders at Vanderbilt, in 1947 becoming the backfield coach. Prothro married his second wife in Memphis, Shirley Seagle, who helped him raise Ann, his daughter by the previous marriage.

When Sanders was enticed to UCLA in 1949 he brought Prothro with him, and they coached together through the highly successful early fifties, including one Rose Bowl appearance after the 1953 season and a National Championship in 1954.

Prothro made the transition to head coach at Oregon State in 1955 and was an immediate success, coming in second to UCLA that first year and taking the Beavers to the Rose Bowl the year afterwards, and only the no-repeat rule kept him from Pasadena in 1958.

When the Pacific Coast Conference disappeared in 1958, Oregon State became an independent. Prothro brought it a successful trip to the Liberty Bowl in 1962, plus quarterback Terry Baker won the Heisman Trophy. When the Beavers joined the Athletic Association of Western Universities in 1964, Prothro then guided them to another appearance in the Rose

Coach J. Thompson "Tommy" Prothro, who jarred the UCLA football program back into national prominence.

Prothro during his days as an assistant coach under Red Sanders at UCLA during the early 1950s.

Bowl. He had only one losing season in Corvalis, compiling an overall 63-37-2, the winningest record by any major West Coast team in that ten-year period.

Prothro, like Sanders, could bring forth Herculean feats from lesser endowed players, and knew that if he could tap the talent-laden Los Angeles area there would be no telling what he could accomplish. Concurrently, UCLA athletic director J.D. Morgan sorely wanted Prothro as the replacement for Barnes. Morgan was the kind of bullish, determined individual who in almost all cases got what he wanted. Prothro made it easy for him to make the pitch, as he had to be in Pasadena for his Beavers' appearance in the 1965 Rose Bowl. Morgan landed

142

him.

Tommy Prothro was another innovator, the first to use backs and others familiar with ball handling on the front lines of his kickoff receiving teams, just in case an onsides or squib kick was employed. The 4-3-4 defense was early in its development when he decided to go with it, and he experimented with wider spacing between his defensive front. His off-balance winglike offensive formation was almost a pro-set with a split end and occasional flanker back, capable of shifting from sweeping end runs to stunning pass plays with relative ease.

When Prothro arrived in Westwood he discovered that, unlike some programs when a coach departs under fire, Barnes did not leave the cupboard bare. He had had a highly successful recruiting year before the 1964 season, and Prothro inherited a wealth of sophomore talent, defensive guard Larry Agajanian, linebacker Don Manning, defensive end Wade Pearson, offensive tackle Larry Slagle, defensive right tackle Alan Claman, and a player who despite his six-foot-one-half-inch height and 196-pound weight made up for it with drive and heart to make the team as a walk-on defensive left tackle, Terry Donahue.

There was another notable sophomore. Prothro had in quarterback Gary Joseph Beban another opportunity to mold the kind of winner who could earn the honor Baker received at Oregon State. They came to call Beban "The Great One." He was. As Prothro's "Sprint-Out T" offense resembled at times a modified wing formation with its sweeps and end runs, Beban's prep experience with the single wing primed him to run this run-pass attack with confidence. He did.

Plus there were upperclassmen who blossomed under Prothro. On offense there were juniors place-kicker Kurt Zimmerman and backs Ray Armstrong and marvelous Mel Farr, and seniors ends Kurt Altenberg and Bryon Nelson, tackle Russ Banducci, guard and co-captain Barry Leventhal, halfback Dick Witcher, and fullback Paul Horgan.

The lightly regarded defense included juniors end Erwin Dutcher, guard John Richardson, and safety Tim McAteer, with linebacker Dallas Grider and defensive back Bob Stiles recruited from the junior college ranks. The senior stopmen were end and co-captain Jim Colletto, guard Steve Butler, linebacker Jim Miller, and defensive right half Bob Richardson

(John's brother).

Prothro once outlined his basic winning methodology into three parts: "One, mental and physical ability of the players. That is a result of recruiting. Two, the techniques taught. Not plays or formations but the fundamentals of the hitting position. Three, morale. It you've got any two of those, you can win."

For Prothro, that first one was the major hurdle. It was not enough finding players with talent and the academic credentials to be admitted to UCLA. They had to be players with character. They might not love him, but if they believed in him, they would win. They were treated like adults, and he expected adult behavior from them.

Rick Purdy, who played fullback under Prothro for three years, deeply respected the man for concrete reasons. "(He believed) that players would perform better if there was that big line between the head coach and the players. Prothro didn't need to be friends with the players. He said, 'Here I am. I'm in charge. You're going to do what I tell you to do, and you're going to do it well, and you're going to win because you're going to do it that way.' He was always consistent that way. Most kids I think respect that quality in a coach. What they don't like is vacillation, where one player is treated this way and another is treated that way. You can't demand respect, you have to earn it, and in my opinion Prothro earned that."

There is no way of knowing in advance if a team is destined for glory. Any expectations for the 1965 Bruins rested through the coach's ability to draw his players out. As the "skywriters" picked the Bruins to finish last in the conference, it was one of those teams that the eternal word "potential" often is applied to, that being a safe way of explaining away things if a team does or does not "live up to its potential." The first game of the season disguised what potential there was.

Hugh "Duffy" Daugherty's Michigan State Spartans needed, unlike the Bruins, only a short term of maturing before hitting their stride. Even so, at season's beginning, they had more than enough of what it took to handle UCLA.

For the Bruins, Beban started revving up slowly until he began to dominate the offensive punch of the team, but his efforts were only good for three points. The Spartans were more

144

effective, relying on the power rushing of sophomore fullback Bob Apisa, who scored the game's only touchdown on the way to the 13-3 victory.

During the year, the Spartans would acquire a luster of strength that would batter opponents into submission, rising to number one in the nation by the end of the regular season. The Bruins became a team releasing emotional bursts of daring that would leave opponents in shock, hopefully unable to recover before game's end and were an exciting team to watch.

UCLA and Michigan State were destined to meet again.

Things began to happen for UCLA. Against a favored Penn State team, after falling behind, 7-0, the Bruins struck for 24 unanswered points by the third quarter. Beban teamed with Farr and receivers Altenberg and Nelson, giving Prothro his first win as the Bruins' head coach, holding on for a 24-22 victory.

The Bruins hosted tough Syracuse, 4-0 in the series, having so far defeated UCLA by an aggregate score of 116-22. It was finally UCLA's turn. The first two Bruin plays of the game resulted in a touchdown apiece. Syracuse fumbled the first possession over to UCLA on the 27, and Beban swept his way right for the needed yards and a touchdown. Next, downing a Syracuse punt on the 21, Beban unloaded the first of many long bombs to come, this for 35 yards and good for a 79-yard Altenberg romp.

Three minutes into the game, the much-heavier Orangemen found themselves in a permanent hole. Heralded Syracuse running back Floyd Little was held to 27 yards, requiring a sophomore tackle-turned-fullback named Larry Csonka to work overtime to bull his team back into the game. But UCLA's inspired defense kept its opponents on the short end, the Bruins winning it 24-14.

The next big test was a visit to Missouri. Posted as eight-point underdogs, the Bruins once again surprised the odds-making fraternity by forging a 14-0 lead seven seconds into the fourth quarter. But if turnabout is fair play, UCLA got a taste of its own medicine as the Tigers struck for two shocking back-to-back touchdowns from a kickoff return and a punt return, knotting the game at 14-14. Missouri's Coach Dan Devine admitted, "I didn't think we were lucky to tie, and I'm not

145

satisfied with the tie." Prothro had three words for that: "He was lucky."

UCLA was a surprising preseason 2-1-1 against four of the toughest teams in the nation. The first conference battle was Cal, the Golden Bears also considered a surprise team in the AAWU, though once losing badly to Notre Dame. Seemingly even "on paper," the Bruins did not just shock the Bears, they slaughtered them.

Beban's bomb was twice the instrument of doom, and with the sharp-eyed running and stellar sweep blocking of Farr and Horgan, and the pass-receiving talents of Altenberg, Witcher, and Armstrong, UCLA suddenly gelled as an offensive unit capable of scoring on anybody at any time from anywhere on the field. The unsung heroes of this incredible 56-3 victory remained the smallish Bruin defense, performing feats of mind-over-matter magic to stop virtually every Bear scoring drive.

UCLA received its first scare, traveling to Colorado Springs to face the Air Force Academy. As the Falcons had previously fallen to the Bears, 24-7, the game was tabbed to be a breather, but the "nothing to lose" Airmen played havoc with their opponent, whose main concern appeared to be how to get a good seat on the return flight home. The Bruins were lucky to get out with a 10-0 victory after being held scoreless in the first half, in part because they were Farr-less, a minor injury keeping him out that half.

In a home game against maligned but improving Washington, Husky coach Jim Owens introduced an unscouted passing attack, led by quarterback Tod Hullin, who connected for three touchdowns and a 24-12 halftime lead. But the difference became Beban, who in short order in the third quarter ran the opening scrimmage play 60 yards for one touchdown, and on the next exchange unloaded a controversial 60-yard touchdown pass play to Witcher for the final winning margin, 28-24. It was the defense from there on out, with three interceptions, a heads-up fumble recovery by Donahue, and a stout performance by John Richardson.

That scoring pass play controversy was created when Witcher, prior to the play, seemed to rush off the field to the sidelines as if being taken out of the game. Instead of departing he positioned himself just inside the lines. Blending in with his

146

Bruin teammates off the field, he was not spotted by the opposing bench. Unwarned and unaware, the Husky backfield did not pick him up, and Witcher scampered unmolested down the sidelines after the snap and was all by himself when the Beban bomb arrived, making it touchdown time.

Prothro in later years explained what had happened. "Owens teams were extremely disciplined. They were the only team I ever knew that all snapped their heads down together in the defensive huddle and then up all together. At that time the rule required all 11 offensive players to be within a certain distance of the ball in order that the defense could see them all.

"We had 11 in the huddle when their heads went down, (at which time) Witcher left. When their heads came up, our other 10 broke. They never saw Witcher. (They changed their defensive huddle the next week!)"

Owens allowed that he "didn't think it was a sleeper. The guy was just more lined up as a flanker and our halfback didn't pick him up." Still, there were others in the Washington camp who did not feel so magnanimous. The groundworks for revenge were being laid.

Though certainly at this point the coaching brilliance of Prothro and staff can be taken into account for much of the Bruins' success, the unique character of this team was one of the prime motivators toward reaching the top. A word began to crop up in attempts to describe this team: Gutty.

Though in the years that followed it became a term that carried more negative connotations than when first applied, "gutty" seemed to most aptly bring to mind the special quality of the 1965 Bruins. It signified their belief in themselves, belief in their abilities to overcome any obstacle if they tackle it as a team, belief in their ability to draw upon some secret wellspring of strength that belied their size. Like something out of the French Foreign Legion, like the Greeks who snatched victory in the face of an overwhelming defeat in the Trojan War, these Bruins would fight to the last man, would find a way to win, a team that had what it took, The Gutty Little Bruins.

Climbing into the Top 10 going into the game with Stanford, the Bruins threw and ran their way to four touchdowns in the rain and a 30-13 victory. The defensive hero was Dallas Grider, with Bob Stiles adding to the Indians' miseries.

The Rose Bowl decider was then set up. UCLA versus Southern Cal. The Trojans sported a strong defense, an able offensive line, a good quarterback in Troy Winslow, and a fabulous running back, Mike Garrett.

Garrett was dubbed by John Hall, then columnist for the *Los Angeles Times,* as "Iron Mike, the chunky little Trojan bomb." Garrett had twice faced the Bruins yet had never scored against them in those two victories, and had yet to appear in the Rose Bowl with the varsity Trojans. This was his last chance. But he had to be content as the Trojans' first Heisman Trophy winner. He had Gary Beban to blame.

UCLA scored first, Mel Farr running 49 yards for a first-quarter touchdown on a counter play that had the Trojans going right when he cut left. The PAT was blocked. Southern Cal later scored seven in the second quarter, then added nine points in the fourth quarter to take a seemingly insurmountable 16-6 lead, having absolutely dominated the line throughout the afternoon.

As the game neared its end, a portion of the 94,085 in attendance began to reach an obvious conclusion and started to file out. By the time some of them ran back to their seats in panic or incredulity, it was too late.

Beban had struck.

With four minutes to go, Trojan Winslow fumbled the ball, recovered by Bruin Erwin Dutcher. Beban took the snap, rolled to his right, spotted Witcher beyond the lone defender, and let the ball fly, a 34-yard touchdown play. He then passed to Nelson into the end zone for the two-point conversion, pulling the Blue up to 16-14.

As expected, the ensuing kickoff was an onsider, which was successfully covered for the Bruins by Dallas Grider. Shortly, Beban wowed 'em again, as The Great One threw on another rolling run to his right, this time to the streaking (and originally the decoy for intended receiver Farr) Kurt Altenberg, a perfect 52-yard touchdown strike caught and carried in from the five.

Though the try for two failed, the 20-16 margin was more than enough. The Trojans were literally too shocked to recover

Gary Beban at work against Southern Cal in 1965, a game the Trojans led after three quarters 16-6, a lead they would not hold.

in the remaining two-and-a-half minutes. Within the space of 90 seconds, Gary Beban had elevated UCLA past Southern Cal and into the Rose Bowl.

Mike Garrett, who had gained 210 yards rushing on the day, made it a special point to visit the victor's locker room. Entering the melee, still wearing his Cardinal Red and Gold uniform with pride, this great man, his Rose Bowl dream over, spoke to the respectful Bruins: "When a team comes back the way you did, it deserves to go to the Rose Bowl." He wished them luck and told them to make the West Coast proud. He quietly left, tears in his eyes.

Though many Trojan players have shown in victory or defeat the kind of character often associated with the many fine teams that Southern Cal has fielded in its history, to the minds and hearts of every Bruin present that evening Mike Garrett was truly "The Noblest Trojan of Them All."

The ecstasy of having reached the Rose Bowl was temporarily set aside by the Bruins, for there was still one more game, against Tennessee, played in Prothro's hometown of Memphis. It was with certain pride that Tommy Prothro brought his conference champions east to meet the Volunteers. He did not enjoy himself.

After trading touchdowns in the first quarter, the Vols

Left end Kurt Altenberg's game-breaking reception that put UCLA up and over Southern Cal 20-16 and into the Rose Bowl.

steamed ahead to lead 20-7 at the half. Beban led a third quarter Bruin charge good for two touchdowns, and an intercepted fumble by UCLA's Tim McAteer ran in from the 35 put the Bruins on top, 28-20. Tennessee came back with a touchdown and a field goal, and so the Bruins fell behind, 29-28. Back came Beban, back came the Bruins, as he swept his way into the end zone from four yards out to earn a 34-29 advantage with less than four minutes to play.

What happened next would lodge and fester in Prothro's craw for years to come. His diatribe after the game explains: ''It was the worst-officiated game I have ever seen. I'm embarrassed that I'm a Southerner. I was proud before today, but I'm not sure anymore. The pro-All Stars couldn't have won out there today. The officials gave Tennessee *three* extra time outs in their final drive. They threw a lateral and it was called an incomplete pass. But I won't single out any one bad call because I could be here all night.''

As sportswriter Frank Finch of the *Los Angeles Times* understated, Prothro was a "bitter man who felt he'd been jobbed in his own hometown." Tennessee had scored in that final drive and with 39 seconds left threw a two-point conversion and won the game, 37-34.

Thus having lost to Tennessee, one of the participants in the Bluebonnet Bowl, UCLA faced the prospect of meeting gigantic Michigan State, now the number-one team in the nation. The general impression was not whether the Spartans would beat the Bruins, but how bad.

The Spartans had not just become powerful, they were awesome. The 137 rushing yards the Bruins amassed that first

game remained the second most ran up against Michigan State all season. After their third game that year, MSU held every opponent to less than 100 yards per game—Michigan to 29, Notre Dame to -12, Ohio State to -22. As Prothro put it, "You play Big 10 teams as early in the year as you can, before they have a chance to find out who their best boys are. They have so many of them."

Prothro studied the Spartan game films. What he saw did not cheer him. Working closely with offensive coordinator Pepper Rodgers, who had spent the entire season up in the press box with binoculars glued to his eyes as he phoned down suggested plays, they could see few weaknesses.

The Spartan defense featured guard Harold Lucas and the wonderful end Charles "Bubba" Smith. In fact, virtually every Spartan starter that year ended up a pro-All Star in 1970. The Bruins would have to rely on speed. They certainly were not going to push their opponents out of the way.

Still, Prothro believed his team could win. As much as the Spartans had improved during the season, so had the Bruins. Beban was a natural option-quarterback, able to throw accurately while on the move. Plus there was the long pass that had lifted the Bruins past several opponents during the season.

The one unanswerable question rested with the Bruin defense, the no-name, no-weight defense. No one had paid much attention to the defense...except the Bruin offense. The two squads relied on each other like trapeze artists, each re-

Beban scores against Michigan State in the 1966 Rose Bowl. The Bruins knocked off the number-one Spartans 14-12, UCLA's first victory in Pasadena.

quired to do its job in order to make the other's possible. The defense would have to do its job New Year's Day very very well.

January 1, 1966, was a clear, sunny day. Intermittent rains throughout the week had produced less-than-perfect field conditions. But once the ball had been kicked off, nothing mattered but the game.

UCLA and Michigan State sparred with each other through the entire first quarter. Prothro worked to instill a psychological edge for his team right from the start. "The first play, Beban faked to Farr and went around Bubba Smith for a big gain. Only Beban and Farr knew Beban would keep the ball. This was an attempt to make Bubba a little tentative as he was too much for us to handle otherwise."

As the quarter was about to end, Michigan State made the first mistake of the game, fumbling a UCLA punt on the six, John Erquiaga recovering for the Bruins. After rushing the ball to the one, on the first play in the second quarter Beban crashed over for the touchdown, and Zimmerman's PAT made it 7-0 Bruins.

Prothro gambled, having made up his mind to do so well in advance of the game. It was just a matter of timing, somewhere along the line, to try an onsides kick. He had detected a slight tendency in the Spartan front line to automatically turn its backs immediately after a kickoff in the haste to get down the field and set up interference for the return.

Also, Michigan State would probably suck up all the momentum on a "return favor" march, all the more reason to throw an onsides curve. Even if it failed, the sheer audacity of it still might have an unsettling effect on the Spartans.

Caught flat-footed, the onsider worked. Dallas Grider, the man who had turned the same trick against Southern Cal, recovered the kick. Bruins' ball on the 42-yard line.

Mel Farr burst up the middle for 21 through the shocked Spartan defensive front line. Then Beban finally unloaded deep to Altenberg at the six and he carried it to the one. Beban again did the honors and plunged in for the score. Zimmerman's PAT made it 14-0.

Thwarted all game long by a tenacious, anticipating, eager, and determined Bruin defense, the Spartan offense was thrice stopped on fourth and short situations in the second half. It was

The incredible elation from a victory in the Rose Bowl is seen on every face.

not until late in the fourth quarter that the Spartans staged their nerve-wracking rally.

After a 42-yard connection from quarterback Steve Juday to end Gene Washington put the ball on the 38 (though a quick whistle allowed the Spartans to retain the ball after Washington fumbled the ball over to game MVP Bob Stiles), Apisa took a pitchout and ran the necessary yardage for the score. Juday attempted to pass for a two-pointer, but alert Bruin defenders rushed him into an errant throw. At 14-6 Bruins, less than half the quarter remained.

Assuming that the battered Bruins were running out of gas, the Spartans kicked off normally. UCLA failed to move the ball and was forced to punt. Alternating his two quarterbacks, Juday and Jim Raye, who brought in fresh plays with them each time, Daugherty saw his Spartans quickly flash from their 42 down to the Bruin 28, then doggedly fight their way into the end zone from there. A pass from the seven put the ball on the two. A plunge put it on the two-foot spot. Juday finally snuck it over with 31 seconds remaining in the game.

It was time for "The Tackle."

Left with no choice but to go for a two-pointer and a tie, the Spartans elected to go with a power pitchout to Bob Apisa, the bruising 220-pound Hawaiian fullback who had been churning up yardage all season long like a Rototiller gone berserk. Taking in the ball at the seven, he turned with all his might for the goal.

He was met head-on by Jim Colletto at the three, but with a broken hand Colletto could not hold on. Dallas Grider then smashed into the charging Spartan. Bob Stiles hurled himself into Grider's back, knocking himself out in the process. Apisa strained for the goal, a Gulliver pestered by mere Lilliputians, but was shuttled out of bounds, short of glory.

UCLA 14, Michigan State 12.

UCLA finally earned its first Rose Bowl victory after five tries. Michigan State's three appearances in the Pasadena classic had all been against UCLA, and after this first loss Daugherty accepted the defeat with style. "We came from behind to win the other two times. History has a way of evening things up. After those first two games, I never heard any alibis from UCLA. They took it graciously, and if we can't do the same thing, we're not much of a team."

The 1966 Rose Bowl champions.

The entire season might be summed up by a small statement made by Dallas Grider prior to the game with Southern Cal. It was obvious all season long that the smaller, lighter Bruin defenders were playing far over their heads. Game after game, they provided the offense with stirring examples of determination, instilling the entire team with the inspiration and the will that leads to victory. This "unknown" defense had that unmeasureable difference that turned aside any statistical evidence when the Bruins were sized up against their more dominating opponents.

All Grider said was, "They don't weigh our hearts."

The year 1966 was the year the Bruins were gypped. There is no softer way of putting it. The Bruins that were the surprise in 1965 were a surprise no longer. Prothro's quest for a second National Championship for UCLA first rested with this team. The team's fortunes were not entirely decided on the playing field.

Quarterback Gary Beban returned for his junior year, backs Mel Farr and Cornell Champion (who'd sat out the 1965 season) were back as seniors. There was also a surprising sophomore fullback named Rick Purdy who eventually beat out junior Steve Stanley as a starter. With names like Richardson, Donahue, Claman, Dutcher, Grider, Manning, and McAteer back on defense, there was enough continuity from the previous year to make Prothro's high hopes justifiable.

The first game, against Pitt, was a 57-14 rout. The Bruins rose to number two in the nation. Syracuse was next to discover the UCLA team of 1966 was formidable, losing, 31-21. In that game, Floyd Little, who had already passed Jim Brown in the Syracuse rushing record books, gained only 18 yards, the bruising Larry Csonka only 32.

Against Missouri, the Tigers held UCLA to a 3-0 lead at the half, then after the Bruins surged to two touchdowns and a 17-0 lead, Missouri came back to within three (including a successful onsider) before Farr went 13 yards for the icer and the 24-15 final.

Then UCLA went flat against Rice. After trailing, leading, trailing, tying, then trailing again, the Bruins had to score twice in the waning moments of the fourth quarter to pull it out, a 17-yard Kurt Zimmerman field goal with seven seconds remaining doing the trick, 27-24. Of future importance was the fact that, after Beban had the wind knocked out of him, sub quarterback senior Norman Dow stepped in and threw for two touchdowns against the Owls. Things returned to normal the following week against Penn State, UCLA breaking away to a 49-11 victory.

The return trek to the Rose Bowl began against Cal, and after the Bruins carved out a 28-0 lead with touchdown scores in each quarter, the Bears made a ball game out of it, scoring a touchdown and then kicking an onsider that led to another. But that was it, as UCLA won, 28-15.

One last nonconference game remained, against Air Force. Though the Falcons briefly led midway through the second quarter, Beban, Dow, and company salted the game away in the fourth quarter, 38-13. The Bruins were now also leading the country in scoring.

Washington spoiled it all. After winning in Seattle in 1958, the Bruins had lost the following three away games to the Huskies. The 1966 contest made number four. Though an alleged "jinx" would continue through the mid-seventies, as with such coincidences, it was more perpetuated as a promotion angle to drum up interest in each game. Games are played one at a time, and an upset is an upset and a deserved victory a deserved victory. In 1966 the Huskies upset the Bruins by playing the game, not by any "jinx."

It was one of those games that no matter what the Bruins did they could do no right. To say Beban had a bad day statistically does not describe the numerous passes that were on target but inexplicably dropped.

Furthermore, the field was a morass, because, in part, of its being watered prior to a Pop Warner game played that morning, chewing up the natural Husky Stadium turf considerably and helping to slow the vaunted Bruin running attack. If it was planned, it worked. Washington won, 16-3. It had not forgotten the "Witcher pass" from 1965.

The week before Southern Cal, the Bruins had to beat Stanford if they were to keep their Rose Bowl hopes alive. They did. Responsible for scoring the game's only touchdown in the first quarter, Beban was swamped while delivering a pass late in the third quarter and incurred a cracked fibula just above the

157

ankle. Norman "Avis" Dow, so nicknamed because of his perennial number-two spot behind Beban, filled in to lead the team to a fourth-quarter field goal that put the game away, 10-0.

Beban was out for the season, a season with only one more scheduled game. That left Dow, starting his first game ever as a Bruin, to face the Trojans.

The game was touted on all fronts as the Rose Bowl decider. Southern Cal had not enjoyed a spectacular year but had managed to post a 4-0 record against league opponents. Though UCLA had lost a conference game to Washington, a quirk in scheduling had the Bruins meeting only four of its AAWU competitors, Southern Cal playing five. A UCLA victory in this game would still leave the Trojans numerically one up on the Bruins, but the rule of thumb that was supposed to be applied was that the AAWU, in case there was a tie or other extenuating circumstances, was to vote for the most representative team to play for the honor of the West Coast in the Arroyo Seco stadium. Still, to be considered at all, UCLA had to win.

The Bruins got the first part right. Dow came through with flying colors, scoring the first points in the game for the Bruins part way through the third quarter on an end run for five yards and a touchdown. He then brought the Bruins back after Southern Cal had tied the game at 7-7, running one play 26 yards up to the Trojan 38, passing to Ray Armstrong to the 21, and then feeding Cornell Champion into a perfectly executed scissors play that resulted in a touchdown and the final 14-7 victory score.

Then came the conference vote. The Trojans had finished with a 4-1 league to the Bruins' 3-1 (which actually put the Bruins in a second-place tie with Oregon State). But that "most representative" part made things sticky. UCLA on the year posted a 9-1 record. At this point Southern Cal was 7-2, with Notre Dame, the number-one team in the nation, still to be reckoned with.

Southern Cal got the nod. Southern Cal lost to Notre Dame, 51-0, and was defeated by Purdue in the Rose Bowl, 14-13.

The hurt felt in Westwood was deep. Locked out of an opportunity to play elsewhere by the exclusivity clause in the Rose

Right half Cornell Champion on his way to the Bruins' second touchdown against Southern Cal in 1966. The Bruins were voted out of a deserved Rose Bowl visit by the conference the next week.

Bowl pact, the number-five team in the nation was shocked and saddened by the decision of the member athletic directors. Though the conference had expanded to eight members in 1964, so many schedules had been figured years in advance that it was not until 1970 that the full seven-team slate for all members was realized.

The fact that all parties had been led to believe that the UCLA-Southern Cal clash was to be the decider led to the deepest sense of outrage. Whatever the reason behind the specious logic of the AAWU, the decision against UCLA was a bitter pill to take. It was the first time Tommy Prothro was frustrated by circumstances beyond his control while at the helm of the Bruins. There were more frustrations to come.

In 1967, for the first and only time in his career at UCLA, Tommy Prothro had his Bruins begin preparing for a single game during spring practice. It was for the opener in September. He instituted specific plays and running drills with only it in mind. The only thing Prothro did not do was have the scout team don orange jerseys. The target was Tennessee.

The impact from the loss in 1965 to the Vols in Prothro's hometown was unfathomable. It was the only game during his tenure in which Prothro ever lost his composure. He stormed the sidelines, stormed the field, and once incurred a 15-yard unsportsmanlike-conduct penalty.

The postgame statements in which he railed at the officiating were never honestly rescinded. The "shame" he felt as a Southerner upon that occasion was genuine. For Tommy Prothro, this became a game which would vindicate him to his home state. In a nutshell, Joseph Kennedy's maxim best described his frame of mind: Don't get mad; get even.

It would also mark the return of Gary Beban. Now a senior, the slow promotional build-up during his sophomore and junior years towards Heisman Trophy candidacy became emphasized. There were few strong candidates recognizable at the outset of the season posing a challenge, notably Leroy Keyes of Purdue and Larry Csonka of Syracuse.

However, an unheralded entrant made his presence more than felt, a junior college transfer at Southern Cal, a junior running back who went by his first two initials. O.J. Simpson made Coach John McKay's life a whole lot simpler.

Then there were the Bruins themselves, a senior-stacked team that felt particularly good about itself. Their sophomore season brought a Rose Bowl victory, their junior a 9-1 record that was treated with contempt by the conference, and an approaching season against quality competition that might top them all.

Those seniors included tackle Al Claman, end and co-captain Vic Lepisto, linebackers Wade Pearson and Don Manning, right halfs Andy Herrara and Gary Bernstein, and safety Sandy Green on defense, and guard and co-captain Larry Slagle, center John Erquiaga, end Dave Nuttall, and right half Steve Stanley on offense.

The top juniors featured on defense were guard Larry Agajanian, left half Mark Gustavson, and tackle Hal Griffin, and on offense receiver Ron Copeland, halfback Harold Busby, and fullback Rick Purdy. Finally, the rich sophomore class included defensive guard Floyd Reese, tackles Bruce Jorgensen and Vince Bischof, linebackers Mike Ballou and Don Widmer, receivers Gwen Cooper and George Farmer, offensive tackle Gordon

Bosserman, left half Greg Jones, fullback Mike Garratt, and quarterback Bill Bolden. Plus there was a Canadian place-kicker with the unusual name of Zenon Andrusyshyn, a name still on many Bruin football records.

For all of Prothro's preparation, the opener with Tennessee was no cakewalk. The number-eight and the number-nine Vols staged an emotional seesaw battle. UCLA fumbled the opening kickoff and before a full minute had elapsed fell behind 7-0. That set the general tone of the game, as the Bruins could only make it up to 7-3 at the half.

Once tied at 13 early in the fourth quarter, the Vols took a 16-13 lead, only to have Beban construct one of his now-patented late game rallies, capping it off with a 27-yard end run that put UCLA on top for good, 20-16.

With that one out of the way, the rest of the season was supposed to be gravy. The Bruins climbed to number six in the nation.

Against Pitt, Greg Jones ran for 161 yards, including a 43-yard touchdown romp, and was voted the game's MVP. Beban was not too bad either, his first pass (with an injured hand) and the first play from scrimmage for UCLA good to Jones for 34 yards and the all-time passing record for the Bruins. UCLA won it handily, 40-8. UCLA rose again, number four on the AP, number two on the UPI. The number-one team was Southern Cal.

Washington State, with its Veer-T copied from the University of Houston, was no match for the power-oriented winglike team from UCLA, the Bruins crushing the Cougars, 51-23. It was an ignominious way for the Bruins to renew its athletic acquaintance with a school unmet since 1958.

Encountering an emotionally charged Penn State team in University Park, the Bruins could not match the intensity shown by the Lions in the first half, down at that point 7-0 to the 11-point underdogs. But UCLA overmatched its opponent in that second half, putting 17 points on the board for a lead that was not threatened until the closing moments of the game, when Penn State pulled up to the 17-15 final. UCLA, unfortunately, lost Jones for three weeks with a shoulder separation.

Against Cal, with Jones out, the main brunt of the burden was handled by Beban and Purdy, with the golden toe of An-

161

drusyshyn providing kicking and punting support. UCLA, the nation's rushing leaders, racked up another win over Cal, 37-14.

Stanford began to return to its classic aerial format and put on a late-in-the-game rally that almost lifted it over the Bruins' 21-16 advantage, coming as close as two futile passes that sailed over the intended receiver's head in the end zone fired from the 16-yard line. UCLA was now 6-0, heading down the stretch.

Then against Oregon State the Bruins encountered a stirring coaching effort masterminded by Dee Andros, who had a very fine and somewhat underrated Beaver squad that year. He surprised the Bruins with an offense featuring a tight backfield formation close to the line, an old formation called the "Belly-T," relying on smart running options into the line and lengthy ball control, 'a la the Wishbone. It succeeded in earning Oregon State a most respectable 16-16 tie.

This game was further marked by two dichotomous efforts by Andrusyshyn, one a scoring 52-yard field goal and top place for distance in the Bruin record book, the other a mere 37-yard game-winning attempt with 15 seconds to go which was blocked chest high by the Beavers' Ron Boley. One of the contributing factors to the block was that Andrusyshyn was a soccer-style kicker, using the side of his foot, which brought on a low trajectory. It would prove to be his and the Bruins' most vulnerable spot.

The Bruins came back strong the next week to deck a brave but punchless Washington team, starting with the first play of the game and not stopping until it was 48-0. It opened with a 69-yard Beban bomb to trackster Ron Copeland; two plays later Jones scored on a flare pass from the eight, and the Bruins were off and rolling with just three minutes gone. The defense was up too, and for the entire game the Huskies never passed midfield.

But something of much greater impact on the Bruins was occurring at the same time in Corvalis, Oregon. Number-one Southern Cal was suffering a 3-0 loss at the hands of Oregon State. The Big Game was next.

Though the Bruins were then elevated at this point to the number-one position in the nation, the Trojans were posted as three-point favorites, expected to spring back from their loss the previous week. It was expected to be as monumental as it turned

162

out: It pitted for the first and only time the greatest offensive leader in UCLA history in Gary Beban against the one player who was in a position to steal his Heisman Trophy thunder, Orenthal James Simpson.

The 1967 UCLA-Southern Cal game ranks as one of the most exciting college football games ever played. Beban went 16 for 24 yards and 301 yards, passing for two touchdowns in the second half that put UCLA ahead 20-14. But in one of the smarter coaching moves ever employed against the Bruins, McKay stacked the middle of his defensive line with the tallest players on his squad whenever the Bruins were in a point-kicking situation, anticipating Andrusyshyn's tendency toward low trajectories.

It was effective to the point of absurdity. Though Andrusyshyn did miss a "close" field goal from the 16-yard line, two were blocked (from the 25 and 30, again chest high), and he only made the first two out of three PATs, (a tie would have put UCLA in the Rose Bowl), 10 points the Bruins failed to collect.

Shortly after UCLA went ahead for the last time in the fourth quarter, the alert Trojan quarterback Toby Page, inserted for starter Steve Sogge, saw that the Bruin coverage would have stopped the pass play meant to be called and audiblized a weak-side rush by Simpson. O.J. sprang through the line, and once in the secondary the pass-minded Bruin defense was no match for the greatest runner in football history, going 64 yards for the tying points. The successful PAT made it Southern Cal 21, UCLA 20.

For the remaining 10 minutes, the Trojans put a hex on the Beban magic, ends Jim Gunn and the glass-eating Tim Rossovich preventing The Great One from going wide or smothering him when he tried to pass. Southern Cal rebounded to become the National Champions.

Though a final game with Syracuse was yet to be played, the Bruins' season was emotionally over. Syracuse overpowered UCLA, 32-14. The poor Beban performance in his final game as a Bruin, due in part to a rib injury incurred when speared during the Washington game worsened by Southern Cal, fortunately did not affect the outcome of the Heisman balloting.

The scribes and broadcasters had seen enough from the plucky Bruin not only that year but in the culmination of his three years at the controls, leading the Bruins to an aggregate 23-5-2 record. The bowl-less 1967 Bruins fell to number 10, but it marked the third straight year a Beban-led UCLA team finished in the Top 10. Gary Joseph Beban was awarded the Heisman Trophy for 1967.

Upon his acceptance of this award, the first player in UCLA history so honored, Beban publicly acknowledged the forgotten men who he sincerely felt were most responsible for making his selection possible. "Not only in the Heisman Trophy vote but also in all football, the linemen are overlooked. Nobody knows this better than backs. This trophy makes it look like there's one super player in football. There isn't."

He was The Great One indeed.

The first all-Prothro squads began to emerge by 1968, when the freshmen he recruited in 1965 survived to become seniors. There was just one problem with the starting seniors that year. Mickey Mouse could have counted them on the fingers of one hand, and he's got a digit missing.

Because there were only four senior starters, for the first time in UCLA history Prothro decided that it would not be fair to pick the traditional team captains, so he abandoned the yearly honor for "designated game only" captains for the purpose of the coin toss this year only. With leadership at a premium, it inadvertently added to the slightly demoralized atmosphere.

Based upon Prothro's deserved reputation as a worker of wonders, the preseason pundits declared UCLA the number-four team in the nation. The Bruins finished 3-7. Oops.

Greg Jones, the junior starting left halfback, had sophomore great Mickey Cureton, nephew of Bruin defensive All-American from the fifties Hardiman Cureton, breathing down his neck. Fullback Rick Purdy and quarterback Bill Bolden were the primary senior returnees, junior tackle Gordon Bosserman, end Mike Garratt, and halfbacks Glen Cooper and George Farmer lending their talents when they could.

Other steady Bruins who returned on defense were seniors left half Mark Gustavson, left tackle Larry Agajanian, and right end Hal Griffin, and juniors linebacker Mike Ballou, safety Dennis Spurling, left end Vince Bischof, and tackle Pete Kranske. The prime underclassmen were defensive back Danny

164

Graham, fullback Bob Manning, and Steve Frietas at offensive tackle.

In the opener, a home game against a hapless Pitt team, Bolden put on a brilliant performance, showing he was more than up to the task of running the option offense, having spent a brave junior season behind Gary Beban. It did not take long for the first heartbreak of the season. Eighteen minutes into the game, Bolden injured his arm. Junior college transfer Jim Nader stepped in to continue the romp started by Bolden's two touchdowns, one a 53-yard pass to senior receiver Ron Copeland, and Nader passed for four touchdowns in the 63-7 throwaway.

With Bolden in and out of the lineup all season, Prothro shifted the talented Jones over to quarterback behind Nader. Forced, therefore, to spend some of his time on the bench because Prothro did not want to risk losing him to injury playing tailback and leaving the team without a practiced replacement for Nader, Jones was somewhat frustrated, but he stuck by the team.

The windy Athletic Association of Western Universities was at last officially scrapped for the more catchy Pacific-Eight, or Pac-Eight as it was quickly shortened. The Bruins' conference opener was an uneasy 31-21 victory over Washington State. Though the Cougars scrapped their ineffective T formation for the shotgun, the Bruins managed to survive the unusual attack, though neither Nader nor Jones particularly shone at quarterback.

UCLA then began to slip into oblivion. Playing a cold and muddy game in Syracuse and partially returning Jones to tailback, the slippery footing and the hard play of the Orangemen subdued the Bruins into a 20-7 loss. Bolden came back for only three plays against number-three Penn State, and a blocked Andrusyshyn punt by future Pittsburgh Steeler star Jack Ham was good for a Lion touchdown, UCLA losing, 21-6, and disappearing altogether from the top national rankings.

Even Cal managed to take advantage of UCLA's miseries, as the Golden Bears shocked the faltering Bruins with points, 35-15, and injuries. The Bruins incurred a broken leg (Farmer), separated shoulder (Bischof), and three other minor but debilitating casualties. Bolden came back and was responsible

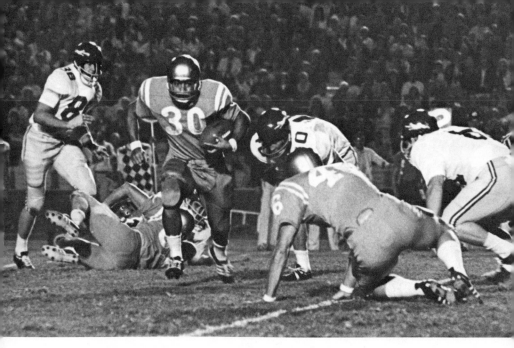

Tailback Mickey Cureton (30) finds running room against Washington State, as right half George Farmer (46) clears the way, in this 31-21 1968 Bruin victory.

for the Bruins' points, until he left the game with a twisted ankle.

For one week, Bruin hopes were revived, as they staged a typical cardiac-kids comeback against strong Stanford, winning it late in the fourth quarter, a touchdown set up by a 50-yard Nader bomb to the three after he replaced interception-prone Bolden, UCLA taking it, 20-17. Indian sophomore quarterback Jim Plunkett would have increasingly better luck against the Bruins in the future.

In Knoxville, against Tennessee, more and more injuries hit the team in a 42-18 loss. The saddest injury to ever befall a Bruin was to back-up center sophomore John Chrestman, who suffered a neck injury on the then-rock-hard Neyland Stadium turf so severe he was paralyzed from the neck down. Rick Purdy, was the first to reach him: "You could just tell by the glazed look in his eye that something was very very wrong. That was the one time I was frightened on the football field."

Through intense therapy at the UCLA Medical Center and private care at his home in San Diego, Chrestman was able the next year to return and continue his studies and therapy at

UCLA. Though unable to ever play again, his scholarship remained intact, which he later voluntarily relinquished, having made a tremendous recovery.

UCLA finished out the season with straight losses to Oregon State, Washington, and Southern Cal. It was the only losing season for Tommy Prothro at UCLA.

Like a Phoenix rising out of its own ashes to become a majestic being again, the Bruins of 1969 were the team Prothro had dreamed of creating all along. For whatever recruiting failures made for the dearth of seniors in 1968, this squad returned a corps of seasoned varsity men *everywhere* and stands as one of the most gorgeously constructed teams in UCLA history.

The defense was employed in a modern 4-3-4 system from the previous 4-4-3 alignment, and included two All-Americans, seniors right tackle Floyd Reese and middle linebacker Mike "Cat" Ballou (consensus). Other senior stars were left linebackers Don Widmer and Vince Bischof, right end Wesley Grant, and right safety Dennis Spurling. Juniors right cornerback Raynaud Moore and left cornerback Danny Graham plus sophomores left end Jim Berg and left safety Ron Carver made important contributions.

Then there was the offense. Senior halfs Greg Jones and George Farmer were joined by junior fullback Mickey Cureton to form a rushing backfield of speed and daring. Senior ends Mike Garratt and Gwen Cooper were accomplished receivers. The line featured seniors right guard Dennis Alumbaugh and left tackle Gordon Bosserman, junior right tackle Steve Frietas and sophomore center Dave Dalby to power the incredibly versatile attack. Prothro's offensive ace-in-the-hole was the incredible long-distance kicking ability of senior Zenon Andrusyshyn.

Finally, there was the quarterback, junior Dennis Dummit, "The Man With the Golden Arm." A transfer after playing two incomparable years at Long Beach Junior College in which he threw 30 touchdown passes, Dummit represented the final piece to a perfect season puzzle Prothro had been planning since he returned to Westwood. This was a fabulous team.

The Bruins opened by devouring Oregon State, 37-0. Dummit's first pass went to Cooper for 60 yards and a touchdown, the third play of the game. The UCLA triple offense worked like the wonderful machine it was from the outset. Andrusyshyn kicked three field goals, one more than he had the entire 1968 season.

On Pitt's opening kickoff, Ron Carver ran it back 71 yards to the 22 and UCLA immediately scored. Though the Panthers put up a stirring fight, the Bruins marched and slung to a 42-8 victory. Against Wisconsin in the first away game of the season, the Bruins revealed a disarming tendency to fumble, five times, all lost, making it 11 such lost miscues already in the season. Still, the uninspired Uclans managed to stumble to a 34-23 victory.

Playing in Chicago against surmountable Northwestern, UCLA trudged to a mere 10-0 lead at the half in smoggy weather so bad Lake Michigan might as well have been the Mediterranean though it was only a half mile away. The second half was another matter, the Bruins exploding with long runs and long bombs to an easy 36-0 win.

In a crazy game against Washington State played in Spokane, the Cougars and the Bruins played giveaway, the Bruins losing three out of eight fumbles, the Cougars four out of seven. However, the chilling UCLA defense held Washington State from doing much damage with the gifts (all within the 10), and the Bruins smoothed things out to a 46-14 laugher. Dummit so far had thrown for nine touchdowns in five games, 999 yards, and was 52 for 94, a little better than 55 percent. Best of all the Bruins were back in the Top 10 at number eight in the nation.

The Bruins surprised the heady Bears of California, 32-0, posting their third shutout in six games. A trampling ground attack and a swirling passing attack accounted for 570 yards to the Bears' 197.

Then a piece from that perfect season puzzle came loose.

A confident, poised Bruin team traveled to The Farm to face an equally confident and poised Indian squad, led by Bay Area product quarterback Jim Plunkett. The tall Stanford star, teaming with nervy little Randy Vataha, perforated the Bruin secondary in the first half.

The Bruins began the game with a devastating opening drive, passing, pitching, and running with ease for 77 yards in 11 plays for a touchdown. But when Andrusyshyn shanked the PAT, it was as if a spell had been broken. The Indians stormed back, Plunkett leading his troops to a 17-6 advantage by the intermission. UCLA had bungled the ball away five times during all this and looked for all the world like a team asking to get beat.

The Bruins regained their composure for the second half, offensively and defensively. Dummit scored two touchdowns on one-yard keepers, the second capping an 80-yard drive in 12 plays. The defense had been told to come back and put the heat on Plunkett and to largely ignore the run. They stunted, they juked, they harrassed, and they got to Plunkett, sacking him four times after he had gone all season with but one, with Reese, Ballou (nine solo tackles), and Grant the overall standouts. A Stanford field goal with just under five minutes remaining in the game made it 20-20, that failed Andrusyshyn PAT looming ever larger.

UCLA came back, and pushed its way to set up a 27-yard field goal try. The man who held the record for the longest field goal in UCLA history at 52 yards kicked it short, wide, and out of bounds. The Canadian who kicked "Z-streaks" would never be the same as a Bruin. The game ended in the tie, and the perfect season was scarred at 6-0-1.

Once again Prothro leveled hard charges against the officiating, citing a pass interference call when no Indian had been touched and a nonexistent holding call. Eighty-one yards in all were assessed against UCLA to only 10 for Stanford. Prothro was not endearing himself and UCLA to the Pac-Eight officiating corps.

Washington was the next opponent. The volatile conditions on Coach Jim Owens' Husky team, 0-6 so far and destined for but one win for the season, exploded on the eve of the UCLA game. The entire black playing squad and the lone black coach, either voluntarily or coerced through extenuating circumstances, quit the team. The defection of these 12 players increased the likelihood of the Huskies' sustaining another loss. They did, 57-14.

Then the Bruins had one last tune-up before the Big Game with Southern Cal, against Oregon. UCLA had a tough time getting out of Eugene with a 13-10 victory. Five-foot-nine Bruin defender Ron Carver saved the day, single-handedly stopping two separate Duck drives in the closing moments of the game to

Dennis Dummit, UCLA's record-setting quarterback, showing his form against Washington in 1969, a 57-14 Bruin victory. The "100" on the helmets honored the centennial of college football.

preserve the victory. Like another pound added to an ever-increasing Sisyphean rock, Andrusyshyn missed another PAT, making it six for the year.

The game with Southern Cal was gripping. Both defenses played spectacular games. Both offenses waited until virtually the last five minutes of the game before shooting off fireworks that still are discussed, still argued, still recalled with anger or a wink.

The Bruins scored in the first quarter, a touchdown pass on a Dummit shovel to Jones who started on an end run, put on the brakes, and fired a pass to Farmer for 41 yards and a touchdown. Andrusyshyn's number was not called, and the decision to go for two points failed, Dummit's pass deflected.

The Trojans pulled ahead to a 7-6 halftime lead, Clarence

Davis taking it in from the 13 after Trojan ace defender Jimmy Gunn had intercepted a Dummit pass. Gunn was part of a defensive framework billed as "The Wild Bunch," Charlie Weaver, Al Cowlings, Tody Smith, and Willard "Bubba" Scott, and they certainly lived up to that image in this game, as Dummit was sacked 10 times.

All remained quiet on the Western front until two-thirds of the fourth quarter was over. Dummit, who put on one of the gamest performances, knocked senseless time and again yet alway drawing upon his competitive spirit to continue, forged a 10-play, 80-yard touchdown drive to put the Bruins ahead, 12-7. Once again, Dummit lead an attempt for two, this time a sack stopping the Bruins from increasing their lead.

In one of the more frustrating episodes in Prothro's career, his decision not to use Andrusyshyn for that first PAT was compounded when the Bruins faced their first opportunity to kick a field goal. Called to confer with Prothro, Andrusyshyn eagerly offered to serve as a decoy in a fake field goal attempt. Prothro, shocked, realized his kicker feared risking another failure and did not *want* to kick. He was through for the game. With him went that extra punch UCLA would need to beat Southern Cal.

The piece to that perfect team puzzle had fallen out for good.

It was minutes later that Trojan quarterback Jimmy Jones, completely ineffective all day, surprised the nation by taking the Trojans 68 yards for the winning touchdown, culminated by an amazing play that followed on the heels of one of the most controversial plays in UCLA-Southern Cal history.

With the Trojans stopped on the Bruin 43, fourth and 10, Jones attempted a desperation pass to receiver Sam Dickerson which soared high over his head out of bounds, incomplete. But Bruin defender Danny Graham, who had slipped and in righting himself had taken his eyes off the play, arose and found Dickerson right on top of him and "tackled" him.

In a judgment call still the subject of heated debate, Graham was called for pass interference, and Southern Cal kept the ball, first down on the 32. One play later, Jones hit Dickerson in the farthest corner of the end zone, a play also tainted by an "out-of-bounds-when-caught" opinion. Southern Cal was miraculously in the Rose Bowl with this cloudy 14-12 victory.

171

Jerry Long, Bruin assistant coach at the time, believed, "Tommy Prothro was never the same. Something snapped." Never having courted favor from the conference, the officials, the fans, or his critics, Prothro had seen the team he believed was his finest achievement come up one victory short. His frustration at being in a conference where a team with a 9-1 or an 8-1-1 record went unrewarded with postseason play added to his discontent.

Shortly after this final game, Prothro stood firmly behind his creation. "I still think this was my greatest team. And the second best team, whichever one it was, wouldn't even be close." The players knew it, too. Dennis Spurling, when someone apologized to him for the Southern Cal loss, said, "Sorry nothing. This is the best team I ever played on. No reason to be sorry."

And there was not.

The senior-stacked team of 1969 meant that the 1970 squad would have a hard time of things. Prothro barely avoided a second losing season, going 6-5, as the Bruins played their first 11 game regular season schedule since 1941.

To believe that Prothro was simply going through the motions during this season is unfair. But whatever joy he had derived in the past from the planning and winning of games at the college level was not fully present. It was no secret that he loathed the proselytizing nature of recruiting, which also added to his diminishing fervor. Nevertheless, Prothro was too much the professional. His commitment to his players, to seeing them through another season, was his primary motivation. He did them proud.

Prothro had the prospect of facing a season with 17 departed starters, worsened when a malingering injury to the supertalented Mickey Cureton forced his permanent retirement from football. In a freak tackling accident during the 1969 Stanford game, his neck had been twisted and a ligament behind his right ear was stretched to twice its normal length. It was not until the following January that he finally sought specialized help for the nagging pain that would not heal. Cureton finished his education, however, and entered into a successful teaching career.

Unfortunately, there was no one to decidedly replace

172

Cureton on the team. Suddenly Prothro's Bruins were forced to rely on one offensive arm—Dennis Dummit's.

There were only 10 seniors on this squad, among them fullback Bob Manning, offensive right tackle Steve Frietas, defensive left tackle Tim Oesterling, and right safety Doug Huff. Picking up the slack were junior defenders Bob Pifferini at left linebacker, Ron Carver at safety, and on offense right end Bob Christiansen, center Dave Dalby, and halfback Marv Kendricks.

The sophomores on this team were plentiful and good, including cornerback Allan Ellis, linebackers Rob Scribner and Vincent Mok, safeties Paul Moyneur and Alan Lemmerman, offensive guards Randy Gaschler and Russ Leal, and end Jack Lassner. This was a team for the future.

The Bruins traveled to open against revenge-minded Oregon State. Beaver coach Dee Andros, nicknamed "The Great Pumpkin" because his visage so resembled a smiling jack-o'-lantern, plotted an eight-man defensive front to hopefully stifle Dummit's passing attack. It worked at first, causing a second-quarter safety at Dummit's expense.

But the running attack UCLA did possess, tailbacks senior Art Sims and sophomore Randy Tyler with soph fullback Gary Campbell mixing time with Manning, ran inside the ends for steady gains, as the Bruins bounced back from a 9-0 halftime deficit to set up two Dummit touchdown tosses to Christiansen and win the curtain raiser, 14-9.

UCLA staged a similar second-half comeback against Pittsburgh, the visiting Bruins presenting Prothro with his one-hundredth win as a college head coach, 24-15, and keeping the head man's record against the Panthers 5-0. The next week, the Bruins staged still another comeback victory, this time at home against surprising Northwestern, using a fourth-quarter fourth-down 53-yard touchdown pass, Dummit to sophomore right half Terry Vernoy, to win, 12-7. At 3-0 so far, the Bruins had developed an unexpected team image as winners who won when they had to.

The first stiff challenge to their fresh expectations came the next game out. For the first time the Bruins were to meet the Texas Longhorns, number one in the nation, coming off a national championship year and heading toward another. And

173

UCLA had to travel to Austin for the privilege.

What transpired was the greatest single-game performance by a Bruin quarterback in UCLA history. Dummit completed 63 percent of his passes for a record 340 yards. The UCLA defense stopped the crushing Wishbone offense with seeming impunity, holding a rushing attack that had averaged 437 yards a game to a "mere" 235. And, in keeping with their seasonal tendencies so far, the Bruins put together two comeback touchdown drives that put them ahead in the fourth quarter, 17-13.

Time started to run out on the Longhorns, as the Wishbone offense is not particularly a "catch-up" formation. There were finally only 12 seconds left, Texas at the UCLA 45 and needing a touchdown to overcome the Bruins' four-point lead. The more than 65,000 in attendance, the coaches, the players, and the concessionaires knew exactly what had to be done to keep the Longhorn's 22-game winning streak intact.

Texas quarterback Eddie Phillips reeled back and let one fly. Longhorn receiver Cotton Speyrer made the catch of the game, as both Bruin defenders played the ball instead of the man, and he ran it in untouched from the 20 as the stadium trembled with its approval. It was Texas over UCLA in a miracle, 20-17.

This miracle was quickly bettered. One week later, in just over the four minutes remaining in the game, Oregon Duck quarterbacks Dan Fouts and Tom Blanchard combined for *three* touchdowns to overcome a 40-21 UCLA lead and win, 41-40, as the Bruins inexplicably disintegrated before the hometown fans.

Though the Bruins finally did a bit of last-second scoring themselves again to wrest a 24-21 victory away from Cal at Berkeley, Rose Bowl-bound Stanford finally evened Plunkett's record against UCLA at 1-1-1 using three Steve Horowitz field goals to boost the Indians over the Bruins, 9-7. Plunkett and Horowitz would later put on a clutch performance to lift the underdog Indians to victory over heavily favored Ohio State in that year's Pasadena classic, 27-17.

UCLA was on the giving and receiving end of two lopsided games, the first a smashing Bruin victory over Washington State, 54-9, marked by five straight and six total successful two-

"The Golden Arm" of Dummit unsprings against the number-one Texas Longhorns in Austin, 1970. Dennis passed for a single-game school record of 340 yards in this 20-17 losing cause.

point PATs.

The tables were turned two weeks later (after a bye) as Washington purposefully poured it on in a 61-20 victory to the joy of the Seattle audience who through the fourth quarter chanted, "We Want 100." Unlike the times when UCLA had routed the Huskies in their two previous Coliseum meetings which featured extensive use of second and third-string players, Husky coach Jim Owens employed his top players throughout the contest.

In a wild conference closer for both schools, and in what would be Prothro's last appearance in the Coliseum in the college ranks, the Bruins and the Trojans played for nothing more than the city championship. As every Prothro/McKay match-up had been as entertaining as hell, this proved no exception.

The Bruins shocked a strong Southern Cal defense by scoring a touchdown just barely three minutes into the game and followed it up with a fumbled kickoff recovery that led to a field goal and a 10-0 lead. The Trojans responded with a touchdown, but Dummit struck with a 39-yard touchdown pass to Christiansen, followed by another fumbled kickoff present resulting in touchdown number three and a 24-7 UCLA lead. Southern Cal came back for another touchdown, and the 78,773 fans in attendance and a national TV audience were treated to a marvelous first quarter in which 38 points in all were scored, neither team required to punt.

In the second quarter, UCLA began to salt it away, with two touchdowns on drives of 49 and 76 yards to take a substantial 38-14 lead into the halftime locker room. The scoring relays stalled in the second half, Southern Cal trading its third-quarter touchdown with UCLA's fourth-quarter answer, the final tote at 45-20. The chain-smoking Prothro had evened his record with the cigar-chomping McKay at three games apiece, which kept the Trojan coach from compiling the first-ever four-game string of victories against his cross-town rival.

Prothro's last game was as a visitor at Tennessee, after waiting through another bye. The Volunteers were headed for the Sugar Bowl in Coach Bill Battle's first year. UCLA played the first half as if the season was already over, netting but nine yards rushing and 25 passing. True to form, the Bruins stormed back to take a 17-14 lead with less than four minutes to play, but a fluke play in which an umpire accidentally maneuvered himself in the thick of a passing play allowed the Vols to make a key fourth-down bid successful and score not long thereafter. A gift loss-on-downs turnover was then cashed in by the Southerners for the 28-17 final.

When Dan Reeves, then owner of the Los Angeles Rams, made the offer of the head coaching spot to Prothro, UCLA's tenth coach departed for the pro pastures for good. He finished with an overall 104-55-5 record, 41-18-3 while at UCLA for a .686 record, second at the time only to his mentor, Red Sanders.

Prothro's career at UCLA had been a memorable one. He returned UCLA football to the national prominence once enjoyed annually in the fifties. He guided the varsity career of

176

Gary Beban, earning him and the school its Heisman Trophy. He led the Bruins to their first victory in the Rose Bowl.

His teams were predictably unpredictable. He would creatively punt on third down throughout this period, yet was just as capable of going for it on fourth down whether leading, tied, or behind. His experiments were calculated, and a failed play did not necessarily mean a mistake, as it might be just setting up the defense for a killer that looked just like its "failed" counterpart.

He remains one of the most complex men ever to have stepped into sports notoriety. Still, his ties with UCLA run deep and strong, and he remains a friend of the university to this day.

A scrawl chalked on the locker room blackboard just prior to the 1970 Southern Cal game by the Bruins' beloved trainer Ducky Drake might sum up the six years Prothro guided the Bruins:

"A Lifetime To Remember."

CHAPTER 10

1971-1973

A tradition of selecting either a current or an ex-assistant coach or an ex-player as head coach had begun in 1939, broken only by the hiring of Sanders. In Prothro's case, he had left UCLA to become the head coach at Oregon State, had driven his teams into excellence and two Rose Bowl visits, and had returned to Westwood an established winner. If it worked once, it might work again, and UCLA athletic director J.D. Morgan relied on the same process in seeking Prothro's replacement.

He was Franklin Cullen Rodgers, Jr., born Oct. 8, 1931, in Atlanta, Georgia. A grandfather had been so taken by the World Series exploits of St. Louis Cardinal pitcher Pepper Martin that he dubbed his grandson "Pepper." Seldom has he been called anything else.

Pepper Rodgers, forceful, dynamic, with boundless energy, sharp wit, has an always positive outlook on life. Raised in Georgia, he matriculated at Georgia Tech, where his brash confidence in himself and his abilities as quarterback created an almost mystical aura. Rodgers *caused* victories to happen. When his team would fall behind, the jaunty Rodgers would trot by his coach, the similarly luck-endowed Bobby Dodd, wink, and tell him to "watch this!" And Rodgers would score.

If there was anybody whom the song "Mr. Touchdown" fit, it was Pepper Rodgers. He really *could* run and kick and throw. Rodgers' list of prep and collegiate honors is impressive. He earned All-State fame in football, baseball, and basketball; the MVP award for the 1954 Orange Bowl (in which he passed for three touchdowns, kicked four PATs, and added a field goal as well); and was already in the Georgia Tech Hall of Fame when he came to UCLA.

He graduated from his alma mater in 1954, and after a brief spring coaching stint as an assistant at Virginia, he entered the Air Force, where the next five years were spent playing and coaching, including two years with Coach Ben Martin at the Air Force Academy. Captain Pepper Martin left the service and next staffed at Florida for four years (60-64), the Gators visiting the Gator Bowl twice during that period.

He joined Prothro's staff at UCLA in 1965. As the offensive coordinator, Rodgers manned the binoculars in the press box, relaying plays and suggestions from his aerie, and was directly responsible for many of the game-breaking successes enjoyed by the Beban-led Bruins in the 1965 and 1966 seasons.

Rodgers rose to the head coaching ranks in 1967, taking on a tough rebuilding job at Kansas University. Rebuild them he did, and a 9-2 second-year record was the most games the Jayhawks had won in a single season in 60 years. The Orange Bowl visit this earned was a loss to Penn State, 15-14, marking the first time he'd ever been involved in a losing bowl game in 11 trips.

A long-established offensive reputation and a casual rapport with players, plus his previous and successful stint at UCLA, made his choice as head coach of the Bruins one of promise. Rodgers fulfilled that promise—and how.

But not at first. Inheriting the wing-ish T formation from Prothro, Rodgers fielded a team coming off an unsteady year. Though it contained the biggest offensive line in UCLA history, averaging 235 pounds, without a clear choice for a quarterback replacement for Dummit, and with a young crop of running backs behind the stalwart senior Marv Kendricks, the team lacked a central scoring focus.

The offensive line was charged by seniors left tackle Greg Pearman and All-America Dave Dalby at center and juniors left guard Randy Gaschler, right guard Russ Leal, and right tackle Bruce Walton (basketball Bill's brother). Kendricks and juniors Gary Campbell and Randy Tyler were the primary backfield punch, and senior and All-Coast right end Bob Christiansen was the top receiver.

The defense was the part that was going to keep whatever Bruin hopes there were alive when things got darkest. By and

Bruin head coach Pepper Rodgers relaxes on the sidelines with quarterback Mark Harmon.

large, they did. Senior Mike Pavich and sophomore Rick Baska filled up the middle guard spot, sophomore ends Cal Peterson and Fred McNeill, and linebackers junior Vince Mok and senior Bob Pifferini covered the midground, and juniors safety Paul Moyneur and cornerbacks Rob Scribner and Allan Ellis provided deep coverage.

The schedule Rodgers inherited was enough to give even a seasoned team the heebie-jeebies. The opener at home was against virtually the same Pittsburgh team that had given the Bruins such a tough time in 1970. With the lead changing hands throughout the game, a UCLA turnover late in the fourth quarter set up Pitt's game-winning touchdown in the 29-25 loss.

Then crushing Texas came to Los Angeles, the number-three team in the nation. The Bruins kept it close for three quarters, after surprising the Longhorns with an early 7-0 lead and barely missing another touchdown opportunity, but the Texas Wishbone rolled on to win, 28-10. Next traveling to a number-four Michigan, the Wolverine defensive line put in a magnificent performance, preserving the 38-0 shutout.

Returning to Westwood, an exhausted Rodgers began to reassess his players, position by position, hoping to strike upon some untried and unthought-of combination that might snap this horrendous start, the longest opening losing streak since 1943.

Junior college transfer quarterback Mike Flores was enjoying only fair success (though a considerable number of his passes were dropped rather than poorly thrown), and back-up junior Clay Gallagher was also unproductive. Rodgers dipped down to number three, junior Scott Henderson, and started him against visiting Oregon State. Rodgers also installed the I formation during the week for good measure. The Beavers won, 34-17.

Traveling to Spokane to play Washington State, the Bruins were faced with a Cougar team eager to take advantage of the Bruins' misfortunes. The Blue presented its anxious head coach with a much-appreciated fortieth birthday present, his first UCLA victory, 34-21. The following week, UCLA's new I formation ground out a 28-12 travel trip over Arizona, the first meeting between the schools since 1928. The most glaring weakness shown these last three games had been an inability to cover on punt and kick returns, with Oregon State and Washington State each scoring a 100-yard kickoff return and Arizona taking a punt in from 94 yards out.

UCLA next faced Cal, a team that had been slapped with a no-postseason game penalty by the NCAA for having on the squad "illegal" Isaac Curtis, who was delcared ineligible for taking one of his entrance exams after a specific deadline had passed (there were extenuating circumstances). Cal's protest was unsuccessful, and the entire season was declared null-and-void in advance, with or without Mr. Curtis. The Bears played him, and the Bears were winning. Cal beat UCLA, 31-24.

The Bruins entered into a fumblathon in losing to Washington the next week, hampered by the loss of both starting backs, Kendricks and Johnson, plus a strong performance by Husky quarterback Sonny Sixkiller. It was the visiting

181

Huskies, 23-12. Stanford completed UCLA's losses on its way to a second consecutive Rose Bowl trip, beating the Bruins, 20-9.

Meeting fellow injury-laden Southern Cal, both teams could only muster enough energy to score a touchdown apiece, and the game ended in a 7-7 deadlock. But a portentious public change in the Bruins had transpired this day.

Although the freshman squad had been practicing it all year, and the varsity had relied on it whenever a scoring drive neared the end zone, Rodgers officially scrapped an offensive formation for the second time this season and used this third attack virtually the entire game, sort of "trying it on for size."

UCLA's Wishbone T had been born.

Almost unique in the West, the UCLA Wishbone figuratively and emotionally set apart the Bruins from their coastal counterparts. The sizable offensive line Rodgers had at his disposal was tailor-made for this offense, one far ahead of the typical defenses of its day. When it was operating at its full potential, the Wishbone could be phenomenally devastating. The UCLA division would provide spectacular examples of its crushing power.

Briefly described, the quarterback essentially forms with three "yoked" backs a "Y" or, poetically, a Wishbone-like curved T. After the snap, the quarterback first has the option to fake or give the ball to any one of his three advancing backs directly into the line.

Or then the fun begins. The quarterback might keep the ball, moving laterally down the line with backs trailing or preceding him, with the option of slicing into the line open to him at all times. If a defender moves in to tackle the QB ("commits"), the ball is pitched to one of the accompanying backs, who then either proceeds into and through the line or continues the option ploy with the backs still at his disposal. Optimally, this all transpires at breakneck speed, driving defenses crazy.

Unfortunately, this optioning is also extremely fumble prone, as clean timing of every pitch is absolutely mandatory. Another factor is its tendency to be an extremely time-consuming process, as most run-oriented offenses are. If a Wishbone team is in control of a game, no problem, but when it is forced to play catch-up late in the fourth quarter, its chances

182

of staging a whirlwind pass-induced game-saving drive are virtually nil.

The team's composition was not without its question marks. The four seniors on defense, right end Paul Moyneur, linebacker Vincent Mok, safety Alan Lemmerman, and future pro star Allan Ellis at left half, meant a long line of juniors would bear most of the assault. Rick Baska manned the right guard spot, Fred McNeill was posted at right end, Cal Peterson split time with sophomore Fulton Kuykendahl at left end, Jimmy Allen was at right half, and Jim Bright was also at safety.

The offensive line featured seniors right tackle Bruce Walton, center Randy Gaschler, left guard Russ Leal, and tight end Jack Lassner and juniors Steve Klosterman at right guard and Ed Kezirian at left tackle. The backfield was junior rich, with right half Kermit Johnson teamed with his Blair High School partner James McAlister at left half, and junior college transfer quarterback Mark Harmon, son of Michigan Hall of Famer Tom Harmon, set to call the signals. Plus, there was the tremendous kicking ability of junior Effren Herrera to add his points whenever possible.

Rodgers needed another sharp, offensive-minded assistant, as he had been to Prothro. Homer Smith was that man. The fact that Smith was one of the nation's premier passing coaches did not deter Rodgers from seeking him out, as Smith was deeply familiar with a run-oriented game as a player and graduate assistant from operating Princeton's single-wing attack.

Between the 1971 and 1972 seasons, long hours were spent by the two of them drilling the nuances of the Wishbone into each other's head. With just the same intensity, they were to drill it into the Bruins.

"Pepper drove that thing through like a wagon master driving 'em through the West," Smith recalled. "That was his main strength. He *made* it. I've received some credit, along with (assistant coaches) Tony Kopay, Terry Donahue, Billie Matthews, and the others, but the power of Pepper's will is what made it happen. He thought it would work immediately. And it did. It worked in the first game (that season)."

That first game was against unsuspecting Nebraska, number one in the nation, defending National Champions for two years straight while enjoying a 32-game unbeaten streak, begun with a win against Rodgers' Kansas team. Pepper started it, and Pepper ended it.

On the strength of McAlister and Johnson, along with Harmon who threw a 46-yard surprise bomb for a first-quarter touchdown, plus the defensive brilliance of Allen and Peterson, UCLA never trailed. Herrera helped the Bruins jump to a 10-0 lead, but Nebraska tied it by the half, as Husker Heisman candidate Johnny Rodgers lived up to his publicity, along with the great play by defensive middle guard Rich Glover, who was literally a one-man gang.

In the second half Harmon put his Bruins ahead with a short touchdown run set up by Allen's interception of an errant pass by Nebraska quarterback David Humm. The Cornhuskers tied it one more time at 17. Then UCLA entered into its most impressive drive of the evening, mainly because it was not set up by any of Nebraska's many turnovers, driving 57 yards to set up Herrera's game-winning 30-yard field goal with 22 seconds remaining to play. The Bruins shocked the nation with this 20-17 upset victory.

Pepper Rodgers went home that night and, fully clothed, jumped into his pool. The machine that would be the UCLA scoring monster for the next two years had just been switched on. It popped and sputtered, but it had bumped up against one

Two-time National Champion Nebraska was stunned by UCLA's Wishbone in the 1972 opener, this game-winning field goal by Effren Herrera doing the trick for UCLA, 20-17.

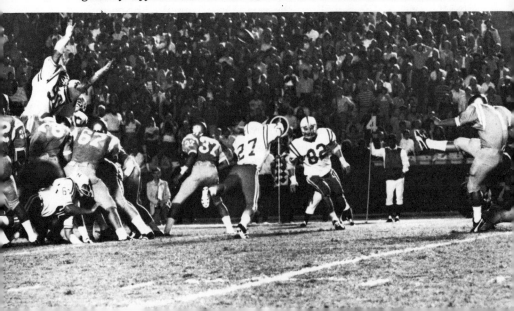

of the best defensive teams in the nation and had survived, survived a winner. It worked! It won! Coaching was fun again!

Visiting Wishbone-ish Pittsburgh, UCLA rushed for 406 yards, including a game-opening 99-yard march to score. Johnson later sprinted 80 yards for one touchdown, and back-up quarterback Rob Scribner, who had selflessly agreed to move from his previously starting cornerback spot, chalked off a 63-yard keeper of his own for another. With this 38-28 victory, the Bruins nosed into the Top 10.

Then the Wolverines came to Los Angeles, and they brought with them Bo Schembechler's "Meat Grinder" offense. Though the game marked the only time young Harmon faced his famous father's alma mater, Michigan was simply too well stocked at this stage, knocking the Bruins out of the Top 10 with their 26-9 victory over UCLA.

Like a train momentarily sidetracked, the engine was restoked against Oregon the following week, UCLA chugging to a 65-20 home victory. The Ducks, fresh from a similar 68-3 wipeout against Oklahoma, saw three Bruin quarterbacks run free, Harmon, Scribner, and freshman wildcat John Sciarra (freshman now declared eligible for varsity play this year).

Arizona next came to the Coliseum, putting up a strong fight before succumbing after Johnson's 69-yard touchdown run in the last two-and-a-half minutes of the game. The Bruins had actually been behind in the first quarter, 21-7, but along the way amassed an incredible 505 rushing yards, setting a new school record, and Johnson set a single-game rushing record of his own, 183 yards for 15 carries, tops during the Wishbone years. It was UCLA 42, Arizona 31.

Dry weather greeted the Bruins for their game in Corvalis against Oregon State. Turning over all four fumbles, the Bruins started slowly then revved up to an easy 37-7 win, as they rose to third in the nation in rushing. Next to face the machine was Cal, led by fine quarterbacks Jay Cruze and Steve Bartkowski. The Bruins reset the single-game team rushing record at 532, as Johnson ran for touchdowns of 45 and 55 yards, Scribner tallied one from the 48, and UCLA renewed another string of victories over Cal with this 49-13 victory. Though losing five of its seven fumbles, the Bruins now found themselves leading the nation in per-game rushing, one yard more per game than Oklahoma.

Against Washington State, UCLA once again had a tough time getting the machine warmed up in the first quarter. It was not until McAlister scored from two yards out almost five minutes into the second quarter before the Bruins clicked off 21 unanswered points to cruise in from there, beating the Cougars, 35-20.

Stanford was forced to stop calling itself the Indians. The overreactive board of trustees succumbed to a minor campus demonstration staged to protest the "demeaning" team name and, until a more suitable alternative could be selected, had chosen the ultrasafe "Cardinals" as the replacement.

Hosting Stanford, UCLA's defense quickly found quarterback Mike Boryla carried on the Red passing tradition admirably, his aerial show more than justifying his position as that season's Pac-Eight offensive leader. Harmon had a hand in every Bruin score, running for two touchdowns and passing for two more.

The Bruins led 28-23 with just under four minutes left to play. Boryla brought his team down to the 29, but after overthrowing his first-down target, UCLA defenders McNeill and sophomore right tackle Tom Waddell shut off the passing on the following two plays, the second a fumble recovered by junior linebacker Steve Hookano to put the game on ice.

The conference race for the Rose Bowl was now down to two teams, UCLA and Southern Cal. With technically a game to waste, an "it doesn't matter if we win or lose" Bruin team visited Washington and paid for it. The Bruins lost three fumbles. Reliable senior legman Bruce Barnes shanked a punt. There were two interceptions. A bobbled punt return once forced the Bruins to begin operations from the one. It was one of *those* games.

After hurrying to 7-0 and 14-7 leads, the Bruins let up, and the Huskies turned on. With their wide attack shut off, the Bruins were funneled into a stifling Husky defensive front, the Wishbone as ineffective as possible. Washington continued the string of Seattle-based victories, 30-21.

The unheralded Bruins had flashed onto the national scene, creating an offensive furor that at any time would have focused undivided attention on their doings. However, 1972 belonged to Southern Cal. The number-one Trojans were, by

186

most accounts, one of the greatest college football teams ever created. With breakaway runner Anthony Davis, rock-solid fullback Sam "Bam" Cunningham, the release valve passing combination of quarterback Mike Rae and flanker Lynn Swann, to some they were *too* good to be a college team!

Like Washington the week before, Southern Cal took away UCLA's mandatory wide game, forcing the Bruins up the middle into one of the most punishing defensive lines in Trojan history. Sometimes even presenting the Bruins with a nine-man front, it was felt that UCLA's fortunes might have been brighter had Harmon passed more than the two times he did in the first three quarters, desperately resorting to the air for three of seven in the fourth.

Though the Trojans' perfect season continued, 24-7, UCLA set the conference team rushing record at 3,810 yards, passing Howard Jones' 1929 Thundering Herd of Southern Cal by two.

The Bruins expected to be even stronger for 1973. Only one starter, cornerback Allan Ellis, departed the defense. The offensive backfield was remaining virtually intact.

On offense were seniors place-kicker Effren Herrera, right guard Steve Klosterman, tackles Al Oliver and Ed Kezirian, tight end Gene Jones, right half Kermit Johnson, fullback James McAlister, and quarterback Mark Harmon. Juniors included right guard Myke Horton, fullback Charlie "Choo Choo" Schuhmann, left guard Gene Clark, left half Russel Charles, center Art Kuehn, and split end Steve Monahan, and sophomores were quarterback John Sciarra, split end Norm Anderson, left half Eddie Ayers, center Randy Cross, left tackle Phil McKinnely, and punter-fullback John Sullivan, plus freshman running back Wendell Tyler.

Defensively, the upperclass roster featured seniors left tackle Gerry Roberts; right tackles Bill Sandifer, Pat Sweetland, and Gerald Peeke, ends Cal Peterson and Fred McNeill; cornerbacks Jimmy Allen and Alton McSween; left linebacker Rick Baska; and safety Jim Bright. Left end Fulton Kuykendahl, nose guard Greg Norfleet, linebacker Gene Settles, and safety Greg Williams were the junior returnees, bolstered by transfers cornerback John Nanoski, safety Kent Pearce, and middle guard Mike Martinez.

They were going to be quite a team. Pepper Rodgers set the tone for the coming season, understating, "Yes, we should be stronger. But we close against Southern Cal, the nation's number-one team, and do you know who we open up against next season? Nebraska at Lincoln. Here we go again!" Rodgers' assessment of the future described the exact nature of the 1973 season. Nebraska and Southern Cal represented two rock-hard bookends with a stack of paper-thin opponents in comparison between them.

The Cornhuskers were about as high for their opening opponents as a team could possibly get. It is roughly estimated that any football team gets radically emotional only once or twice during a regular season. Nebraska used up one right away. This was factor number one in its favor.

Nebraska also presented UCLA (and the nation) with a new defensive development. As conceived by Husker assistant Monty Kiffin, the linebackers are prevented from being blocked by varying charges by the down linemen, freeing them to shift along or "scrape" the line as a play develops and always be in the right place when the line is threatened by the ballcarrier. (This became known as "The Arkansas Package," or in some coaching circles as "The Universal Defense.") This was factor number two for Nebraska.

Finally, an army is only as good as its boots. Due to a mix-up back home, the Bruins arrived in Lincoln with the wrong shoes, footgear not suited to run on the rain-slicked artificial turf. Factor number three, and the Bruins stumbled into a 40-14 Cornhusker ambush. UCLA had all season to recover until the game with the Trojans.

Recover the Bruins did, with hapless Iowa the first to fall. Sciarra stepped in midgame in this home opener to replace a stuttering Harmon and shifted the Wishbone into high gear after a dismal 7-7 first quarter to lead the Bruins to a solid 55-18 victory. Sciarra repeated the same feat the following week in East Lansing, as the Bruins outpowered an underrated Michigan State team, 34-21. Still, a glaring tendency for all the ballcarriers to fumble sent mild shockwaves through the coaching staff.

The following week, Utah was trampled in the Coliseum. The Bruins scored three touchdowns in the first three minutes

188

and continued to mount up the second-highest score ever by a UCLA team, 66-16. In this game, Sciarra and Harmon reversed roles, as Harmon came in to relieve a semi-successful Sciarra to personally demolish the Redskins, the battle for the number-one quarterback spot now neck-and-neck between these two close friends. All this, plus Johnson was fast tearing toward the career rushing mark held for 34 years by Kenny Washington.

Opening the Pac-Eight race against Stanford in Palo Alto, the Bruins caught a still-rebuilding Cardinal team too soon, rushing for yet another team record of 621 yards, adding 29 more through the air, to cap off this 59-13 win. But after scoring three touchdowns himself, churning fullback James McAlister left the game with a severely bruised knee and did not travel to Spokane the following week to play Washington State.

Schuhmann filled in and broke the game open after a superhuman stunting and gambling Cougar defense had kept UCLA to only a 3-0 halftime lead. "Choo-Choo" broke out for 53 yards to score and give the Bruins a comfortable 17-7 lead late in the third quarter. This victory brought Johnson the all-time UCLA rushing record with five games still to go; Harmon was set (for now) as the top quarterback; and Kuykendahl, Peterson, and McNeill were the defensive standouts, as UCLA finished with a 24-13 advantage.

Sad California was next to face the Bruin juggernaut, the third consecutive game to be missed by McAlister. Harmon's arm was responsible for 185 passing yards of the team's 545 total, and Bruin cornerback Jimmy Allen snagged Bear quarterback Vince Ferragamo's end zone-bound pass at the goal line and ran it back the full 100 yards for the longest scoring interception in UCLA history. Cal lost big, 61-21, yet with all these repeated lopsided victories UCLA was surprisingly ranked only thirteenth in the nation.

The following week the Bruins were pegged as prohibitive 35-point favorites over one of the weakest teams in Washington history. The odds-makers missed by 14. The Bruins gained 671 yards in total offense, still the UCLA record. Sciarra carried five times for 130 yards, after spending most of the week in the hospital with a strained back. Johnson picked up 141 more yards, including a 57-yard touchdown popped through left tackle. Freshman Tyler scored three touchdowns in the fourth

The UCLA Wishbone juggernaut of 1973, here grinding out a 62-13 victory over Washington, quarterback Harmon initiating the option sequence.

quarter, the Bruins stretching out to an incredible 62-13 victory.

Though there were still a few players and coaches around who remembered the Huskies' all-out 61-20 victory in 1970, UCLA had the courtesy to play out its bench in this one. Possibly more than any other game for UCLA, this full-team participation game showcased the awesome power of the Wishbone working to its full potential. Coach Smith recalled, "The offense got ahead of the defense. They couldn't catch up. They didn't know what was coming. The machinerey got ahead of their machinery. And everything worked."

A strange chapter opened and quickly closed with this game as well. In a day when kickers were bent on field goal distance, UCLA's especially fine kicker Effren Herrera was becoming frustrated. His four field goals against Washington in 1971 stands as the school record for most in one game, (since tied), and his nine successful PATs against Utah that season tied the Bruin record set in 1968 by Zenon Andrusyshyn.

But now that he was a part of a Wishbone team that so seldom stalled midfield, he began to feel his field goal talents were going to waste. In a fourth-and-two situation on the Husky 23, the team clicking off six yards a play, Rodgers opted to go for it. It is possible that had the Bruins made it nothing would have happened. But they did not, and Herrera resented not being given the chance to kick another field goal at the time.

190

He then purposefully shanked an extra point try on the Bruins' final touchdown, and afterwards made it a point to tell the public about it as a protest over what he felt was a lack of respect for his talents by the coaching staff. It did not take long for him to realize he had momentarily placed himself above the team and once again returned to the fold, completely forgiven and the incident forgotten.

However, it did end up with a sad, ironic twist. His protesting PAT miss resulted in his only tying the NCAA single-season PAT mark at 60, a national record still unbroken, instead of breaking it.

The Bruins had a relatively tough time in defeating the Ducks in Eugene, Oregon, even though UCLA managed to only fumble once throughout the traditional downpour. After skidding to a 7-0 halftime lead, the Bruins broke it open in the third quarter, Oregon scoring a mop-up touchdown well into the fourth quarter to avoid the shutout, making it the 27-7 final.

In the last game before Southern Cal, the Bruins served as rude hosts to Oregon State. On the first play of the game, UCLA on the 18, Harmon faked a jam into the middle, drawing in every Beaver linebacker and d-back. By the time his pass reached streaking freshman end Ray Burks, with not a Beaver within 25 yards of him, there was a moment's hush as everybody in the Coliseum realized the Bruins had already scored, 15 seconds into the game! Johnson became the first player in UCLA history to rush for 1,000 yards in one season, and a thoughtful Pepper Rodgers inserted him late in the fourth quarter to ensure Johnson scored touchdown number 15, guaranteeing another Bruin single-season record.
UCLA simply crushed Oregon State, 56-14.

Directly after that season's Washington game, senior defensive tackle Bill Sandifer, after musing about not taking the remaining games before Southern Cal seriously, gave a most psychic warning: "I just hope nobody on this team gets too cocky." Directly after the Oregon State game, directly before Southern Cal, the Bruins got cocky.

"There is no way in hell anybody is going to stop us—that's our feeling now," said James McAlister, adding, "I think they'll be more concerned about us than we'll be with them." Johnson piped in, "I don't see how they can defense us.

They will be so conscious of our running game that the pass will sneak up on them and it will be over.'' Sciarra joined the chorus, ''I'm looking forward to it because we're bigger, stronger, and more experienced.'' Such comments are, of course, a locker room decorator's dream.

Southern Cal did defense the awesome UCLA offense. The Bruin coaching staff was completely stymied during the game by the defensive antics of Trojan linebacker James Sims. Furthermore, 8-1-1 Southern Cal, laden with mistakes and penalties all season, played an almost flawless game against UCLA, including no turnovers, while the Bruins handed over the ball six times, with four fumbles and two interceptions.

It was not a game UCLA should have lost. The coaching staff admittedly took a ''take what the opponent allows'' approach to this game, and once having decided that it was pointless to run wide—the bread-and-butter for the Bruins all season—the team instead was directed to flail at an unbending Trojan defensive line.

Coach Smith admitted that, ''We let them throw a monkey wrench into our Wishbone. We should have handled it as a machinery problem, corrected it, and gone right on about out business. We didn't. We came in at halftime, we started trying to do something else, and then a third attack plan (creeped in), and we shouldn't have done that. We should have taken our Wishbone machinery and applied it as intensively as we could, and if something went wrong we should have repaired it right on

John Sciarra starts a play against Southern Cal in 1973, with lead man James McAlister and fullbacks Russel Charles and Kermit Johnson on the move.

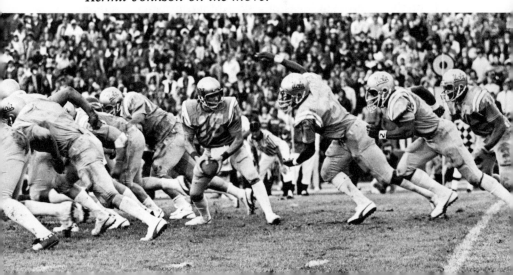

the spot."

The Trojans had essentially dismantled the Bruins. Favored by three, the Bruins lost, 23-13. Finishing out the season at 9-2, the Bruins fell to number nine in the nation but were unable to accept any bowl bids due to the still-intact exclusivity clause with the Rose Bowl. Even so, UCLA had reset its own conference rushing record at 4,403 yards and with 5,177 total offense yards had broken Southern Cal's 1970 Pac-Eight record by 22 yards.

The season of bookends was over. Still, Rodgers had a promising year ahead of him. He had a strong recruiting showing, fine players were returning, and he was looking forward to getting over that final hurdle and into the Rose Bowl. There was only one thing that could possibly pry him away from UCLA.

That one thing was the opportunity to return to his alma mater as its head coach. When Georgia Tech made the offer, the grateful Yellow Jacket could not refuse. "I guess I'm a vagabond at heart," he explained. "I really do not have any place I have more loyalty to than UCLA, except I am loyal to Georgia Tech. I really love UCLA and wouldn't leave except to go to the place where I ushered at football games, went to school, and have a multitude of friends."

With Rodgers went UCLA's two-year love affair with the mighty Wishbone. Its effect had been far reaching: After a dismal 3-7-1 1971 season, Rodgers, like a smug poker player who always manages to come up with an ace-in-the-hole, resurrected a faltering UCLA football program into impressive 8-3 and 9-2 seasons, good enough for two bowl bids in any other conference.

Though his stay at UCLA was relatively brief, his impact is still felt. The teams and players Rodgers fielded are plastered throughout the Bruin record books. His sharp wit and brash smile pixilated those who came into friendly contact with him while at UCLA. He fought for his Wishbone and saw to it that his Western brand led the nation in rushing with 400.3 yards per game in 1973 and was right up there in scoring and total offense for both years as well. He remains one of the greatest offensive football minds to ever coach the UCLA Bruins.

CHAPTER 11
1974-1976

In the search for a new head coach at UCLA in 1974, one individual began to stand out. He was a California product who had risen abruptly through the ranks of some of the most offensively exciting teams in the nation—and never left the state. His name was Richard Albert Vermeil, and he was to synthesize the offensive promise of the Bruins and propel them to brilliance.

Born October 30, 1936, in Calistoga, California, a small town in Napa County, one of the state's premiere wine centers, Dick Vermeil grew up to star on that town's high school football team, also excelling in basketball, track, and baseball. He played quarterback for two years at Napa Junior College, then transferred to San Jose State, playing two seasons and graduating in 1958 with a bachelor's degree in physical education, continuing there for his M.A. in 1959.

From the role of a high school assistant in San Jose that fall of 1959, he moved to the head spot at San Mateo's Hillside High School for three years. His college experience began as the head coach back at Napa College for the 1964 season; then he moved onto John Ralston's Stanford staff for four years, each successive season rising and taking on greater responsibilities until he was offensive backfield, quarterback, and passing coach by 1968.

After spending a year on George Allen's staff with the Los Angeles Rams, he joined Tommy Prothro's last corps at UCLA in 1970 as offensive coordinator, and moved with Prothro back to the Rams in 1971. In 1973 the new Ram owner, Carroll Rosenbloom, terminated Prothro's job, but Vermeil remained to assist the new coach, Chuck Knox, working with the backfield runners and the special teams.

Ralston, Allen, Prothro, Knox, four superior coaches who all felt that Dick Vermeil was, at 37, one of the finest young coaches in the nation and would do an outstanding job for UCLA. Selected as the Bruins' twelfth coach, he had driven himself by sheer force of will from relative obscurity into one of the top coaching positions in the nation in just 15 years.

Vermeil was not enthusiastic about inheriting the Wishbone. Hoping to find a happy medium between the Wishbone-trained veterans and a more pass-capable format, he selected the Veer attack as the best for him and the program.

The Veer, as created at the University of Houston by Coach Bill Yeoman, operates with split right and left halfbacks positioned and operating similarly as their Wishbone counterparts, but without that fullback. This allows for two receivers and forces the defense to respect the passing threat this T-like formation presents while still allowing a team to option-pitch run as with the 'bone (making it also just as fumble-prone).

Though quarterbacks are generally willing to run, most *love* to pass, and junior quarterback John Sciarra was a happy Bruin when Dick Vermeil came on board. His line was solid, with seniors left tackle Gene Clark, center Art Kuehn, and right guard Myke Horton and juniors right tackle Phil McKinnely, left guard Randy Cross, tight end Gene Bleymaier, and split end

The indefatigable head coach Dick Vermeil.

Norm Andersen providing interference. Senior left half Russel Charles and sophomore right half Wendell Tyler were the starting split backs, senior Steve Monahan was the flanker, and junior transfer Brett White manned the punting and place-kicking chores.

Seven senior defensive starters were expected to help buffer the expected rough spots during the transition between the two offensive sets. Inside linebackers Tom Waddell and Fulton Kuykendahl, nose guard Greg Norfleet, outside linebacker Russ Ball, left cornerback John Nanoski, and safeties Herschel Ramsey and Kent Pearce were those seven. Juniors left tackle Cliff Frazier, outside linebacker Dale Curry, and right cornerback Matt Fahl and sophomore right tackle Bob Crawford filled out the starting stopmen.

Vermeil's debut was a real barnburner in Knoxville, Tennessee. UCLA opened the season as the nation's number-12 team, Tennessee number 16. The Volunteers had a one-man explosion in their backfield, quarterback Condredge Holloway, whose electric performance in this nationally televised game sent the 57,000 fans in Neyland Stadium literally out of their minds.

Tennessee shocked the Bruins with a Holloway quick-count touchdown pass on the second play of the game and increased its lead to 10-0 in that quarter. UCLA was able to pick up just three points by the half, this after Holloway had been sent to the hospital for X rays of an injured shoulder.

In the second half, a Bruin touchdown on a fumble recovered in the end zone by senior nose guard Rick Kukulica brought the teams even at 10-10. Sciarra was having a brilliant game, once going 71 yards on a keeper while heading for a rushing total of 178 yards and passing for 15 of 21 and 212 yards. Sciarra located Andersen in the end zone for a 13-yard touchdown pass and a 17-10 fourth-quarter lead.

But just before this go-ahead Bruin drive, Holloway flamboyantly returned to the arena, making a grand entrance into the stadium with a clean bill of health, sending the sea of orange in the stands into a frenzy. When he finally took over the controls of the Tennessee team, he screamed them down the field to the tying score.

Then, as cool as if he had been a master of the Veer for seasons on end, Sciarra guided the team down the field,

196

watching the clock, successfully bringing them down to the Vol 23 with but seconds to go. Kicker White unfortunately missed from 40 yards out, and the game went on the books at 17-17.

As Vermeil put it, "I'd rather tie than lose, and all we can do is grow. I think some of the things we've been selling our players will mean more now. Two weeks from now (after a bye), you won't recognize our offense."

Vermeil was a master at making such statements that promoted his team without ever containing inciteful remarks that future opponents could use on their lockers. Unfortunately, after spending two weeks attempting to work out the fumble-bugs, the Bruins visited Iowa with the same all-too recognizable offense, fumbling six times and losing three. The Bruins lost to the Hawkeyes, 21-10. "I thought I'd started to develop discipline on the practice field that would carry over against anyone we played in a game," he remarked. "I guess you can see, I haven't."

Receiver Norm Andersen keeps a tight grip on the ball in the 1974 Tennessee game, UCLA's first with the Veer, a 17-17 tie.

Discipline was the cornerstone of Vermeil's coaching style, and that translated into extra hard work if he suspected a loss was the result of its lack. The Bruins steamed into the home opener with Michigan State, and their work began to pay off. Exploding against the weaker Spartans, UCLA thundered to a 56-14 victory, scoring two touchdowns per quarter, with virtually every player contributing to the win.

At 1-1-1, UCLA was a qualified mystery at this stage of the season. In another bumbler one week later in Salt Lake City, UCLA looked anything like a world beater in defeating the Utah Redskins, 27-14.

Vermeil, to his credit, was staging virtually a one-man campaign to drum up local nonalumni support for his Bruins. Southern California is an area slightly sports jaded by the Dodgers, Rams, Lakers, Kings, Trojans, tennis, soccer, surfing, track, auto racing, volleyball, bicycling, hang gliding, over-the-line, sailing, you name it. Just prior to the conference opener against Stanford, Vermeil told the world, "I expect Stanford (0-3-1) will have to play its best game of the season to beat us because UCLA is going to play like you've never seen a Bruin team play."

The Cardinals did, but the Bruins did not—at least not the way Vermeil intended. Stanford sophomore quarterbacks Mike Cordova and Guy Benjamin built two first-half touchdowns into a 13-10 lead that almost stood up the entire second half. Fortunately, White kicked a 37-yard field goal with no time remaining and pulled the Bruins up to a face-saving 13-13 tie.

Now the Bruins were 2-1-2 and *still* a qualified mystery. Underrated Washington State was next to give the Bruins fits. In a crowd-pleasing show of solidarity, the defense prevented the Cougars from scoring a go-ahead touchdown four straight times from the one, preserving the 17-13 fourth-quarter advantage that brought Vermeil his first conference victory. It looked as if the Bruins were finally coming together.

The following game accidentally turned UCLA's season back around in the wrong direction. The Bruins traveled to meet their interuniversity brothers in Berkeley, the Bears still enduring an NCAA probation from the Isaac Curtis affair from the 1971 season.

It was an important game for Cal for many reasons. The Bears were enjoying one of their finest seasons, 5-1 at this point, behind the combination of quarterback Steve Bartkowski, receiver Steve Rivera, and running back Chuck Muncie. Bear head coach Mike White was Vermeil's best friend. Countless players on the Bear squad, as always, were from the Los Angeles area. Finally, Cal's record against its southern brethren was fast getting out of hand, having lost to UCLA 12 times in the past 15 years.

The Bruin defense put on a tremendous show, keeping the Bears to just three points, while Sciarra led his team to two touchdowns in the first half, the first a 69-yard scoring strike to Andersen. But while attempting a second-quarter pitchout, Sciarra's foot was firmly planted when he was hit by Bear tackle Dave Frey, a clean and legal tackle that just turned Sciarra the wrong way, and snap, his ankle broke. The multidimensional quarterback, vital to the team's continued success, was lost for the season.

The back-up quarterback, sophomore Jeff Dankworth, stepped in and most ably led the team for the rest of the game, including two touchdowns in that second half, as the Bruins coasted to a 28-3 victory.

But further injuries began to accumulate, most notably to Kuykendahl, Frazier, Clark, and freshman inside linebacking wonder Frank Manumaleuna. (Manumaleuna's neck injury was such that UCLA had to, in good conscience, release him from the team, the diagnosis indicating that another such blow would be fatal. Manumaleuna defied the odds, continued his college playing career with San Jose State, and went on to a fine pro career.)

Ironically, shortly after Dankworth replaced Sciarra he too suffered an injury to his ankle when it accidentally was stepped on by center Kuehn. Though he was able to finish the game in spite of the pain, his injury worsened immediately thereafter.

Dankworth was not able to start the following week in a crucial game against Washington in Seattle. Getting the call was freshman Steve Bukich, who opted to attend UCLA even though his father, "Rifle" Rudy Bukich, had been a star with Southern Cal (and the Rams).

It was too much to expect from any player with but one

full week's worth of practice on the first team. The Huskies won, 31-9, continuing the Seattle "jinx" as well. Vermeil allayed some of Bukich's pain by allowing, "He isn't the reason we got beat. He made some mistakes...but he didn't play on defense."

The following week, the team bounced back over the Oregon Ducks. Dankworth was able to go the distance, and the defense stopped two Duck drives, one at the seven and the other at the one with timely interceptions, and accomplished UCLA's first shutout since 1969 with this 21-0 victory. But again, another key injury hurt the team, this one to Wendell Tyler.

The offensive line creatively sought recognition by referring to itself proudly as "The Huge Corporation." The partners did their job against Oregon State. After a 7-7 tie at the midway point, they began to blow open the holes that let Dankworth, left halves Charles and junior Eddie Ayers and right half senior Charlie Schuhmann dart their way to five touchdowns to make it a 33-14 runaway.

With an increasing number of players watching the season slip by them from the sidelines, the Bruins had mustered enough talent among the reserves to defeat lesser opponents. Healthy and talented Southern Cal was another matter. With the Trojans boasting the likes of quarterback Pat Haden, receiver J.K. McKay (son of head coach John McKay), freshman star defender Dennis Thurman, and the super back Anthony Davis, the Bruins suffered the same kind of day as they had in Washington, falling 34-9 and finishing the season at 6-3-2.

The most disheartening thing about the 1974 season was the constantly unsettling atmosphere the parade of injuries brought. The many superb athletes on the squad were sometimes overburdened with the need to overcompensate for not just one teammate but for whole squad sections that fell by the medical wayside. Young replacements for the veterans were getting rude baptisms instead of slow seasonings.

Over the years UCLA has been blessed with players of character, who allow for the uncertainties that playing such a hard contact sport brings, and who rarely dwell on the "might have beens." Vermeil's Bruins believed in themselves, in what Vermeil was drilling into them. They would take the lessons learned in 1974 to heart and would make the 1975 season a most unforgettable year.

The defense was thick with experience, starters and reserves alike, with four freshmen also making the grade. The line included left tackles junior Tim Tennigkeit and sophomore Pete Pele, nose guards senior Cliff Frazier and sophomore Steve Tetrick, and right tackles freshman Manu Tuiasosopo and junior Bob Crawford.

Inside linebackers included senior Terry Tautolo; sophomores Raymond Bell, Willie Beamon, and Jeff Muro; and freshman Brad Vassar. Outside linebackers were senior Dale Curry, junior Raymond Burks, sophomores John Fowler and Frank Stephens, and freshman Steve Shoemaker.

The deep men included cornerbacks junior Harold Hardin, sophomore Levi Armstrong, senior Barney Person, and freshman John Lynn. Moving from corner to strong safety midseason was junior Oscar "Dr. Death" Edwards, joining sophomores Pat Schmidt and Mike Coulter and seniors Matt Fahl and Jeff Smith.

The offense was decidedly upper division. Right tackle was manned by senior Jack DeMartinis and junior Rob Kezerian, right guards were senior Randy Cross (who alternated at center) and junior Keith Eck, the center junior Mitch Kahn, left guards senior Phil McKinnely and junior Greg Taylor, and left tackles sophomore Gus Coppens and senior Bob Reyes.

Junior Rick Walker and sophomore Don Pederson split time at tight end, senior Norm Anderson held the split end spot with sophomore James Sarpy filling in, and junior flanker Wally "Hollywood" Henry teamed with sophomore Severn Reece.

Senior Brett White performed the point-kicking duties, while junior John Sullivan handled the punting. In the backfield were right halves senior Eddie Ayers and junior Jim Brown and left halves junior Wendell Tyler and senior Carl Zaby. The quarterback was senior John Sciarra, returning 100 percent from his broken ankle and receiving some notice as a definite Heisman Trophy candidate.

Dick Vermeil, the master quotesman, made a simple declaration early in the season, namely that the Bruins could score on *anybody*. It was unique as challenges go. It did not say his team was going to win, it was just going to score. At its worst, it was a challenge to see if any defense they faced could shut out the Bruins. At its best, every UCLA opponent was put on notice that the Bruins *were going to score.* In pure subtlety, it ranks as one of the most clever pronouncements in college football, a tremendous challenge made in simple human terms.

The Bruins opened at home against lightly regarded Iowa State. Problem was, the Cyclones packed a punch comparable to their name. Coached by future Ohio State head man Earl Bruce, Iowa State also operated with a Veer offense, though without the manpower at UCLA's disposal.

UCLA quickly went up 7-0 after Wally Henry set up a short 32-yard touchdown drive after running back the kickoff 62 yards. What then happened was not a case of the Bruins going "flat" after scoring easily, it was a fired-up Cyclone defense that heartily pounded the unsuspecting offense. The Bruins were only able to cash in an Iowa State pass interference turnover in the second quarter for a White field goal and the 10-0 halftime lead.

The second half was another matter, as the Bruin offensive line took charge, and when Sciarra connected on a couple of big-play passes the rush-keyed Cyclone defense was forced to loosen up. When that happened, the Bruins took command, as Tyler and especially Sciarra ripped off large chunks of yardage to increase a tenuous 17-7 advantage to a 31-7 lead. Two Cyclone scores during the fourth quarter made for the 37-21 final.

UCLA moved up to number 12 in the nation and next played host to number-10 Tennessee. In an attempt to acclimatize his Volunteers to hot and sunny Los Angeles, Coach Bill Battle brought his team in a day early. It was hoped that his Vols would be completely rested and ready to go wild on Saturday.

Tennessee went wild, all right, collecting a total of 458 yards...but the Bruins countered with 486 of their own. Tyler ran 82 yards for a touchdown, Sciarra connected with Sarpy for 47 yards to set up another, Henry ran a counter for a 45-yard touchdown, and UCLA was never headed, the Blue defense putting a lock on the Volunteer scoring in the fourth quarter to hold onto the 34-28 Bruin victory.

The Bruins were 2-0 and seemingly on their way up to a brilliant season, with 0-2 Air Force Academy next in Colorado.

Vermeil told the *Los Angeles Herald-Examiner's* Tom Singer,' "We've told (the players) we're two-and-oh because we have concentrated on the team we were playing. We're not so good that we can overlook anybody," referring to the upcoming game with Ohio State.

In a faltering performance that found Sciarra playing with an injured and heavily taped shoulder, the Bruins were hard pressed to score. Three touchdowns on carries by Tyler, Sciarra, and Brown were not enough to keep down an opportunistic Falcon team. The Birds had in their arsenal Dave Lawson, a kicker who at the time held the NCAA long-distance field goal record at 62 yards, and in this game he successfully scored from 58 yards out.

The Bruin defense was able to stall a last-second fourth-quarter drive, the Falcons foregoing an attempt for a 68-yard field goal against the wind. A 20-20 tie was the outcome, and more trouble was just around the corner.

The true odds-on favorite for that year's Heisman Trophy was Ohio State's senior tailback Archie Griffin. As recipient of the award the previous season, he was tabbed to become the first two-time winner in history, a feat that had eluded four earlier junior honorees. Part of Griffin's seasonal resume would come from a performance he and his teammates would give against UCLA in the Los Angeles Coliseum on a sultry Saturday night in October in front of 55,482 fans and a national television audience.

The Bruins put on an impressive show the first nine minutes of the game. First Frazier caused Griffin to fumble on UCLA's 26 to stop a strong opening Buckeye drive. Then Sciarra went to work, smartly moving his team down the field, Ayers picking up 34 yards on one clip, the drive completed when Sciarra found Sarpy open for a 13-yard touchdown pass, the Bruins traveling 73 yards in seven plays to go up 7-0. The ensuing kickoff pinned the Ohioans on the eight. All seemed well.

Whatever defensive smokescreen UCLA had theretofore employed was blown away, as the Buckeyes marched those 92 yards to score, including a 48-yard keeper by senior quarterback Cornelius Greene, and the visitors were off and running. When a penalty allowed the Bucks to kickoff with an extra 15 yards tacked on, Coach Wayne Woodrow "Woody" Hayes surprised

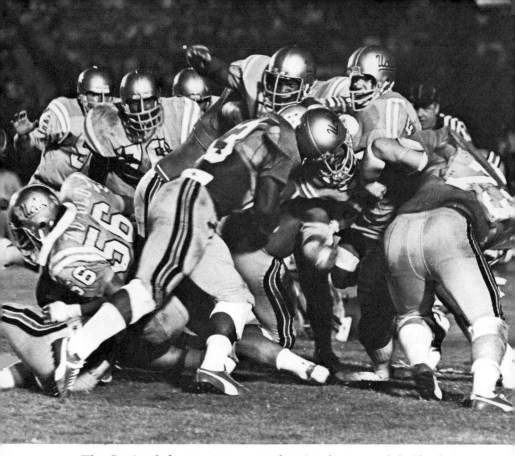

The Bruin defense comes together in the second half of the regular-season Ohio State game in 1975, here stopping two-time Heisman Trophy winner Archie Griffin. UCLA lost, 41-20.

no one by going for an onside kick, which was successfully recovered, and immediately Ohio State punched in for another touchdown and assumed full control of the game. It was 28-7 by halftime, 38-7 with 20 minutes to go.

In those last 20 minutes, the first plateau in the maturing process for the 1975 Bruins was reached. The defense began to miraculously harden from that point on, in spite of the brutal punishment the Buckeyes had been meting out all evening. Those minutes belonged to UCLA, scoring two touchdowns against one Tom Skladany field goal for Ohio State. All tallied the score became 41-20, in favor of the Midwesterners.

On the plane trip back to Columbus, Hayes reportedly made an eerie prediction to his Buckeyes, utterly convinced they would rocket into the Rose Bowl. He told his men that the team they would face on January 1, 1976, would be the UCLA Bruins.

The Uclans were now 2-1-1. Next stop, Palo Alto, to face a typically "flaky" Stanford team capable of winning or losing against all odds. The Cardinals were extremely intermittent, partially from having one too many quarterbacks legitimately qualified for the job, juniors Mike Cordoba and Guy Benjamin.

No matter which one Stanford coach Jack Christiansen played that season, there was an opposing vocal faction among the fans and students who vented their displeasure. As Christiansen related, "It's too bad when you hear your players say at halftime that it sounds like they're playing in a visiting park because of the way the students boo." Though Cordoba played the entire game for the Reds, Mal Florence of the *Los Angeles Times* said it best, "Sciarra was easily the best quarterback on the field."

In a slow developing game from a Bruin standpoint, UCLA was held to a 7-0 halftime lead and 17-14 going into the fourth quarter. Then Sciarra and Company smoothed out the Veer, as the option run began to baffle the Cardinal defense. Four hundred eight of UCLA's 472 yards were earned through the rush, as the Bruins rambled to a 31-21 victory.

The week before Vermeil had received in the mail one of the more ineffective attempts to instill fear in an opponent, "The Package." It was a block of turf allegedly taken from the Stanford end zone. A note signed by the Cardinal defense informed Vermeil that that was all he and his Bruins would see of it during the game. "Sure I showed it to the team," Vermeil said later. "How do you think they reacted? Just like I did. I brought the sod with me to give back to them. In their ear!" After the game, there was a run on Q-tips in Santa Clara County.

Next facing Washington State in Spokane, the Veer-oriented Cougars lost starting quarterback John Hopkins early and unveiled sophomore reserve Jack Thompson, a passing phenomenon nicknamed "The Throwin' Samoan." The success of the Bruin Veer this day rested with the run and with Sciarra who led his team to a comfortable 30-7 fourth-quarter lead which the Bruin reserves frittered away to the 37-23 final.

Cal met the Bruins in the Coliseum. Knowing the key to

205

the Bruin offense was John Sciarra, a Bear defender became overzealous in his desire to literally knock the quarterback out of the game, à la 1974. The second time he slammed into Sciarra well after he was morally allowed to do so, John asked him, "What's your problem?"

His problem was Cal's problem: It was losing to UCLA again, in spite of the fine performances by Bear junior quarterback Joe Roth and powerful senior running back Chuck Muncie. The final score was UCLA 28, Cal 14.

Don James was in his first year as head coach at Washington and was beginning to lay the groundwork for the successful Husky seasons to come. Though they started this season poorly, the Huskies had one of their finest games of that year in the Coliseum against UCLA.

They habitually presented the Bruins with a disguised eight-man defensive front, concentrating on the run. The time it took the Bruins to finally recognize this defense was long enough for the Huskies to beat them 17-13. Never in UCLA history would a loss prove so valuable.

UCLA then faced Oregon and Oregon State in succession. The Bruins ran all over the Ducks for a 50-7 victory in Eugene and turned to a passing attack in Los Angeles to down the Beavers, 31-9, this aerial attack meant to give the Trojans "one more thing to think about."

But well before their meeting, strange things had been happening in Exposition Park. Trojan coach John McKay announced midseason he was leaving to head an expansion pro team in Tampa Bay, Florida. The Trojans inexplicably became a very talented team that had no business losing but was. It formed the worst slump in John McKay's tenure, three straight Pac-Eight losses, after not having lost a conference game since 1971.

The play that the Bruins used to hurt the Trojans the most was the option counter pass. Sciarra would fake to the right half who plunged into and through the line, with the quarterback then threatening to pitchout to the advancing left half. If the cornerback acted to cover the run, releasing his man-to-man coverage on the tight end, the ball was immediately passed to the now undefended receiver.

The Trojans posted a 7-0 lead, then the two teams traded

touchdowns to make it 14-6. The Bruins staged a second-quarter surge that brought them an 18-14 halftime lead. UCLA's second touchdown was a startling 57-yard run by Tyler; the third was that option pass play, 18 yards to tight end Don Pederson. The third quarter was more UCLA, as a fumble by Southern Cal's Mosi Tatupu recovered by Hardin set the Bruins up on the 19. Immediately, Sciarra used another option counter pass again to Pederson to score, putting the Bruins ahead, 25-14.

Southern Cal scored barely into the fourth quarter to draw closer at 25-22. Then the Bruin defense was asked to perform a succession of miracles. Tyler turned the ball over with his fourth fumble of the game. The defense held. White, also punting for this game, fumbled a snap, and it was lost. The defense held. Back-up junior left half Kenny Lee, who had never fumbled even in practice, coughed the ball up. The defense held. Through it all, until the final gun sounded, the defense held the score at 25-22; this critical Bruin victory over the Trojans was preserved.

Tied with Cal in the Pac-Eight with identical 6-1 records, the Bruins' victory over the Bears plus a one-half game better overall record earned them the right to play in the Rose Bowl.

This UCLA-Southern Cal game created several new records for both schools. UCLA's 11 fumbles with eight lost each formed single game records. Southern Cal had for the first time lost four conference games in a row since joining the original Pacific Coast Conference in 1922. Though Trojan record-setting tailback Ricky Bell was kept six yards shy of over-taking the NCAA single-season rushing record set in 1971 by Cornell's Ed Marinaro, Bruin Wendell Tyler broke Kermit Johnson's single-season school rushing record set in 1973, with the bowl game still to come.

The Bruins were asked to once again go up against Ohio State, now 11-0 and Big-10 champ, long ranked number one in the nation, and a team that had improved considerably from its convincing victory over UCLA earlier in the season. The same set of circumstances marked UCLA's visit to the Rose Bowl in 1966, only the prospect of the Bruins' staging another shocking upset was even less conceivable.

The undefeated Buckeyes were averaging 34 points a game

as the nation's leader. Griffin had won the Heisman Trophy again. Ohio State had the finest combined offense and defense in the nation. Plus Woody Hayes was bent on making this fourth-straight appearance in the Rose Bowl a winner, having previously lost two of three against Southern Cal.

But, as in 1966, the Bruins were not the same team as they had been in the beginning of the season. Future all-pro center and offensive guard Randy Cross admitted, "Being waxed by those guys was the best thing that happened to us all year." Just like the team a decade earlier, the Bruins firmly believed they could and would win.

On January first, 1976, a bright, clear day in Arroyo Seco Canyon, UCLA faced Ohio State, all the fantastic hoopla and festivities that are a part of this New Year's Day tradition amplified by its also being the official "Bicentennial Opener" in celebration of the United States' two-hundredth birthday. On this day of days, UCLA was to make its own kind of history.

It did not seem that way for much of the first half. UCLA, the team that could score on anybody, was held scoreless for this half. Yet the Buckeyes were similarly just as ineffective in scoring against the inspired Bruin defense, held to just three points by the intermission. Through it all, UCLA had gained but nine yards rushing to Ohio State's respectable 155.

It dawned on the UCLA coaching staff what was going on. Ohio State had apparently studied the UCLA-Washington game films and had imitated the Huskies' disguised eight-man defensive front. Once it registered that this was what the Bucks were up to, the entire Bruin offense became electric, knowing what it would take to score. It was that old equalizer, the pass. The whole team reacted and began to peak. The second-half kickoff could not come too soon.

White kicked a 33-yard field goal to tie the game as the second half began. Then John Sciarra went to work. He uncorked for two touchdowns to junior flanker Wally Henry, a 16 yarder and an exciting 67-yard connection that opened up a 16-3 third-quarter lead over the dumbfounded Buckeyes.

Ohio State refused to fold and powered 65 yards to a well-earned touchdown, fullback Pete Johnson doing the honors from three yards out as the game crossed over into the fourth quarter. But the Bruin defense kept its poise, as quarterback

Right half Wendell Tyler breaks a tackle against Ohio State in the 1976 Rose Bowl, won by UCLA 23-10.

Receiver Wally Henry scores one of his two touchdowns in the Rose Bowl.

Cornelius Greene was twice intercepted to muff any chance of a further Ohio State comeback.

The final blow was administered by Tyler, who never fumbled all day, as he broke into the open from midfield, cut across the grain at the precise moment he should, and scored, a 54-yard touchdown run that put the lid on the Buckeyes for the day. UCLA had done it again.

Final score: UCLA 23, Ohio State 10.

Woody Hayes admitted to *Columbus Dispatch* sports editor Paul Hornung, "We got outcoached and just got beat. Our defense played magnificently for the first half, but our offense didn't play good all day. This staff just outcoached us." Vermeil answered certain pregame Bruin critics with unprecedented heat, "I'd like to tell a couple of those Northern California writers who said that we didn't belong here to go to hell. I knew we could beat Ohio State, and our players knew we could beat Ohio State!"

Vermeil became a national quantity with this victory.

There were justifiably high hopes that the teams he subsequently would bring forth at UCLA would carry the same stamp as this one, teams composed of talented players capable of following the expert coaching of Vermeil to its logical victorious conclusion. All would be deeply motivated and would know how to win.

"As far as I'm concerned I hope I'm here the rest of my life," he had said not long after. "I can't think of a better place to be and I appreciate the fact that I was given the opportunity to coach here. I'm not big headed enough to think that an offer better than the one I have will be given me. My number-one concern is my obligation to UCLA. I would never apply for any other position."

But one came applying for him. The owner of the Philadelphia Eagles, suffering under a continual rebuilding program for the past 15 years, saw in Dick Vermeil the caliber of man to succeed where others had failed. He was a winning college coach with highly regarded experience in the pros. In the parlance of the times, Vermeil was given an offer he couldn't refuse and accepted the Eagles' job. Within five years he would have them playing in the Super Bowl.

Though his stay in Westwood was extremely brief, he remains a devoted friend to UCLA. Two years may not seem much, but the impact of this man on the UCLA program was profound, from the reemphasis on the pass to the consciously positive promotion of Bruin football to woo the public. He meant business, and the results backed him up. The sheer energy he brought to his position is something that is long remembered.

Athletic director J.D. Morgan would be fortunate indeed to find a man willing to work as tenaciously for UCLA as Dick Vermeil.

CHAPTER 12

1977-1979

Real-life stories abound about how certain individuals start out in the corporate mail rooms and through diligent work and almost divine timing wind up as chairmen of the board. On the college football scene, the walk-on player is metaphorically starting out in the mail room. He usually represents a player the staff either did not think was worth recruiting or, more often, did not know existed.

Terrence Michael Donahue began his UCLA football career as a walk-on. Though told in no uncertain terms that his chances for success were almost nonexistent, he went on to prove that not only did he belong on the varsity, he deserved to be a starter. There were many, many more surprises in store for UCLA from Terry Donahue.

Born in Los Angeles on June 24, 1944, he prepped at Notre Dame High School in the San Fernando Valley and played linebacker. He played one year of frosh ball in 1962 at San Jose State then transferred to Los Angeles Valley College and *did not play*. Making it to UCLA in the fall of 1964, he red-shirted that season as an offensive lineman.

When Tommy Prothro became the head coach in 1965, he saw that Donahue had the kind of character he was hoping to build into his program. Donahue made the varsity as a defensive left tackle, and before the season was over, six-foot-one-half-inch, 190-pound Donahue was a starter and helped the Bruins shock the nation in UCLA's first victory in the Rose Bowl, defeating the number-one Michigan State Spartans.

Donahue also played in 1966, on the UCLA team robbed of a Rose Bowl appearance by a scheduling quirk that had it playing one less conference game than Southern Cal. He received his degree in history in 1967.

One of Prothro's assistants, Pepper Rodgers, was hired as the head man at Kansas and brought Donahue with him as the freshman coach, this at the ripe age of 23. Rising to the varsity staff by the next year, Donahue coached the defensive line, and helped Rogers bring the Jayhawks a Big-Eight cochampionship and a trip to the Orange Bowl. When Rodgers was hired as UCLA's head coach in 1971, Donahue returned with him to Westwood, having by then married the lovely Andrea Sogas of Prairie Village, Kansas.

Switched to coaching the offensive line, Donahue was one of the key people on Rodgers' staff who made the UCLA Wishbone offense in 1972 and 1973 the national wonder it was.

The third UCLA player to become its head coach, Terry Donahue.

When Rodgers was enticed to return to his alma mater, Georgia Tech, Donahue remained to aid new Bruin coach Dick Vermeil and developed a frontal unit justifiably calling itself "The Huge Corporation." The Rose Bowl victory of 1976 meant Donahue became the first person in UCLA history to appear in the Arroyo Seco classic as both a player and coach.

Then Westwood was shocked by the sudden departure of Vermeil to the professional ranks, days before letters of intent were to be signed by that year's recruits. A slate of prep prospects hung in the balance. To conduct an extensive search to find a "name" coach to head the Bruins would take valuable time. Furthermore, athletic director J.D. Morgan was growing weary of the lack of continuity the program was developing, as this would make the fourth head coach at UCLA in seven years. Optimally, someone who would remain at UCLA and be relatively immune to outside enticements would be a godsend.

More and more, regardless of his age, Terry Donahue began to add up as the logical choice. Donahue, like Vermeil, had risen fast to become one of the top young coaches in America. The departing Vermeil and Tommy Prothro with the San Diego Chargers already had offered him jobs.

Terry Donahue was simply in the right place at the right time with the right qualifications. In slightly more than a decade, he had developed from a walk-on player to become the head coach at one of the nation's premier football programs. At the age of 31, Terry Donahue was hired as the head football coach at UCLA.

Donahue had the good fortune to assume command of a team rich in returning players, many who played on the victorious Rose Bowl team that January. The offense was extremely strong in starting seniors, as right guard Greg Taylor, left guard Keith Eck, center Mitch Kahn, right tackle Rob Kezirian, tight end Rick Walker, flanker Wally Henry, left half Wendell Tyler, and quarterback Jeff Dankworth gave proof.

Junior offensive stars included split end Homer Butler, left tackle Gus Coppens, and punter/place-kicker Frank Corral. Sophomore strength came from starting right half Theotis Brown, left half James Owens, and left tackle Jim Main.

The defense was spread across the classes. Seniors were strong safety Oscar Edwards, right corner Harold Hardin, and outside linebacker Raymond Burks, with alternates Wilbur Harden at left cornerback and Tim Tennigkeit at left tackle. Juniors up were nose guard Steve Tetrick, inside linebacker Raymond Bell, left tackle Pete Pele, outside linebacker Frank Stephens, left cornerback Levi Armstrong, and free safety Pat Schmidt. Sophomore starters were right tackle Manu Tuiaso-sopo and inside linebacker Jerry Robinson.

Donahue's first game as a head coach was nothing if not pressure laden. First of all, it was a Thursday night away game. The opponent was Arizona State, still number two in the nation from having defeated Nebraska in the Orange Bowl. Matching wits with Donahue across the field was Frank Kush, National Coach of the Year in 1975. To top it all off, Donahue's curtain raiser was on national television. The now 32-year old lamb was to be slaughtered by a 56-year old wolf before an audience numbering in the millions.

The lamb would turn out to be a fox.

A Bruin turnover in the first quarter gave the Sun Devils the first points of the evening, when ASU settled for a field goal after being unable to locate receiving gem John Jefferson, who was playing with a severely injured foot, twice in the end zone. Then the Bruin offense took over.

Two Dankworth touchdowns in the second quarter and two Brown touchdowns in the third humbled Arizona State. Along the way, an impressive performance was submitted by the offensive line, taking charge of the game for its backfield. The depth of Brown, Tyler, and back-ups sophomore Owens and senior James Brown as rushers overwhelmed the Devils, with Dankworth making the fake-oriented Veer ground attack click, risking as he did only three passes for two receptions, the prevalent notion "why throw if you don't have to" at work. Arizona State finally scored again in the fourth quarter, a Jefferson reception in the end zone, bringing about the 28-10 final.

Frank Kush admitted afterward, "UCLA completely intimidated us. We were mentally and physically dominated like a Sun Devil team never has been before." Donahue's start was nothing short of spectacular, and, to add spice, an incredible slate of Top-10 upsets across the nation shot the Bruins up to number three. Just what a rookie coach needs!

There was still the championship for the state of Arizona

215

Quarterback Jeff Dankworth hands off the ball to back Theotis Brown in the Bruins' 1976 opener against Arizona State, a 28-10 UCLA win.

to dispose of, as the Bruins met the Arizona Wildcats in Los Angeles. Though UCLA was a decided favorite, both offenses were held at bay in the first half. It took a flashy 75-yard pass interception run-back for a touchdown by Armstrong on the last play of the half to put UCLA on the boards with a fortunate 7-3 lead.

Four touchdowns in the third quarter later, the Bruins had smacked the Wildcats silly, Brown scoring two, Tyler one, and junior back-up Steve Bukich stepped in for a most successful Dankworth, passing for one as well. The difference between halves was a blocking adjustment made to counteract the Arizona free safety who was charging the scrimmage line and disrupting the option. That was all it took, as UCLA whisked its way to a 37-9 breeze.

The 1976 Bruins notched all-time UCLA victory number 300 the following week against Air Force, as Tyler surpassed Kermit Johnson as the most prolific rusher in school history. Again, the Bruins played in a fog at first, letting the outmatched Falcons score first, UCLA obtaining a half-time lead of only 13-7. Another second-half four-touchdown boom blew it open, as UCLA won, 40-7.

Terry Donahue then faced college football legend number two, Wayne Woodrow "Woody" Hayes. Ohio State's own General George S. Patton, now in his twenty-sixth season, had compiled an awesome 183-52-8 record up to this game. At its completion, Hayes would have a great deal of respect for the coaching ability of young Terry Donahue.

It was a game of spectacular defensive work from both teams. The Bruins entered the game with Tyler and Brown both less-than-100 percent but were balanced by the fact that the Buckeyes' big back Pete Johnson was also slightly injured. Though the Bruins outgained the Bucks in the first half by 2-to-1, with Ohio State held to 0 yards the first quarter, the favored Buckeyes drove 46 yards for a touchdown in the second quarter to grab a 7-0 halftime lead.

The Bruins staged another second-half upsurge, including a daring fourth-down midfield fake punt, the snap going not to Corral but to Brown, who kept the Bruins going with a first down toward an eventual touchdown, UCLA taking a 10-7 lead into the fourth quarter.

After Ohio State tied it up at 10-10 with a Tom Skladany field goal with 7:39 to go, it got down to a serious chess match between the two coaches. On a fourth-and one decision on the Buckeye 43 with just under four minutes to play, Donahue called for a punt. Then, when the Buckeye return drive stalled on the UCLA 47 with 35 seconds left, Hayes called for a punt. With it UCLA's ball on the seven with 24 seconds to go, Donahue called for Dankworth to fall down on the ball and run out the clock.

Hayes was booed as he walked off the field, and both coaches received considerable criticism for apparently accepting a tie rather than trying to luck into a win at all costs. Donahue and Hayes knew better.

"People said that neither team at the end of the game tried to win," Donahue remarked. "That's not correct at all. The fact was that Coach Hayes and I put tremendous pressure on each other, trying to force the other team to make a mistake, and neither one of us would make that costly mistake."

Donahue further analyzed the game, "People said I was conservative. Well, I didn't think running the fake punt in our

Ohio State in Columbus in 1976, as Jeff Dankworth rolls out from the Veer to find a receiver in this 17-17 tie.

own territory on national TV against Woody Hayes and Ohio State was conservative. I thought that was insane! And yet we did it, and it worked.

"That to me was one of the real scary coaching decisions I've ever had to make. I knew that game would disintegrate right in front of us (if it failed). Ohio State was beginning to dominate the game, and we had to change the momentum of the game and we did it with a fake punt. It was, to me, a classic football game, one of the great football games I've been involved in."

The fun and games of the preseason over, the Bruins faced their first conference opponent. As always, the Stanford game was a tickler.

Guy Benjamin, another in the string of Red passing artists, had led his team to a seemingly firm 20-10 lead late in the third quarter. Then the heretofore stellar UCLA defense reaffirmed itself and began to harrass and pester Benjamin into throwing one interception which was run back for a touchdown, throwing another interception to set up another Bruin touchdown, fumbling to set up still another touchdown, and a coup-de-grace interception run back by Robinson for 69 yards for one more touchdown. The final score was UCLA 38, Stanford 20, one of the more impressive comebacks in recent Bruin history.

A large dose of fan support was pegged as a critical factor in pulling the team together to overcome Stanford in the second half. A special section in the Coliseum had been developed for the alumni, including their own band, cheerleader, and pompon supply. The students and these alums began to compete to see who could boost the team's morale more than the other. Credit goes to an ex-Bruin assistant coach under Prothro, Rodgers, and Vermeil, Jerry Long, who created this innovative alumni "Spirit Section," which became the model and envy of college programs nationwide.

The Bruins enjoyed a much-needed breather against one-punch Washington State. Virtually the only thing going for the Cougars was the arm of junior quarterback Siaki "Jack" Thompson, who was the Pac-Eight's total offense leader, fourth in the nation. The Bruin defense simply smothered Thompson, snagging six interceptions and one fumble on the way to a 62-3 blowout.

On the eve of their game against Cal, the Bruins well remembered hearing how the defending co-champion Bears allegedly had deserved more than the Bruins to represent the Pac-Eight in the 1976 Rose Bowl. This game was expected to be a tight affair, as Cal returned a goodly number of players from the previous year.

Dankworth led the Bruins to two easy touchdowns but then injured his back. Taking over, understudy Bukich was unable to maintain the strong Bruin momentum and Cal sprang back to score a touchdown and two field goals to pull near at 14-13. Dankworth was able to return for the now-traditional second-half explosion, and from there on out it was all UCLA. The lead was built to 39-13 before Cal scored again late in the fourth quarter to make the 39-19 final.

It must be mentioned that the Bears were operating without their star quarterback, Joe Roth, as well as flanker Wesley Walker. Though it was a football-related injury that kept senior Roth out, the plucky Bear quarterback, recognized as one of the best in the nation, would tragically lose his life to

219

Quarterback Rick Bashore in action against Iowa in 1977.

melanoma cancer after this season. He never allowed his condition to affect his desire and determination to excel in sports, and each year a game in Cal's Strawberry Canyon is dedicated to this inspiring player.

Terry Donahue faced still another psychological test this first year, when asked to break the Bruins out of the long-standing "jinx" of biannually losing to Washington in Seattle, as established in 1960. Tyler, suffering from a sore ankle, was replaced by James Owens, who teamed up with roommate Theotis Brown as the split backs to rush the Bruins past the Huskies. Brown set a new single-game rushing record in the process at 220 yards, Owens netted 123 yards of his own.

Though UCLA never trailed, Washington was never truly out of it, as they kept the game as close as 14-13 at the half and 24-21 midway through the fourth quarter. Then Brown popped a 51-yard touchdown run up the middle, which brought the Bruins their 30-21 final score.

In preparing for this game, Donahue had essentially ignored the "jinx," and it worked. "I'm glad the legend is dead. We only talked about the jinx down there (in Los Angeles) because it was played up in the press. We didn't discuss it once we got up here." And that took care of that.

For the next two weeks, the number-three ranked Bruins faced relatively easy teams, Oregon and Oregon State, defeating them both, 46-0 and 45-14 respectively. Of note in the Duck game, Corral kicked a 55-yard field goal to set the still-existing UCLA record for distance. The Bruins rose to number two in the nation. However, hot on their heels was crosstown rival Southern Cal, who rose from number four to number three right behind them.

Both teams entered the Big Game as virtual equals on paper, though Tyler was hampered by a painful shoulder injury. Head Coach John Robinson's first Trojan team had lost only one game, upset in the season opener by Missouri, then ran off nine straight victories. UCLA had the lone tie against Ohio State to mar its otherwise perfect record. It looked like it was going to be a titanic struggle.

For the first quarter it was, as both teams spent an agonizingly long time just feeling the other out. Finally, UCLA began to move the ball offensively, and the momentum shifted its way. Then the unbelievable happened, completely altering the game for good. On a handoff from Dankworth, as Brown reached the line just as a hole opened, a Bruin lineman accidentally punched the ball right out of Brown's arm, sailing it like a wounded duck into the surprised hands of Trojan defensive back Dennis Thurman, who ran the unexpected gift back 47 yards for a score to ignite the Southern Cal machinery.

The Trojans began to roll from that point on and built a 24-0 lead into the fourth quarter. Then two solid Bruin touchdown drives were constructed, one for 60 yards, the other for 47 after the Bruins recovered an onside kick. But after Dankworth was unable to successfully hit for a second two-point conversion, the ensuing onsider was covered by the Trojans. (If UCLA had been able to score three eight-point parlays to tie, it would have put it in the Rose Bowl.) All this action took place in the last four minutes of the game, leaving no hope for further Bruin scoring chances. Final score: Southern Cal 24,

UCLA 14.

As Bob Oates of the *Los Angeles Times* saw it,"The Trojans smothered the Bruins with their defense, wore them down with their offense and consistently got the big breaks, outlucking them on five or six decisive plays, including a questionable interference call on the 1-yard line."

In the locker room, UCLA was asked to face improving Alabama in the Liberty Bowl in Memphis, Tennessee, five days before Christmas. In spite of the disappointment of not becoming the first team in UCLA history to make back-to-back visits to the Rose Bowl, Donahue convinced his team it should make the trip East.

"I felt that it was imperative that UCLA begin to build a bowl tradition like other teams throughout the country had," Dohahue recalls. "It was one of the aspects that was missing from our program that we needed, and I thought that if we went, we'd try to have as much fun as we could and at the same time end our season with a big win over Alabama."

The Liberty Bowl was not a pleasant evening for UCLA. The weather had been a warmish 60 degrees-plus through the first two days of pregame preparation, then on the day of the game the temperature dropped, an icy wind cropped up, and it became achingly cold.

Alabama stomped UCLA, 36-6. Looking back on it, Donahue revealed, "It was a difficult loss, because I hated to see our football team lose like that; we were a better team than that. And unfortunately people began to remember the Southern Cal game and the Liberty Bowl as opposed to remembering a heck of a lot of other good victories throughout the course of the season. We ended 9-2-1, and at that point it was disappointing. As I look back on it, it was an unbelievably successful first season."

Jim Murray, the celebrated syndicated columnist from the *Los Angeles Times*, had words of praise for Terry Donahue during this first year. "Who is this young whipper-snapper and why is he doing those terrible things to older, wiser, balder heads? There are some people who think Terry Donahue was born 60 years old. Terry Donahue has yet to rip out his first yardline marker, slug a photographer, or bar the press from practice. The only thing he has done like a 60-year old coach is win. So far, he's the Grand Young Man of Football. But, if he keeps it up, they may have to start to call him 'Pop.'"

The following spring, Donahue engineered one of the finest recruiting forays in recent UCLA history, making a concerted effort nationwide to attract players to Westwood. Not only were there many high school All-Americans and assorted Blue and Gold Chips signed, but, as is so seldom the case, the majority developed into superb contributors to the Bruin cause.

Freshmen select included Kenny Easley from Virginia, Arthur Akers from Massachusetts, Scott Stauch from Oregon, Billy Don Jackson from Texas, Larry Lee from Ohio, Brad Plemmons from Washington, Mike Mason from Michigan, plus a host of Southland products as well, Michael Brant, Ronnie Dubose, Chris Elias, Glenn Windom, Gregg Christiansen, Dave Otey, and the biggest nugget of all, running back Freeman NcNeil.

They formed the backdrop to a team that would require, if not rebuilding, at least restructuring. The bevy of starters on the offensive line had graduated, dictating more open-mindedness as to their replacements. The front five were formed by junior Max Montoya at left tackle, senior Bryce Adkins at left guard, juniors center Brent Boyd and right guard Jim Main, and senior right tackle Gus Coppens.

Seniors split end James Sarpy, tight end Don Pederson, and flanker Homer Butler comprised the receiving corps. Juniors Theotis Brown and James Owens were the split backs, and sophomore Rick Bashore beat out junior Steve Bukich as the starting signal caller. Steady senior Frank Corral was the punter/place-kicker.

The defense was similarly balanced. Senior nose guard Steve Tetrick was flanked by left tackle junior Manu Tuiasosopo and right tackle freshman Jackson. The inside linebackers were senior Jeff Muro and junior Jerry Robinson, the outside covered by seniors John Fowler, Frank Stephens, and Raymond Bell. Left corner senior Levi Armstrong, right corner junior Bobby Hosea, strong safety junior Johnny Lynn, and free safety freshman Easley composed the deep men.

UCLA's opener was against Houston, a nationally televised Monday night game. Houston also ran the Veer coached by the man who invented it, Bill Yeoman. Played in the great indoors of the Astrodome, the Bruins were about to be hit by two of the worst pieces of bad luck, two key injuries that would have a heavy effect on the early part of their season.

UCLA outplayed Houston for most of the first half, as the strength of the Bruins outmatched the finesse of the Cougars. Six points from two Corral field goals in the first quarter were halved by one Cougar three-pointer early in the second quarter. Then, after a punt, Corral saw the Cougar receiver begin a good runback, and the Bruin moved in to support the defense. A block by a Houston tackle broke Corral's jaw, and he was sidelined indefinitely. Unfortunately, number-two kicker sophomore Peter Boermeester had been left in Los Angeles, and

Bruin linebackers All-America Jerry Robinson (84) and Jeff Muro (81) zero in on a Trojan in the 1977 game, won by Southern Cal 29-27.

senior safety Mike Coulter was pressed into duty, his lack of seasoning as such becoming an important factor.

Four plays later, after Houston had fumbled the ball over to UCLA, Brown landed obliquely on his left arm and pulled it slightly out of the shoulder socket. He was also sidelined indefinitely.

Though the Bruins did score a touchdown without Brown just before the half ended and went into the locker room leading Houston 13-3, the loss of their two top point scorers caught up with them in the final 30 minutes. Houston, though fumbling seven times and losing six, came back to score two touchdowns and win, 17-13.

The Bruins barely had enough time to catch their breath before playing Kansas the following Saturday in Los Angeles, with only two full days of practice. In what was evaluated as a sloppy game, UCLA mounted a 17-7 lead in the third quarter and kept a grip on it until the game was over.

In a total offensive breakdown, UCLA was throttled by underrated Minnesota in Minneapolis. One of the unusual reasons was the almost theatrically timed rain, that seemed to unload on the Bruins whenever they had possession, then miraculously abate when the Gophers had the ball!

But the Bruins' offensive woes in this 27-13 loss were not so easily attributable to just the weather. Something was off-kilter. Sooner or later, the coaching staff would put its finger on it. The following week, back home against Iowa, the Bruins had a much easier time of it, defeating the Hawkeyes, 34-16.

The Bruins entered conference play at 2-2, having been considerably hurt, not only by the loss of point-getters Brown and Corral, but by a raft of injuries elsewhere, Robinson's knee, Plemmons' leg, and back-up tight end Kent Brisbin's ankle, among others. But the injuries did not tell the whole story. One of the most critical junctures in Bruin football under Donahue occurred at this point, one that would affect the program for the following two and a half years.

A glaring statistic became obvious: Bashore had carried the ball more than any back on the team, yet was averaging only 2.5 yards per carry. Donahue realized, "We were trying to run a Veer offense without a Veer quarterback. It was at that time I made a decision. I would no longer continue to run the Veer.

225

We were going to have to get into some other offensive approaches if we were going to win with our quarterback situation the way it was.''

It was decided to gradually replace the Veer with the I formation, but a rapid change would be difficult. Juniors Brown and Owens formed a rushing backfield highly geared for the Veer, and neither could be replaced in order to insert the blocking fullback needed to enjoy the greatest benefits found in rushing from the I. The UCLA Bruins were literally caught between offenses, and only one thing was going to completely clear the decks—graduation, 1979.

Stanford was also having its internal problems. The Cardinals' star quarterback, Guy Benjamin, had to be replaced by untried freshman Steve Dils, with freshman Darrin Nelson, out of Los Angeles' Pius X High, also starting in the backfield. Played in Palo Alto, it reestablished this long rivalry as one of the most heart-stopping, last-one-with-the-ball-wins series in college football.

Dils performed with poise, and Nelson simply burned up the ground, as Stanford built a 16-0 lead just into the second quarter. Then Donahue inserted a returning Theotis Brown, who seemed to lift the spirits of the offense and sparked the Bruins to two touchdowns, the second a 75-yard sprint by Brown, with fellow returnee Corral kicking both PATs. Stanford's star kicker Ken Naber tagged on another three-pointer for the Reds, and at halftime Stanford led, 19-14.

In the second half, things went wild. McNeil ran 78 yards to put the Bruins ahead, 21-19, then Stanford scored to take a 25-21 third-quarter lead. It quieted down for a span of just more than 15 minutes, then started up again. Bashore connected with Brown on a 21-yard pass play to give UCLA a 28-25 lead with just 2:20 left in the game. Then Dils set to work, found his best receiver James Lofton twice, the first a controversial catch that safety Easley swore Lofton did not make, the second a 27-yarder good for a touchdown, which gave Stanford a 32-28 lead with all of 37 seconds left in the game.

That was almost enough time for UCLA, downing the kickoff on the 27 and, like lightning, speeding the ball down the field. At first and 10 on the 24 with 12 seconds left and no time outs, Donahue called for Owens to run the trap up the middle, but he was tripped up at the ankle, gained only nine yards, and the clock ticked away to end the game.

"Owens had run a hundred-and-some-odd yards on the trap that day," Donahue explained, "and was killin' em. The off-linebacker came over and made a diving shoestring tackle and Owens came up short. If James would've gotten away from that one tackler, he probably wouldn't have just made the first down, he would've been in the end zone."

The Bruins had lost their first conference game. Unable to truly begin to implement the contemplated changes after the Iowa game in time for Stanford, the coaching staff now began to restructure the UCLA offense away from the pure Veer and into whatever it would be. With these changes came a complete turn-around in the Bruins' fortunes.

Washington State was coming off an impressive victory over nationally ranked Cal, thanks in part to the brilliant passing arm of Jack Thompson, and looked like a team ready to give the Bruins fits. Bashore was virtually not allowed to run and began to pass, completing only seven of 19 passes for 108 yards, but one was a 56-yard scoring completion to Butler.

The Blue defense, led by Tuiasosopo (one of Thompson's Samoan cousins!), so stifled the Cougar offense it was unable to generate any real points until just into the fourth quarter with the game well out of reach. It was a good win at a good time, 27-16.

Cal next expected the Bruins to repeat the previous week's performance and geared its defense to stop the Bashore pass. Like a bait-and-switch ploy, the Bashore run became a surprise factor, as he earned a career game-high 90 yards, including a 41-yard touchdown run, while passing only nine times with three completions. Once again, Cal fielded a team that was deserving of high consideration only to come up against a UCLA team that simply would not let itself lose to the Golden Bears.

Exchanging the lead twice in the first half, Cal then posted a 16-7 lead by the end of the third quarter. Then UCLA struck for two scores, one a short five-yard pass to complete an 80-yard drive, the second a miracle recovery of a blocked punt, blocked and recovered by junior nose guard Marvin Morris who dashed into the end zone from the 26 to put UCLA ahead,

21-16. After Cal mustered a fourth field goal to pull within two, neither team was heard from for the last five-and-a-half minutes, UCLA holding on to the 21-19 final score.

With this win, UCLA found itself suddenly thrust back into the Rose Bowl race with some credibility at 2-1, while Cal's hopes faded at 1-2. But the Bruin opponent the following week in Los Angeles was heavily up into the race at 3-0—Washington.

Once again, the UCLA defense was the shining light, as it forced an opponent for the second week in a row to rely on the field goal as its major point getter, in this case exclusively. Tied at 6-6, UCLA took the second-half kickoff and solidly moved the ball 74 yards to score the first touchdown of the game. Two field goals later the Huskies pulled up to 13-12.

In the fourth quarter, after a poor punt allowed UCLA to get excellent field position on the 35, the Bruins drove to the 13 when the drive stalled fourth and one. Instead of going for the automatic field goal, Donahue daringly sent Brown off right guard. He popped it and scored to ice the game at 20-12.

That play and that win was crucial for UCLA. Just before it was run off, the Coliseum crowd had reacted to the news flashing on the scoreboard that Cal had upset Southern Cal. Realizing that a score would put the game prohibitively out of reach for Washington, Brown turned to his teammates in the huddle and said three simple words: "This is it."

It was. That win, plus the Trojans' loss, threw the Rose Bowl race into turmoil, with Stanford on top at 4-1 and a three-way tie for second among UCLA, Washington, and Southern Cal. With the Bruins facing the two Oregon schools before the final bash with the Trojans, hopes for that Pasadena visit became extremely high.

The next week against a rebuilding-from-the-bottom Oregon team, now coached by ex-Donahue assistant Rich Brooks, the Bruins had a relatively easy time of it, winning 21-3 in rainy and near-freezing weather. Bashore knocked around the slippery turf, cracked his ribs, and Jackson and Tetrick also suffered minor hurts. This, plus a full logbook of assorted injuries throughout the team, was not helping matters. But adding spice, the Trojans had knocked off Stanford to eliminate the Cardinals and turned the Rose Bowl race into a three-team affair.

The Bruins nailed Oregon State, as Buckich started for Bashore. Though three years had elapsed since his last starting assignment, Bukich scored one touchdown rushing and one passing, leading the Bruins to a large 48-18 victory.

One more bizarre twist to the Rose Bowl race took place. Southern Cal disintegrated against Washington in Seattle, losing 29-10, leaving only the Huskies and the Bruins in contention. On a Friday night, the day after Thanksgiving, the Bruins and the Trojans had themselves a ball game.

Bashore, the first sophomore quarterback since Beban to pass for more than 1,000 yards in a season, returned for this game, as both teams enjoyed an extra six days of preparation via a bye. In all estimation, Rick Bashore played the best game of his Bruin career that night against Southern Cal, quickly leading his team to a 10-0 lead. Then, in a total shift in momentum, the Trojans rapped out 26 unanswered points to dominate the second and third quarters.

Then it was UCLA's turn to control the game, as Bashore mixed up the Trojans time and again with misdirections, bootlegs, and some gut-wrenching passing. A 63-yard drive was culminated in a 32-yard pass completion for a touchdown to Owens, Corral planted a 20-yard field goal to draw his team to within six, then a time-consuming game-controlling 80-yard drive ended with Bashore throwing a one-yard pass to Pederson to put the Bruins on top 27-26 with just under three minutes left to play.

Then the Trojans engineered one of the most talked-about return drives in the history of the rivalry, harking back to their controversial score that ended UCLA's 1969 season. Trojan quarterback Rob Hertel started from the Southern Cal 37-yard line and moved his team down to the UCLA 28, where with two seconds left on the clock Frank Jordan kicked the winning field goal for the Trojans that sent Washington to the Rose Bowl, Southern Cal to the Bluebonnet Bowl, and UCLA home until 1978.

The sting of this loss was made more bitter by an unfortunate judgment call made on a key third-and-ten play that kept the last Trojan drive alive. Pass interference was called against Bruin defender Johnny Lynn, even though it is contended he had not touched the receiver but had actually deflected the ball.

"Whether it was or wasn't interference will be argued for as long as people are interested in UCLA football," Donahue reflected. "There's no question in my mind that, if it was interference, interference should have been called all evening long.

"That isn't to take anything away from S.C., because they had a fabulous two-minute drive, fabulous. (But) this was purely a judgment call and it obviously had a tremendous impact on the football game. Decisions in games like that should be made where there is no judgment, it should be obvious to all involved that either there is or there isn't interference."

By the beginning of the 1978 season, there was no use ignoring the obvious, and UCLA's offense was officially dubbed "The Multiple Veer." Tom Singer in the *Los Angeles Herald-Examiner* fingered it as "a multiple-set featuring the single-wing and I." It may have been complex, but it worked.

The offensive legs were senior James Owens and junior Theotis Brown, who was granted an extra year of eligibility by a new NCAA ruling. Senior starters were left tackle Max Montoya, right tackle Bruce Davis, split end Severn Reece, and center Scott Reid. Juniors included quarterback Rick Bashore, right guards Jim Main and Ron Davis, place-kicker Peter Boermeester, and punter Matt McFarland. Sophomores figuring in were Larry Lee at left guard, Michael Brant at flanker, and running back Freeman McNeil.

The defense proved to be senior deep, led by nose guard Manu Tuiasosopo, inside linebackers Jeff Muro and two-time All-America Jerry Robinson, right tackle Don Hopwood, outside linebacker Ken Walker, cornerbacks Johnny Lynn and Bobby Hosea, and strong safety Mike Molina. Dropping to the sophomores, Billy Don Jackson held down the left tackle spot, Glenn Windom, Chris Elias, and Brad Plemmons served as outside linebackers, and the incomparable Kenny Easley began to generate his credentials as UCLA's second sophomore concensus All-America.

It was fast becoming a Donahue trademark to continually evaluate each and every player in the program for possible reassignment if it appeared another position would be more productive. Whatever is best for the team is paramount.

For example, Michael Brant was moved from quarterback to wide receiver, Manu Tuiasosopo from defensive left tackle to nose guard, Larry Lee from nose guard to offensive left guard, Johnny Lynn from strong safety to left cornerback, Bruce Davis from defensive left tackle to nose guard to offensive right tackle, and on and on. As most gladly realized, it was better to be a shifted starter than an unmoved reserve.

In shades of 1976, the Bruins opened with another televised blockbuster, Washington. As the game was to be played in Seattle in September, at least the likelihood of rain was diminished...but it rained anyway. It was, of course, a conference game for both teams, and with due respect to the Huskies coming off their astounding 27-20 victory over Michigan in the previous Rose Bowl, it was expected that the loser of this game would have a tough time making it to Pasadena.

Arizona and Arizona State had been admitted to the conference, making this the first football game in Pac-10 history. On Saturday, September 9, 1978, the Bruin defense defeated the Husky defense. It was one of *those* games.

All the scoring in the wet cold game occurred in the first half. UCLA scored first on a 37-yard field goal by Boermeester 10 minutes into the game, set up by a recovered fumble on the UCLA 40 by left cornerback Lynn. Then, six minutes into the second quarter, UCLA scored a touchdown as Easley successfully blocked a Husky punt, the ball recovered in the end zone by reserve strong safety junior Brian Baggott.

Owens fumbled the ball over to Washington's Bruce Harrell and the Huskies had to go but 31 yards for their only score. The second half, as indicated, went scoreless, the game ending at UCLA 10, Washington 7.

The surprise of the game was Bruin punter McFarland, who kept his team out of danger all game long and managed to overcome Seattle's ripping elements to average 40 yards per kick. The defense so overshadowed its Bruin opposites, it remained to be seen whether the UCLA offense was going to be effective at all.

For their second game, the Bruins traveled to a most unfavorite haunt, Knoxville, Tennessee. UCLA had yet to win a game in the Volunteer State, and possibly its time was due.

The men in orange sported another quarterback in the blistering Condredge Holloway mold, Jimmy Streater. The Bruins, especially interception-minded Easley, hoped that if they keyed on his run they could make him throw, as passing was not Streater's forte.

It was the Vols' season opener, it was 1976 Coach of the Year Johnny Majors' second season after replacing the alumni-beset Bill Battle, and hopes were high that his team would arise from a sad 4-7 season into the light of glory. Spirits were up, Majors having a banner recruiting year in the South. But any benefits the Vols might enjoy from their incoming personnel would be much further down the road. The UCLA defense did it again.

Brown broke a scoreless tie in the third quarter with a touchdown run for 54 yards. The early tone of the season was being set, the defense keeping an opponent at bay until the offense could figure out how and where to move the ball.

Games are sometimes turned around by emotional lifts or failures just before halftime, and this game was a classic case in point. It was UCLA's ball on the Volunteer four-yard line with less than 30 seconds to the half. A Southeastern Conference official assigned to the game, whether he thought he was doing the Vols a "favor" or not, refused to allow the Bruins a time out when Bashore's signals could not be heard over the incredible din raised by the 85,000 screaming fans.

Ninety-nine and 44 one-hundredths of the time that requested time out would be granted, but Bashore was coldly forced to return to the line, the time out refused, with 14 precious seconds consumed pleading with the "deaf" official. After his plunge netted but two yards, there were still three seconds left, yet the officials managed to somehow not see the frantic hand-formed "T" from almost every Bruin on the field.

That was the last straw. The game in 1965 was about to be avenged. There were still 30 minutes of football left, and the Bruins were not about to allow the officials to play foot-loose with them again. With Brown's score, UCLA took the game out of the officials' hands, and a Bashore plunge from the one for another touchdown in the fourth quarter put the game out of reach, the defense notching the first shutout in almost two years. UCLA won it outright, 13-0.

The Bruins rose to number eight in the nation and faced the easy task of disposing of winless Kansas back in Lawrence. A concerned Terry Donahue took his team to the site of the only non-UCLA coaching grounds he had been involved in for the past 11 years, concerned because his unsettled and unsettling Bruins seemed so downright flat during that week's practice.

Donahue was discovering the hard way how tiring three straight road games can be. Adding its weight, Jerry Robinson, the leader on the defense, was out with a sprained ankle. The last thing Donahue needed was to get upset by Kansas, a team Washington had demolished the week earlier.

An upset is what he got.

Nothing went right for UCLA in the first half. Two kickoffs were fumbled and turned over within the 20 for two Jayhawk scores. The heretofore impeccable Bruin defensive secondary allowed a 51-yard bomb to get away, setting up another Kansas score. A Bruin punt was returned 66 yards to set up Jayhawk TD number four. Before the Uclans could clear their heads, they found themselves behind, 28-7, the lone Bruin tally the second score of the game late in the first quarter.

Things went considerably better for the Bruins in the second half; they were able to pull up to within four points with just under five minutes to go, and fully expecting that, when next with their hands on the ball, they could rally for the touchdown that would win it for them. The Jayhawks were then stopped on the 29 and punted, so the Bruins did get it back, back on the 17, as that punt went for a game-best 58 yards, allowing only a four-yard return. The rally did not materialize.

In every statistical area UCLA simply dominated the game. But three minutes of special team and defensive breakdowns brought an exceptional Bruin team to its knees. UCLA lost, 28-24.

Finally, with Minnesota, the Bruins got to play a game in Los Angeles against another team not expected to be a tough opponent. But Minnesota had been the "Kansas" from the year before, and those kinds of things are remembered.

In the midst of one of the poorest general offensive shows of the season, sophomore tailback Freeman McNeil, pawing the turf along the sidelines in his reserve role, began to assert himself more and more, pressing James Owens for the starting spot. He sparked what offense there was to the Bruins' 17-3 victory.

The Bruins had endured four games without a bona-fide scoring offense. The only option was to tinker here, tinker there, striking positive combinations of the split backs and the I quarterback that might effectively move the ball. Terry Donahue had to weather ugly criticism in the press, from the alums, students, and faculty. All they could see was that the Bruins were not winning, winning, winning to their satisfaction.

Even so, the Bruins were 3-1, had defeated the defending conference champion, and had the potential in sheer terms of quality personnel to do a great deal of damage.

Stanford came to town and brought aerial circus master quarterback Steve Dils. As a counterpoint, the UCLA backfield reshifted back into the full Veer offense and turned James Owens loose. The Cardinals scored first, a Dils three-yard run that capped a 50-yard drive initiated by a blocked Boermeester field goal attempt. UCLA found itself when it found Owens, as the Bruins capitalized on a poor Card punt and later a fumble for two scores and a 14-7 halftime lead.

Then all hell broke loose.

Stanford scored a touchdown and a field goal to assume a 17-14 lead, Dils bombing 55 yards for the tying touchdown, kicker Ken Naber scoring a 21-yard field goal after a Bashore pass was intercepted. The Bruins countered with Theotis Brown's electrifying kickoff return for a touchdown, the first in 10 years, this one for 98 yards and a 21-17 Bruin lead.

Back came Dils, and after a 13-yard toss to receiver Ken Margerum and a 33-yard dash by back Darrin Nelson, he hit Gordon Banks from the 12 for six, Naber missing the PAT. So much for the third quarter.

Bashore engineered a field-goal scoring drive, once completing a 16-yard fourth-and-six pass to freshman tight end Tim Wrightman, to get the Bruins ahead by one midway through the fourth quarter. With less than four minutes to play, the Cardinals marched 75 yards to kick a field goal from 30 yards out, Dils sprinkling three passes to Margerum for 38 of those yards.

Then Bashore, playing perhaps the second-best game of his career, pulled it out for UCLA, once scrambling for 16 yards in a third-and-five situation back on the UCLA 30. With 27 seconds left on the clock, Beormeester was asked to kick a 37-yard field goal. The Coliseum shook when 54,000 voices screamed their reaction as Boermeester and the officials raised their arms over their heads to signal "good!" Final score, UCLA 27, Stanford 26.

The Bruins faced the second air-minded master the following week in Wasington State's Jack "The Throwin' Samoan" Thompson, again in the Coliseum. Thompson had yet to lead his Cougar teammates to a victory over UCLA in three tries. A legitimate Heisman Trophy candidate, his talents had taken him to the number-two place in the NCAA passing record books, directly behind Stanford's Jim Plunkett.

It was not to be for Mr. Thompson. The UCLA defense, led by Tuiasosopo and Jackson, stymied the Cougar leader time and again, and he did not throw a touchdown pass. Even so, Washington State did manage to construct a 24-14 lead over UCLA by the half, thanks more to the power running of fullback Tali Ena than to Thompson's passing.

Then Owens, Brown, and McNeil ganged up on the Cougar defense, as the multiple's shifting offenses kept the Cats baffled throughout the second half. The Bruins strung together scoring drives of 72, 78, and 89 yards before Washington State scored again to tie it at 31 all. Then the Bruins socked it away with drives of 80 and 69, the last a one-play burst by Brown in the final minute of the game, and UCLA completed the total comeback with a 45-31 victory.

The Bruins traveled for yet their third aerialist opponent in as many weeks, this time facing California's heralded sophomore quarterback Rich Campbell. Cal had a good team, was undefeated in conference play, and looked to be the only team besides Southern Cal that could get in UCLA's way to the Roses.

So much emphasis began to be placed on this game that it was tabbed as the nationally televised game for that week. For the first time in *years*, the Golden Bears were climbing out of the sports obscurity brought on by extensive probation and the years of campus unrest in the sixties and early seventies, and this TV exposure was proof positive that their dark days were over.

There was one left.

Tailback James Owens streaks through no-man's land against Washington State in the Bruins' 41-35 victory over the Cougars in 1978.

Ten Bear passes were intercepted, setting a Pac-10 record. Three of those interceptions were returned for touchdowns, tying an NCAA record. One of those interception/touchdowns was by tackle *Jackson,* as all 240 pounds of him ambled over for the score from 16 yards out. The other two scoring interceptions were by cornerback Baggott, which also tied an NCAA record.

UCLA waited until the second quarter before beginning the onslaught, both teams playing close to the vest for the opening quarter. Then UCLA scored four touchdowns in 11 minutes, alternating scoring runs by Owens and McNeil with scoring interceptions by Baggott and Jackson.

The second half brought more of the same, as Cal just would not stop handing the ball over to the Bruins. In all, out of the seven scores tallied by UCLA, only one was a start-at-the-20-and-go-80-yards effort. When the scoreboard cooled off, it read 45-0, UCLA.

Against Arizona, after piecing together long march after long march, just before halftime, center Scott Reid was lost for the season with a knee injury. The Bruins' offense then simply dematerialized, with the defense holding on to the 24 points scored in that first half to last through the second, UCLA winning, 24-14. Of equal concern was the benching of Jackson for disciplinary reasons.

The game with Oregon took only one quarter to decide, but it was the fourth. With UCLA down 6-3 with just over a minute gone in the fourth quarter, Brown went wide to the right after having gone up the middle all day and turned on the afterburners to run 74 yards for the go-ahead touchdown. When Boermeester added a field goal, the Ducks responded under the guidance of journeyman quarterback/defensive back Tim Durando and scored a touchdown to narrow the gap.

Brown went to work again and via an audible from Bashore caught the Duck defense expecting him to go wide and burst up the middle for another long touchdown, this for 68 yards. His efforts earned him not only the number-two spot in UCLA total rushing behind Wendell Tyler, his UCLA record 274 yards on the day was the most single-game yards rushing in the history of the Coliseum, college or pros. UCLA won, 23-21.

Then next against Oregon State, in the words of Terry

Safety Brian Baggott during his 61-yard interception for a touchdown against Cal in 1978.

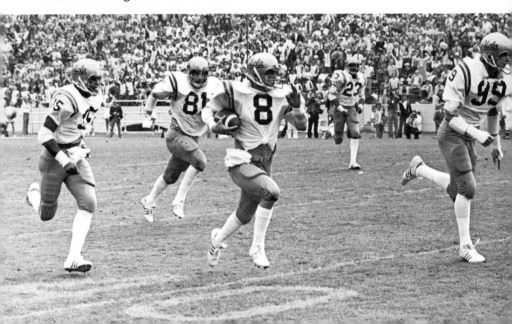

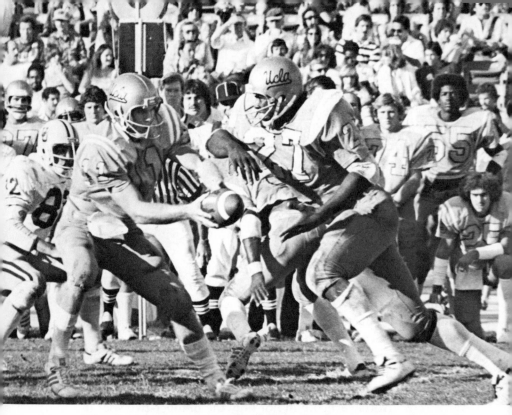

Theotis Brown on a handoff from Bashore against Oregon in 1978, as he set the single-game school rushing record at 274 yards in this 23-21 UCLA victory.

Donahue, "We played bad, the quarterback went cold, and they did good. It was extremely cold, (and) anybody that tries to minimize the effects of weather is not very smart."

The Bruins made but two first downs in the entire second half, Bashore was 0-10 in passing, and UCLA lost right guard Jim Main, the sixth offensive lineman to be felled on the season. Losing 15-13 was not the way to go into the Big Game with Southern Cal.

The 1978 Trojans, undefeated and up for the National Championship (they split with Alabama) were remarkably predictable. They scored, almost without exception, all their points in the second quarter and then let the defense cover it the rest of the game.

Though there's no disguising the fact that Southern Cal did have a very good team, UCLA's chances were considerably lessened when a pinched nerve in Brown's shoulder made it virtually impossible for him to lift his arm past his shoulder. Brown admitted, "Any other game I probably wouldn't have played. It bothered me throughout the game. But that's no excuse. I tried to play and help out. But I couldn't get my arm up and I didn't have all my strength to grip the ball."

The Trojans played to form against UCLA, scoring 14 of their 17 first-half points in the second quarter, and held on while UCLA netted its 10 in the second half. Brown netted a total of 18 yards, gave up a fumble on the 17 that was cashed in by the Trojans for their final points, and could not hang on to the kickoffs that were aimed his way. Southern Cal won, 17-10.

In the locker room, the Bruins were tendered an offer from the Fiesta Bowl, to face equally thwarted (by Alabama) Arkansas. At first it was only halfheartedly accepted. Then the spark of challenge began to enter into their thoughts once more, and the sting of this loss to Southern Cal was soothed.

Brown spoke for the team. "Consolation? I don't look at

Three-time All-America linebacker Jerry Robinson sets the 1978 Bruin defense for a goal-line stand.

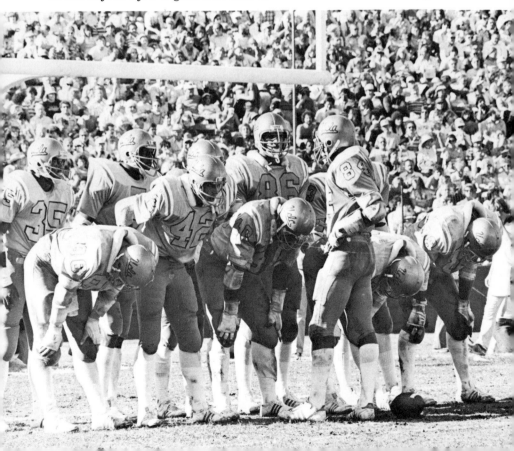

it that way. I look on it as an honor, a reward for the seniors. It's one last chance for us to bounce back, to get our act together.''

Donahue summed up the Fiesta Bowl as being just what its name implies, "We went down there and had about as much fun as I think kids can have at a bowl game. We worked very hard for the game, yet we had fun and really enjoyed it. The players liked Arizona, the weather, the facilities, and everything went fine.''

It showed. Steve Bukich, the senior who had for two years played behind the younger Bashore at quarterback, was given the starting assignment, and though there is no storybook performance to relate, he played the game effectively.

After posting a 10-0 halftime deficit, UCLA stormed back with 10 points of its own, the final score of the 1978 season earned by Mr. Bukich himself on a 15-yard run. The game ended in the 10-10 tie, both teams performing about as evenly as they come.

Donahue's final comments on it noted, "It was one of the hardest hitting and most physical football games I've coached in. The Arkansas players prior to the game appeared almost cocky, and I knew that *we* were really going to play well, that we were really going to hit them. I thought eventually that we would break Arkansas, and Arkansas never broke.''

Many seniors from the 1978 Bruins continued their playing careers in the pros, as Johnny Lynn of the New York Jets, Max Montoya of the Cincinnati Bengals, James Owens with the Tampa Bay Buccaneers, Theotis Brown and Manu Tuiasosopo of the Seattle Seahawks, Bruce Davis of the Oakland Raiders, and Jerry Robinson of the Philadelphia Eagles attest. Robinson became UCLA's first three-time consensus All-America, the first player since Doak Walker of SMU (1947-49) so honored.

During the spring, a new assistant coach came on the scene at UCLA, a young man in charge of the quarterbacks and receivers. Mike Mikolayunas was one of those active, vitally alive people who sometimes comes along to inject a fresh kind of enthusiasm into a football program. The greatest beneficiary was quarterback Rick Bashore, whose positive response to "Miko" brought renewed faith in his ability to lead.

Incredibly, halfway through the spring workouts, the

30-year-old Mikolayunas was struck down by a massive coronary and died. Practice was suspended for a week, and though it was resumed and completed, it was apparent the Bruins had been adversely affected by this tragedy.

The 1979 Bruins were riddled with question marks, and an amazing number of injuries deepened the problems as the season wore on. The young offense was headed by seniors Bashore, right guard Jim Main, center Brent Boyd, and place-kicker Peter Boermeester.

The juniors were right guard John Tautolo, left guard Larry Lee, left tackle Gregg Christiansen, flanker Michael Brant, and tailback Freeman McNeil, plus punter Matt McFarland, who had set the UCLA single-season punting record in 1978 with 3,130 yards. Sophomore starters included tight end Tim Wrightman, split end Dokie Williams, right tackle Luis Sharpe, and fullback Toa Saipale.

The even younger defense was topped by lone senior starter left cornerback and then strong safety Brian Baggott. The juniors covering the field were linebackers Arthur Akers, Billy Don Jackson, and Avon Riley, outside linebackers Scott Stauch, Brad Plemmons, Chris Elias, and Larry Hall, and defensive leader free safety All-America Kenny Easley.

An all-sophomore line featured right tackle Joe Gary, nose guard Ray Robinson, and left tackle Mark Tuinei. Freshmen cornerbacks Tom Sullivan and Lupe Sanchez and nose guard Mark Ferguson were midseason starters as well.

All told, the Bruins of 1979 shaped up as good but not great. Unfortunately, they faced a schedule featuring five bowl-bound teams, and after the season it was rated the toughest schedule in the college ranks for that year. For a team trying to break in players at almost every position, though at least now the I formation was set for good, life was not going to be easy.

In the first games of the past few seasons, whenever the offense was having a difficult time finding itself, the defense carried the burden and usually saved the day. Opening at home against the pure Veer of Houston, the Bruins discovered they no longer enjoyed that freedom.

The first half looked familiar, however, as the Cougars never made it past the UCLA 42-yard line. Even so, the Bruins could only muster three Peter Boermeester field goals for the 9-0 halftime lead.

The Cougars successfully started going outside on the Bruin defense in the second half, and that made all the difference, as they charged to a 21-9 lead. Though Bashore passed for the first touchdown of the year, 22 yards to workhorse tight end Tim Wrightman, Houston closed down the Bruin comeback machine after a field goal to put them up by eight points. In losing, 24-16, it marked the first time Donahue had lost a game in the Coliseum to a team other than Southern Cal.

Regrouping to play host to a powerhouse, the Bruin defense was required to shut down the most prolific passer in the Big-10, Purdue's Mark Herrmann. Under the brilliant coaching of Jim Young, Purdue had returned to the top ranks of not only the Midwest but the nation.

Rolling into Los Angeles to find it shrouded with smog, the Boilermakers were completely surprised by a clever defensive alignment that proved so effective they were never able to counter it. As orchestrated by the intense Bruin defensive coordinator, Dr. Jed Hughes, Easley was stationed at strong safety instead of his normal free safety spot, the nearer to stage a one-man wonder attack on the quarterback—Herrmann wondering how in the world Easley kept smashing into his backfield to drive him bonkers time after time.

On the first play of the game, McNeil churned out 51 yards, and shortly thereafter the Bruins scored. After Easley intercepted Herrmann's first pass of the day, the Bruins scored again. After Jackson sacked Herrmann to bring on a short punt, the Bruins scored again.

Like a whirlwind, it was 21-0 UCLA, just barely into the second quarter. But Herrmann was not to be denied, and he smoothly passed for two touchdowns to bring about a 21-14 halftime score.

In the third quarter, Boermeester kicked a psychologically important field goal, putting UCLA up by 10. When Herrmann was unable to come right back into the game because of shortness of breath, replacement Larry Gates drove his team to a touchdown early in the fourth quarter to pull Purdue up to 24-21.

The defense kept its poise and the offense its push. Bashore led his team on a time-consuming 87-yard march, putting it over himself from the one with only two minutes left to seal the game at 31-21, UCLA.

McNeil came down with a case of the flu to add its misery to a pestering groin injury before the Wisconsin game and watched from the sidelines in Madison. As reserve back senior Glenn Cannon was injured on UCLA's first series, in stepped sophomore Anthony Edgar, and all he did was carry the ball for a school record 39 times for 168 yards, as the Bruins soared to a 37-12 win.

Bashore too had a big day, passing for seven of 10 and 128 yards. But the season-starting outside linebacking corps received the coups de grace as Plemmons joined previously injured Windom on the knee-surgery-is-scheduled list.

Next coach Earl Bruce brought his first Ohio State team to Los Angeles. The venerable Woody Hayes had been forced to retire following an incident in the Buckeyes' game with Clemson in that December's Gator Bowl, in which he lost his head and

Tailback Freeman McNeil in action against Purdue in 1979, a 31-21 win for UCLA.

struck a Tiger player who had intercepted a pass to seal the Ohio State's loss.

Bruce had inherited another seemingly typical heavyweight Hayes team, except he was carrying through in sophomore quarterback Art Schlichter what Hayes had initiated at Columbus that previous year. Hayes at that time replaced then-senior quarterback Rod Gerald with the freshman hotshot Schlichter, guessing that the future of the Buckeyes and the Big-10 rested in the pass.

UCLA stormed out to a touchdown set up by a Jackson-blocked punt attempt downed on the 12, Bashore passing for the score from the 10 three plays later. A 27-yard field goal capped a 55-yard march to put the Bruins on top, 10-0, as the first quarter closed.

Schlichter constructed a 70-yard drive at the end of the second quarter for a touchdown and the 10-7 halftime margin. The *Los Angeles Herald-Examiner's* witty Tom Singer noted, "The difference between today's Ohio State team and the previous 28 (under Hayes) vividly emerged at the end of the first half, when Art Schlichter got possession of the ball at his 28 yard line with 26 seconds to go and promptly threw three passes. In a 10-7 game, Woody Hayes would have had him eat the ball. Earl Bruce advocates a different diet."

Both sides exchanged field goals as a tough defensive second half ensued. When the Buckeyes got the ball on their 20 with 2:21 remaining, the Earl Bruce difference emerged. The UCLA secondary was peppered with Schlichter's pinpoint passes, completing six in a row, the last a two-yarder for the touchdown, and with 46 seconds left in the game, the Bruins found a heartbreaking 17-13 loss on their hands.

Donahue admitted, "Art Schlichter just put on one of the most incredible performances that I've seen a quarterback play. Six straight passes...and he picked on Lupe Sanchez, who was a freshman. Of course, Lupe would learn from that game and go on to become a good player for us...."

Bruin fourth quarter woes were not over, not with Stanford to contend with. In what was rather a sluggish game on both sides in Palo Alto, the two teams found themselves tied at 24-24 with just seconds remaining, Stanford's ball at midfield.

Kicker Ken Naber had already missed two field goals kicking into the stiff wind blowing that day, both from shorter distances, and here he was, trying to kick a prodigious 56 yarder with but four seconds left in the game. It was miracle time. As Naber put his foot to the ball, the wind stopped—completely—just long enough for the ball to fly like a drunk duck, barely gasping a bounce off the left upright to go through. It was a most unlikely 27-24 Cardinal victory.

For the third straight time, UCLA and Stanford had played out the final seconds of their contests, the home team winning each time. As this loss came on the heels of two other major games lost by the Bruins in the final minutes, Donahue had every right to sigh, "It's getting old."

UCLA had not allowed Washington State to win a game since the series was renewed in 1967. In a fine Dickensian manner, Donahue recited the following evaluation of this game played in Pullman:

"There was a total lack of consistent execution. At times the line blocked well, at times it didn't. At times the backs hit the right holes, at times they didn't. At times the receivers

All-America free safety Kenny Easley about to put the clamps on Stanford back Darrin Nelson in the Bruins' 1979 loss at the Farm, 27-24.

caught the ball, at times they dropped it. At times Rick Bashore hit his man, at times he missed him.''

The times all the wrong things happened conspired against the times all the right things did and produced a chilling 17-14 Bruin loss. It was the first time since 1943 the Bruins had opened up conference play with two straight losses, fundamentally putting them out of the Rose Bowl picture right out of the gate.

At 2-4, with many unlucky breaks both figuratively and medically going against the Bruins, the time had come to begin looking to the future. They would need a quarterback to replace the graduating Bashore, and as there were no juniors or sophomores waiting in the wings, attention was focused on three freshmen, Bernard Quarles, Jay Shroeder, and Tom Ramsey. The first experiment would come against Cal.

The Bears, once again, were very, very good. They were ready to play UCLA and *win,* not forgetting that embarrassment in Berkeley in 1978. Unknown to anybody, Donahue had decided that when the second quarter rolled around, no matter what, he was going to insert Quarles.

When it rolled around, the Bruins were down, 20-0. Like Condredge Holloway of Tennessee who electrified his team back to a miracle tie with UCLA in 1974, Quarles sparked the team to a touchdown. He scrambled, he threw, he ran, McNeil ran, Wrightman caught a key pass, and the Bruins were respectable.

The Bears scored again, what might have been the knockout, making it 27-7 at the half. But the Bruins had stormed to the one-foot line before the gun sounded. They knew they would score again.

The decision was made to leave Quarles in for the second half. It was figured Cal would have trouble defensing an obviously effective quarterback whom they had virtually never seen on film. But what all this attention on the quarterback did was distract from the real monster of the Bruins' attack: Freeman McNeil.

McNeil, who scored the first-half touchdown, scored three more in the second half, tying the UCLA single-game record set by Kermit Alexander, also against Cal in 1962, and established an individual record as these scores were all earned on the ground. Furthermore, the Bruin defense completely shut down

Cal's scoring in the second half. Final score became UCLA 28, Cal 27, one of the greatest Bruin comebacks in series history.

Then Washington came to town.

A player on that year's Husky team, punter Rich Camarillo, had actually two seasons earlier tried out to be a member of the UCLA Bruins. According to Pac-10 regulations, he was technically ineligible to play for another Pac-10 team for a period of two full years.

UCLA, in the interest of fair play and to benefit Camarillo, privately advised Washington and the Pac-10 offices of the situation. Technically, every conference game in which he participated as a Husky would be forfeit. As UCLA sincerely wanted to see that proper justice was done both Washington and the player, it relinquished all claims to Camarillo and asked that the Pac-10 grant him full clearance to play. The Pac-10 eventually approved UCLA's request in time for the game, Camarillo was permanently sanctioned as eligible, and everything seemed all right.

UCLA held Washington to a 7-7 tie at the half. Then the bottom fell out, as the Huskies racked up 27 more points to the Bruins' seven. Bashore, with a heel injury, did not start, and when Quarles proved ineffective after scoring one touchdown, in came Schroeder. Not faring much better, Ramsey was inserted, who at least nailed three straight passes to score the second Bruin touchdown of the day. But it ended in a miserable 34-14 loss for UCLA.

The Camarillo episode came out. In Tom Singer's account of the game in the *Herald-Examiner,* it appeared the Washington coaches neglected to inform the team that UCLA had tried to help the Huskies by clearing up the sticky Camarillo matter. Instead, the Husky players were stoked with the false information before the game that UCLA had tried to scuttle the team, get Camarillo declared ineligible and kicked off the squad, and hoped to strip the Huskies of their Pac-10 victories. It allowably contributed to the Huskies' desire to beat the Bruins.

Bruin linebacker Billy Don Jackson was benched for disciplinary reasons for this game, having missed several practices. He did not play again at UCLA. Jackson left school and the following year transferred to San Jose State.

UCLA had been the victim on virtually all last-second deciders this season. Finally, it became the giver, and unlucky Arizona State the recipient. The man most responsible for the Bruins' success was Mr. Tom Ramsey.

The Bruins encountered a Sun Devil team beset with internal problems. Legendary head coach Frank Kush had been ushered out midseason after allegations erupted concerning his harsh training methods, stemming from a court suit initiated by an ex-player. (Kush was exonerated.) To further compound its miseries, a player was found by the NCAA to be ineligible and five of the school's conference games were forfeited.

Even so, ASU fielded a fine team led by excellent quarterback Mark Malone, who had passed for over 1,300 yards the previous season. Initially set opposite him was Quarles, who led the Bruins adequately to a 10-10 tie at the half. But a sock on the knee sent him to the showers, in stepped Ramsey, and a quarterback duel ensued the likes of which was thought only possible with Stanford.

The Devils went up 13-10 via a field goal aided by a 35-yard Malone pass during the strong 76-yard march. Ramsey then jarred the Bruins back into the game with a 63-yard pass completion for a touchdown to freshman reserve flanker Jojo Townsell and a 17-13 UCLA lead.

After Easley ran back a poor Devil punt to put the Bruins in business at the 23, Ramsey scored himself from the 10 on the two-play drive to create a 24-13 lead as the fourth quarter opened. Back came Malone, who engineered two touchdown drives plus a two-point conversion to put Arizona State up 28-24 with 2:03 left to play. Then Ramsey floored the Devils and the Coliseum, moving the Bruins 59 yards to score the game-winning touchdown with nine seconds left to produce a 31-28 victory.

UCLA traveled to play favored Oregon. Rich Brooks was effecting a turn-around in the Duck program, his team number three in the conference and nurturing bowl invitation hopes. But pride more than anything else pumped the Bruins so full of adrenalin, they went out and simply crushed the Ducks, 35-0. Easley went on a one-man rampage, snagging two interceptions that were later cashed in for touchdowns, and the defense realized the first shutout in 15 games.

The one last game on the schedule was Southern Cal,

248

which already had been once declared conference champion, until Arizona State forfeited its victory over Washington to put the Huskies back into the picture. That added just enough incentive for the Trojans to nail the Bruins more than otherwise.

It was, charitably, no contest. Behind the passing of Paul MacDonald and the churning power of that year's Heisman Trophy winner Charles White, they administered such scoring power they simply raced through the Bruin defense to a 35-0 halftime lead.

On the other side of the picture, Trojan defensive back Ronnie Lott and company pressured starter Ramsey into throwing two interceptions. When Donahue replaced him with Bashore for the second half a kind of parity was reached, as both teams traded touchdowns to make for the 49-14 final.

Donahue had some thoughts on that game. "I think that in football, after you've been in it for a while, you learn that you ask no quarter, you give no quarter, as a basic standard, then you make your decisions from there. It depends on the coach's personality, philosophies, and what he's trying to do to the other coach and the other school.

"There's no question in my mind that the fact that it was 49-14 near the end of the game, Paul MacDonald's still in at quarterback, and Charles White's still in at tailback, they were intent on scoring a lot of points.

"They were also going after a National Championship. It wasn't a nationally televised game so a score of more magnitude over your arch-rival will always help you. Charlie White was going for the Heisman so the more yards he gained the better shot he had at it. I'm sure there were some influencing factors in the fact that they kept the troopers in there. You're supposed to be playing with them or you shouldn't be out there." (That year's number-one team was Alabama.)

Donahue was now 0-4 against Southern Cal, setting a series consecutive-loss record, not a comfortable situation within the confines of Los Angeles. The following year would be the start of a new decade. The Bruins were about to arise from this 5-6 season to become one of the most offensively dynamic teams in the nation.

CHAPTER 13
The 1980s

The two recurring problems most affecting the Bruins over the last three and a half years were injuries and offense.

Donahue had continuously pressed the department to institute an "injury prevention" conditioning program. Not surprisingly, the sheer cost of knee surgeries alone did more than any other means of persuasion to convince unsold minds money could be saved by such a program.

The benefits derived from working with weights are complemented with a special diet, positive mental growth, and auxiliary body development and strengthening. Major and many minor injuries dropped dramatically at UCLA during the 1980 season, justifying the faith Donahue had in the potential of such a program all along.

Donahue searched the nation and discovered that one of the best people for this relatively new aspect of football-player-maintenance was a young man named Donn Swanbom. Getting down to the conditioning business in January, Nebraska grad (1976) "Swannie" guided the team's development, and the progress made by spring practice was marked, as the players survived the vernal workouts relatively unscathed. After 1979 that in itself was an emotional lift.

Offensively, the ragged transition out of the Veer and into the I was over. Unrefined as it was, the bulk of the personnel who made it work in 1979 were returning to carry on. The services of a certain offensive specialist, something Donahue had eschewed so far, became available. He was Homer Smith.

As recounted during the Pepper Rodgers years, Smith first came to UCLA in 1972. Though he had gained his early reputation as a passing wiz, he installed with Rodgers the rush-oriented Wishbone-T offense and served as the offensive coordinator.

In its day, the UCLA Wishbone was one of the most potent of its ilk and led the nation in several offensive areas throughout the two seasons it was employed. When Rodgers left for Georgia Tech, Smith subsequently was given the head post at Army.

After a stormy and unpleasant tenure combatting the West Point administration, Smith was terminated in 1978. A growing need to divorce himself from football to study comparative religions drew him to Harvard Divinity School, where he extended his part-time off-season status into full doctorate studies.

Smith kept in contact with Donahue, coaching together as they did under Rodgers, while at Army and at Harvard. He began to miss the challenge and fun of teaching the sport he loved. When he let Donahue know that he was considering a return to the sidelines, that was all it took. Donahue hired him as his first offensive coordinator in time for spring.

Smith's first job was to determine who the next quarterback would be. He had two to choose from, Tom Ramsey and Jay Schroeder, as Bernard Quarles had become academically ineligible and transferred to Hawaii. The competition that Smith orchestrated between them was intense yet, as with Harmon and Sciarra in 1973, full of camaraderie. Ramsey emerged by the fall as Smith's choice by the narrowest of margins.

Sophomore Ramsey had a great team to lead. The tailback was senior Freeman McNeil, UCLA's offensive Heisman Trophy candidate, on his way to becoming the most prolific rusher in Bruin history. Fullback was manned by stocky sophomore Frank Bruno. Split ends sophomore Cormac "The Magnificent" Carney and senior Michael Brant, tight end junior Tim Wrightman and flankers sophomore Jojo Townsell and junior Willie Curran, made the pass a long suit in the Bruins' game plan. Even an alternate "zoom" receiving back was employed on misdirects, featuring senior Ronnie DeBose.

The line was solid, as seniors left tackle Gregg Christiansen, left guard Larry Lee, and right guard John Tautolo teamed with junior right tackle Luis Sharpe to flank centers junior Dave Otey and sophomore Dan Dufour. Norm Johnson inherited the place-kicking duties, with senior Matt McFarland set as the punter.

The defense was wonderful. The free safety was senior Kenny Easley, UCLA's defensive Heisman Trophy candidate, who would become the Bruins' second three-time consensus All-America within two years. Joining him in the deep zones were three experienced sophomores, cornerbacks Lupe Sanchez and Jimmy Turner and strong safety Tom Sullivan.

The entire linebacking corps was top-notch seniors, the inside covered by Arthur Akers and Avon Riley, the outside by Larry Hall and Scott Stauch. The line was suspect only at first. Left tackle junior Joe Gary, nose guards junior Martin Moss and sophomore Karl Morgan, and a sophomore right tackle at six-foot-six and a quarter inch and 257 pounds with the auspicious name of Irv Eatman promptly put any worried to rest.

There was still a wrinkle to contend with before this 1980 season got underway. Back in the summer of 1977, a couple of players received junior college credits for classes they did not attend.

During a conferencewide examination of football this business came to light, and as a result UCLA was placed on a year's probation by the Pac-10, disqualifying the Bruins from any postseason competition.

UCLA was not alone. Oregon, both Arizona schools, and Southern Cal were similarly disciplined. Though there was apparently a wide variance of transgressions involved individually, all five schools were equally "painted with the same brush."

Rather than open a can of worms and fall prey to the bitter counteraccusations that erupted in the old PCC during the midfifties, this blanket grounding was done in hopes that when the inevitable NCAA investigation followed, it would accept the self-policed sanctions by the Pac-10 as punishment enough. (Following its investigation that spring, the NCAA did not take further action against Bruin football.)

Though that created one problem, another had been solved. UCLA had a new athletic director.

J.D. Morgan had undergone open-heart surgery in December 1978, and in October 1979 he announced his retirement.

Associate athletic director Robert Fischer was appointed acting A.D. while a nationwide search for Morgan's successor continued. Prompt decision-making within the department became difficult.

The administration finally realized that Fischer was the perfect choice for the job all along, and the UCLA grad of 1945 was duly appointed as such in May 1980. Fischer has continued to nurture and promote the kind of "Athens of Athletics" at UCLA his predecessor envisioned and has stablized the department through his leadership.

With postseason prospects a dead issue, the Bruins entered 1980 without the primary Pac-10 incentive of the Rose Bowl. Their only recourse was to shoot the moon.

Quarterback Jay Schroeder scores from the 12 against Colorado in 1980, protected by blocks from tailback Freeman McNeil (24), fullback Frank Bruno (42), right tackle Luis Sharpe (67), and right guard Chris Yelich (66).

The Bruins opened at home against Colorado. When Chuck Fairbanks abandoned the professional ranks in New England the previous year, having once been in charge of Big-Eight power Oklahoma, he hit the Rockies just as the Buffaloes emptied of talent. In the face of what amounted to his second rebuilding year, he brought his team to Los Angeles not long after the school had admitted to 50 NCAA violations which would place it on probation for three years. It wasn't expected to be a close game. It was not even a close first quarter.

In all, the Golden Buffaloes lost 10 fumbles. Their quarterback threw a perfect pass to backpeddling Bruin linebacker Larry Hall who was alone in his area. They once stacked a defensive goal-line stand with 13 players.

The Bruins scored four touchdowns in both first half quarters. The second half was filled with many unexposed Bruins getting "valuable game experience," as Colorado was

Fullback Jairo Penaranda on the move against Colorado in the 1980 game won by the Bruins, 56-14.

able to score 14 points that half to close out the fiasco at 56-14.

Then came Big Test Number One. The Purdue Boilermakers had kept East Lafayette clean from loss for 17 straight games, spanning three years. All week long, Donahue admitted that Purdue quarterback Mark Herrmann was noticably improved from the year before and revealed that based on the defensive success UCLA enjoyed against him in 1979, it would take the same kind of defensive intensity, blitzing, and pressure, if the Bruins were going to have any effect on the game.

That is exactly what the Bruins did not do. With the Purdue offensive line constantly on guard for it, it threw Purdue's concentration for a loop.

Though the Bruin quarterback position was still conditionally open, Ramsey was given the starting nod and made the most of it. He outdid Heisman candidate Herrmann, completing eight of 16 for 170 yards and a touchdown, and though Herrmann pased almost three times more for much more yardage, these passes were mainly short bloopers to his backs. When Herrmann did dare the Bruin secondary, it was rough going, and he was picked off twice by cornerback Turner.

In 86-degree weather imported from the coast, the Bruins scored right off the bat, going 52 yards to a Norm Johnson field goal from the Purdue 24. This was followed by a McNeil touchdown six minutes later after nose guard Karl Morgan recovered a fumble on the Purdue 41. Herrmann led his team to a touchdown after a weak Bruin punt, but Johnson came on for UCLA to kick two more field goals to put the Bruins ahead 16-7 at the half.

Psychologically effective was a fake punt call that maintained the drive on the way to the second field goal. Noting on game films that Purdue sometimes stacked the line on punts, blocking defender Easley was instructed to shout the long-favorite Bruin trigger word "Omaha!" to clue his teammates to the alternate play.

Fourth-and-14 from the UCLA 40, on Donahue's behest the team heard Easley bark "Omaha!" moments before the snap. Easley received the snap and, employing remembered skills from his high school quarterback days in Virginia, swung around the right side for 25 yards and the first down!

As both teams exchanged touchdowns in the second half,

255

the game ended in UCLA's favor, 23-14. All Herrmann had done in the process was become the all-time Big-10 leader in total offense and career touchdowns, plus reach sixth place in NCAA completion history. All UCLA had done was win the game. Unranked Purdue stayed unranked. Unranked UCLA moved into the elite at number 14.

For the second year in a row, McNeil missed the Wisconsin game, this time for a hyperextended knee he suffered at Purdue. In stepped freshman Kevin Nelson, brother of Stanford back Darrin, who scampered for 123 yards, one touchdown, and the UCLA single-game rushing record for a freshman.

For a good portion of the first half, UCLA uncovered a no-huddle offense. It effectively unsettled the Badger defense, enabling the Bruins to spring to a sturdy 28-0 halftime lead, easing up in the second half to the 35-0 final.

Ohio State. Columbus, October fourth, 1980. National "ABC Game Of The Week." The Buckeyes were number two in the nation, the Bruins hovering around number 10. Ohio State was undefeated, coming off a 1979 season that was marred only by an upsetting loss to Southern Cal in the Rose Bowl. The Bruins were undefeated, coming off a 1979 season that had gone downhill after being thwarted in the last two minutes of their game with Ohio State. The Buckeyes were confident. The Bruins were confident. It was going to be a classic.

Game day brought early morning drizzles. Fear of the weather crept into some minds, but not Terry Donahue's. As he stood on the balcony of his hotel room, he casually leaned over and stuck out his hand to feel the light rain. "That's Bruin weather," he laughed.

The small contingency of Bruin fans were dwarfed by the overwhelming size of Ohio Stadium. This was Buckeye territory. All the pomp that is college football was on full display. No visiting team enters this stadium without reaction.

Ramsey was ill that morning, a late evening snack the night before turning on him and keeping him up all night. Eatman, from Ohio, had been chided by his friends over the summer for the 1979 loss and decided he would do his utmost to not let it happen again. Easley, for only the second time in his UCLA career, played in front of his parents and family, who had bused all the way from Chesapeake, Virginia.

Left corner back Lupe Sanchez, after an interception against Wisconsin in UCLA's 35-0 1980 victory.

The artificial turf, unaffected by that morning's rain, was *fast.* The Bruins were a fast team, though the natural turf of the first three games disguised it. Their speed was the first surprise.

The Bruin domination on both sides of the line of scrimmage was the other surprise. Eatman sprang into the Buckeye backfield repeatedly, a one-man wall in front of quarterback Art Schlichter, making four sacks and earning network MVP honors.

Both teams slugged it out heavily in the first half, UCLA managing to kick a lone field goal. Ohio State was stopped by a stunting shutout-minded Bruin defense and late in the half a disheartingly easy interception was made in the end zone by safety Tom Sullivan.

The Bruins roared for two touchdowns in the third quarter, the first on a pass from Ramsey to cap an opening

257

Quarterback Tom Ramsey (14) sets the play with his offensive line, from the left Sharpe, right guard John Tautolo, center Dave Otey, left guard Larry Lee, and left tackle Curt Mohl.

56-yard drive in 11 plays, including a fourth-and-one Ramsey sneak on the 36, the second score a solid 65-yard drive with McNeil doing the honors from the one. Both drives were marked by Ramsey passes that seemed to flit all over the field, the host of Bruin receivers thrilled with the chance to show their stuff.

The stunned crowd of over 80,000 watched in disbelief, an eerie silence that seemed so out of place enveloped massive Ohio Stadium. The only note of approval came from the small pocket of Bruin fans in the corner, the occasional sharp chant of "U-C-L-A Fight Fight Fight!" bouncing around the bowl with tremendous effect.

For the last 17 minutes the Bruin defense kept the score at 17-0. The Bruins scored two consecutive shutouts for the first time in 20 years. It was the first time UCLA had defeated Ohio State in Columbus. UCLA was 4-0 for the season, number five in the nation. UCLA was on the way up.

The next week pitted the Bruins against unpredictable Stanford. It was the beginning of a three-set series between two quarterbacks who had battled each other throughout their prep careers in the San Fernando Valley.

Tom Ramsey was leading the Pac-10 in all areas within his domain, yet Cardinal quarterback John Elway was getting all the notoriety. Ramsey was going to state his case with a victory.

It was also a test to see how legitimate McNeil's Heisman candidacy was. But hindering the Bruins, the sensational Easley had incurred a knee injury and would watch the game with the coaches.

After the Bruins struck first, a seven-yard scoring pass from Ramsey to DeBose, Elway and the Cardinals assumed command. Relying on the legs of junior tailback Darrin Nelson to balance its attack, Stanford surged to a deflating 21-7 lead. Elway was sacked five times that half, yet still passed effectively; Stanford for all the world appeared unstoppable.

The second half was another matter entirely. McNeil single-handedly took charge of the game. He thunderstruck the Stanford defense with four touchdowns in that half, two on thrilling bursts of 72 and 42 yards, as he executed perfect pitchout sweep after sweep with devastasting effectiveness.

Just as remarkable was the Easleyless defensive secondary, which rose to the occasion to prevent Elway from doing any further damage on the afternoon, and with the defensive line essentially putting the skids on the Cards' Nelson, the Bruins wound down the afternoon with a stirring 35-21 victory.

McNeil tied his own solo single-game touchdown rushing record and ended up second behind Theotis Brown's single-game record of 274 yards set against Oregon in 1978 with his own 248.

One Bruin play in this game was a daring gamble on Donahue's part with the game still in the balance, UCLA up, 28-21. It was the Bruins' ball, fourth-and-one on the UCLA 14. Donahue felt that, under the circumstances, with Elway having been kept on the sidelines for so long, Stanford was probably ready to bust, and if it got its hands on the ball would probably score and effect a momentum shift.

Not giving the Cards a chance to compose themselves, Donahue had Ramsey go for it. Ramsey got the first down, and a few plays later McNeil burst his 42-yarder to score and put the issue to rest.

Why did Donahue do it? Homer Smith guessed, "I think he's just seen too many close games with Stanford, and he didn't want to lose this one by being conservative."

The team was idle with a bye the next week, something Donahue foresaw as coming at just the right time to bring about a much-needed rest. But dividing the season in half as it did, it somehow dampened the all-out attitude characterized by the first five games. The major achievement had been realized, as UCLA had defeated three of the top teams in the nation to climb up to the number-three spot.

It was a strangely listless Bruin team that faced still another quarterback of national note in Cal's Rich Campbell. Of some

Coach Donahue cheers his team in the Bruins' 28-27 victory over Stanford in 1980. Assistant coach Homer Smith is in the background.

bearing on the game was a raft of Bear taunts in the press prior to the game, implying that the Bears would batter and bury the Bruins under the dirt of Strawberry Canyon.

But the Bruins did to Campbell what they had done to Purdue's Herrmann, giving him everything he wanted underneath the linebackers but nothing in the secondary. When he did test deep waters, he found a vastly improved Lupe Sanchez ready to do him in. Turner picked off one pass and Sullivan doubled that to add to Campbell's frustration. With a fabulous 100-yard kickoff return for a touchdown by Townsell, it was all UCLA, as the Bruins defeated Cal, 35-9.

But the general impression of the team's total performance was oddly negative. There was something disturbing underneath it all, though the Bruins had risen now to number two in the nation as team after team dropped out of the high spots.

According to Donahue, "We won impressively at Cal, and yet to me we appeared sluggish. We didn't appear to have the same fire and zip that we'd had. We appeared to peak, and then we were seemingly on the downswing."

The Bruins swung into Tucson for Arizona, and things went haywire. It was a hot day, and neither team seemed especially excited to play, as the Bruins were heavy favorites to knock off the 2-4 Wildcats

UCLA began with a lightning-fast drive from the opening kickoff, reeling off 78 yards in seven plays, four of which were completed passes, the last a seven-yard scorer to Carney. Then, as if the game were already over, the Bruins went pfffttt.

The Wildcats tied it at the end of the first quarter, finally cashing in on three UCLA turnovers. Then the Bruins collected 10 points and appeared to be back in control, except the last three points were clouded in controversy.

The field goal was kicked in lieu of a touchdown, a 22-yard pass completion to Brant as he skidded out of the end zone, declared a touchdown by the back judge on the scene. But the line judge, who was not near the reception, stepped up and overruled the call.

Sensing the momentum virtually shoved over to their side, freshman quarterback Tim Tunnicliffe, in only his second start after leader Mark Fulcher broke his leg, got hot. The Cats burned up 80 yards, and with 30 seconds left in the half put their team back into it with a touchdown, and suddenly Arizona was down only 17-14 instead of much worse. Taking that kind of momentum into the locker room with them, the Wildcats smelled upset and believed they could pull it off.

Elsewhere across the nation, another upset had just been completed as Mississippi State knocked off number-one Alabama. Donahue and the team were not aware during halftime that, for the moment, they were the heir apparent to that abandoned berth.

Donahue described what happened. "The game was taken to us by Arizona. They sacked our quarterback seven times, our pass protection broke down, our defense gave up some big plays, we had a couple of man-to-man breakdowns.

"Probably the most dominating thing of the whole football game was their punter, Sergio Vega. He probably influenced the football game as much as any punter I've ever seen. Every time it looked like we had them backed up and we were going to get the ball in good field position, he'd kick us back to our own 20."

Vega averaged 54.9 yards per punt and nailed one for 80 yards *in the air*. The Bruins were, understandably, frustrated for the entire second half.

It took Tunnicliffe exactly three plays to move his team 80 yards to score as the third quarter began, putting the Wildcats ahead, 21-17. Still another officiating cross-up cost the Bruins another important chance to turn things around. In the middle of the fourth quarter, Arizona tailback freshman Brian Holland fumbled a Tunnicliffe pitchout that was recovered by the Bruins on the Wildcat 17 and was signaled as such.

The apparent fumble was overruled as a *dropped pass* and Arizona kept the ball. To rub salt in the wounds, Ramsey was tackled in the end zone for a safety with one and a half minutes remaining to give Arizona the 23-17 final.

The 1980 UCLA Bruins were number one in the nation for 30 minutes on November 1. The surprise, the dream was over.

Slipping down to number eight, the Bruins faced the renovated Oregon Ducks in the Coliseum. Dynamic recruiter head coach Rich Brooks had started to enjoy the benefits of his hard work, the Ducks surprising Southern Cal with a 7-7 tie three weeks earlier in Eugene.

Playing a scoreless first quarter, the Bruins lost McNeil for the game with an aggravated bruised thigh. The Ducks traded touchdowns with the Bruins in the second quarter. Then Oregon quarterback Reggie Ogburn drove his team 76 yards for a touchdown, which was followed by a Doug Jollymour field goal to give the Webfoots a healthy 17-7 halftime lead.

The Bruins on offense looked choppy for that first half and most of the third quarter, as nothing seemed to click. Ramsey was performing well, but the team could not seem to shake itself into a sharp offensive unit. Ramsey was relieved of any play-calling duties for the second half, with all plays sent in from the sidelines.

Briefly in the fourth quarter, the Bruins looked as if they had found themselves again, marching solidly down the field behind the straight-ahead rushing of Nelson and Bruno, rushing the team all the way to the six. Down by six with four minutes left, the team appeared poised to power it in for the tie and maybe the lead.

Expecting Oregon to slant into the middle, Ramsey was sent on a sweep—except the Ducks slanted out, a block was missed, and Ramsey was downed for a seven-yard loss. Three passes came up empty, and the game was over, Oregon a 20-14 winner.

Donahue felt that even with the loss, the second half showed him the turn-around was underway. "I thought we'd come back and begin to repeat again. It marked the beginning of when I felt the slump, if that's what it was, was over."

The Bruins traveled back to Arizona to face the Sun Devils, who had so far not lost in Tempe this season. The Bruins performed well at first, but Ramsey was nevertheless pulled in the early goings for Schroeder, who essentially had kept pace with Ramsey step by step throughout the season, and the team adjusted to him quickly. Also, for the second time in the season, McNeil, not completely recovered from his thigh injury, could not play, and any outside hopes for the Heisman were dismissed. Once again, Nelson filled in, and as he had against Wisconsin, Nelson had a field day.

The Bruins went up 10-0 at halftime, padding it to 17-0 at the start of the third quarter with Schroeder's first touchdown pass for 43 yards to Curran. Though Arizona State then scored a touchdown, by the middle of the fourth quarter Nelson salted the game away, scoring from the 13 to give the Bruins an insurmountable lead, ending with 186 yards for his efforts, a school freshman record, and a 23-14 UCLA victory.

As Tom Singer in the *Los Angeles Herald-Examiner* noted, "Pursuing, flowing to the ball, gang tackling and treating passes with their old disdain, they made the evening generally unpleasant for ASU quarterback Mike Pagel and running backs Robert Weathers and Willie Gittens. UCLA's domination was keener than the final score would suggest."

As the Bruins were swinging back up, the Trojans were swinging down, taking a grueling 20-10 loss from Washington (which put the Huskies in the Rose Bowl). Entering the game with the nation's number-two tailback in Marcus Allen, Southern Cal was beset by quarterback problems, as fifth-year senior Gordon Adams had been lost for the season against Washington, forcing sophomore Scott Tinsley into the fray.

Still, the Trojans had their defense and sported one of the finest roverbacks in the country, Ronnie Lott. Yet UCLA had a secret weapon to use against Southern Cal, a walk-on senior fullback named Jairo Peneranda, who simply refused to be tackled all game long.

Southern Cal scored first, a 32-yard Eric Hipp field goal set up by an intercepted Ramsey pass. Schroeder was sent in and constructed a second-quarter 80-yard drive, powered by Peneranda and culminated with McNeil scoring from the six, thanks in part to a block thrown by Peneranda that absolutely leveled Lott. After 30 minutes, UCLA was ahead, 7-3.

When McNeil coughed up the football to Lott early in the second half, the Trojans cashed it in for a touchdown and a brief 10-7 lead. Turning it around, Schroeder drove his team 52 yards in three plays, all pass completions, and the Bruins regained the lead, 14-10.

Earning good field position when a punt exchanged presented them with the ball at the UCLA 43, Southern Cal marched to a first down on the three. It took four crashes by Allen, then a fumble recovered in the end zone by Bruce Matthews, to give the Trojans a 17-14 fourth-quarter lead. It looked very formidable, especially after Schroeder threw an interception that later put the Trojans in business at the UCLA 11.

The Bruin defense stopped Southern Cal cold. Three plays and four yards later, the Trojans settled for a Hipp field goal attempt, but it was wide to the right. The Bruins got the ball on the 20, time running out. They advanced to the 42. Then it happened.

Schroeder peddled back, looked over to the left sidelines where McNeil was supposed to be streaking downfield, and fired. He underthrew it. Defender Jeff Fisher rose up a slight step behind McNeil at the Trojan 40, successfully got a piece of the ball and deflected it.

McNeil spun with the ball, it fell with him as he turned away from the defender, he cradled the ball to his chest and was gone, a second defender left in his wake. Freeman McNeil completed the 58-yard touchdown play to put the Bruins ahead, the missed PAT keeping the Bruin lead at only three points.

Though the Trojans mounted a return drive that brought them conceivably close enough for a tying 46-yard field goal, head coach John Robinson opted for a touchdown pass play that came up empty as time ran out. Donahue had his first victory over Southern Cal, 20-17.

Allan Malamud in the *Herald-Examiner* had his say: "(The Bruins) knew this Trojan horse was a one-trick pony. Allen carried the ball on half of USC's scrimmage plays, 37 of 74. He usually faced an eight-man line and almost everywhere he went he found Irv Eatman, Arthur Akers, Martin Moss, Karl Morgan and Avon Riley." Allen was held to 72 yards, the only time in his regular season collegiate career he earned less than 100.

The probation-fettered Bruins, successful in spite of the restrictions, next enjoyed a rare treat for their last game of the season. It represented a postseason bowl for all intents and purposes, especially as that was what it was being billed as in the host country of Japan, which calls it the Mirage Bowl. Two teams are invited annually to play their last regular season game there. This year Oregon State and UCLA were the honored guests.

To say that the initials "UCLA" are revered in Japan is like saying a beach is sandy. For the many auxiliary groups that traveled with the team to Tokyo and toured the Orient after-

Bruin noseguard Martin Moss stops Trojan Marcus Allen cold during the 1980 victory over Southern Cal, 20-17. Linebacker Larry Hall (41) and right tackle Irv Eatman (75) lend support.

wards, the mere association with the university proved to be a phenomenal calling card into dozens of homes and enterprises throughout the Far East. This awesome global impact of UCLA was brought home to the team members after their sojourn in Japan.

The Mirage Bowl was a godsend to Kenny Easley, who snagged two interceptions, his only for the year, to increase his already-record career tally to 19. The Bruins simply overpowered the Beavers, 34-3.

The season was over, 9-2. McNeil and Easley went number three and number four respectively in the first round of the pro draft, and 12 seniors in all made it to pro camps. Replacing all that strength for 1981 was not going to be an easy task.

It was a cautiously optimistic coach who surveyed the prospects for 1981. While it was not exactly a rebuilding year, it was nonetheless a young team, a "junior" team, one that was expected to be good or possibly very good depending on the breaks. Donahue allowed, "I'd be disappointed if we didn't have an outstanding team."

The defensive line was solid, with seniors Joe Gary and Martin Moss at left tackle, juniors Karl Morgan and Mark Ferguson at nose guard, and juniors Irv Eatman and Jeff Chaffin at right tackle manning the trenches. Replacing four starting linebackers were seniors Glenn Windom (in his fifth year) and Ike Gordon on the outside, junior Blanchard Montgomery, who would set the unit each play, and sophomore Ronnie Butler on the inside.

The deep men were all juniors, left cornerback Lupe Sanchez, right cornerback Mike Durden, strong safety Jimmy Turner, and free safety Tom Sullivan. Then Sanchez broke his arm in practice and was not slated to return for weeks. Turner shifted to the vacated left corner, Sullivan returned to strong safety, and sophomore terror Don Rogers moved up to the free safety spot.

On offense, things were not so promising. The line was originally set with sophomore Don Mahlstedt at left tackle, junior Blake Wingle at left guard, senior Dave Otey at center, junior Dan Dufour at right guard, and senior iron man Luis Sharpe at right tackle. Otey and Dufour wound up splitting time at center. Sophomore left guard Chris Yelich moved over to the right guard hole.

The receivers were top-notch. All-America senior Tim Wrightman was the tight end, junior Cormac Carney the split end, the flanker was junior Jojo Townsell, and the zoom was sophomore Harper Howell.

In the backfield junior quarterback Tom Ramsey became the undisputed number one when classmate Jay Schroeder opted to concentrate on his professional baseball career and left the team. At fullback were juniors Frank Bruno and Toa Saipale. At tailback the sophomore Kevin Nelson was primed to begin his advance on the Bruin rushing record books.

267

Senior place-kicker Norm Johnson, who consistently proved on his kickoffs that if the ball lands past the end zone it cannot be run back, and untried sophomore punter Keven Buenafe rounded out the roster.

It was a young team. It got even younger as the season progressed.

There is no way of compensating for the fatigue, physically and emotionally, of consecutive road games. As in 1978, to open with three straight away games, in this case Arizona, Wisconsin, and Iowa, was asking for trouble. Furthermore, with only two home games in the first eight, the Bruins had every in-flight magazine memorized by November.

It was a soft, sultry night in Tucson for the UCLA-Arizona opener, the site of the Bruins' slide from the top the previous year. If it was anything but Game Number One there might have been some thought of it as a "revenge" game, but there was none of that. It was a conference game for both, and that was enough to worry about.

The Wildcats were somewhat deflated going in. Their starting quarterback, sophomore Tim Tunnicliffe, had been ailing, so there was some question whether he or 1980 starter-till-injured senior Mark Fulcher was going to get the nod. To make matters worse, starting fullback Rory Barnett was felled with a knee injury that week and was lost for the season, and starting tailback Brian Holland and two starting linebackers were hit with a one-game suspension. On the plus side, league leading punter Sergio Vega was back to lift his team's spirits.

The Bruins were relentless, responding to Arizona's opening drive field goal with two touchdowns. Though the Wildcats staged minor comebacks along the way, UCLA continued to pad its lead until the game was out of reach.

The first Bruin touchdown of the year was scored by senior tight end James Forge, a four-yard Ramsey pass to end a 76-yard eight-play drive, Forge's first touchdown ever. Then in the second quarter Carney caught a 10-yard Ramsey pass in the end zone, completing a 94-yard drive in 11 plays. The Cats closed out the half with a 42-yard field goal with no time remaining.

The Bruins increased their lead at the outset of the second half, another Forge reception of a Ramsey pass to score from the four, capping an 80-yard nine-play drive with the opening kickoff, making it 21-6. Arizona scored its first touchdown on a one-yard Fulcher pass, this a 72-yard drive that included a 55-yard pass completion.

UCLA added two more touchdowns, the first a beautiful 30-yard flanker reverse by senior Willie Curran, to produce the respectable 35-18 victory. Unfortunately, number-two fullback Saipale broke his foot and would be lost for most of the season.

The next three games originally were not expected to be too formidable, but then the scores from the rest of the nation came in. Wisconsin upset the number-one team in the nation, Michigan; Iowa upset number-six Nebraska; and Colorado scored a relative upset of its own over Texas Tech.

Donahue could only remark, "Everybody thought we had it made, didn't they? Now our schedule looks like a killer."

Playing the Badgers in Madison, the Bruins struck for two touchdowns before their opponents answered with one of their own to make it a 14-7 first quarter, then exchanged scores for the 21-13 halftime score. Not long after play was resumed, a major mistake on Wisconsin's part accidentally put the game effectively out of reach.

In the middle of the third quarter, a backfield pass thrown by Badger sophomore quarterback Jess Cole to his flanker was unintentionally thrown behind his receiver, making it a lateral. A heads-up play by Sullivan directed enough Bruin traffic its way for teammate Moss to recover the ball on the Badger 23. Five plays later Wrightman scored his second touchdown of the day, and a Johnson field goal later in the game brought a 31-13 UCLA win.

The Bruins moved up to number six in the nation, apparently making the same move to the top as they had in 1980. Road game number three against Iowa would show just how ennervating three trips can be.

The Hawkeyes the past two seasons had been literally reborn under Coach Hayden Fry. The surprise team of the Big-10 in 1980 (finishing fourth) was bringing back virtually intact the same defense that was number one in that conference in prevented yardage, plus an innovative big-play pass-oriented offense.

UCLA was going to learn how to cope without two of its

offensive stars. Nelson injured his right knee against Wisconsin, a hobbling pain that would not go away, Carney had a bruised sternum making it difficult to move, and neither played. Nelson's back-up, junior Terry Morehead, was an Iowa native and planned on a beautiful homecoming to make up the difference.

What transpired in Kinnick Stadium was not pretty. UCLA was tired, ineffective on offense while only somewhat effective on defense. The Hawkeyes were up for the game and sharp. The Bruins gave up two fumbles; Ramsey threw two interceptions (already five for the year) and suffered six sacks, one causing a fumble in the end zone for an Iowa touchdown. UCLA amassed only 121 yards, after averaging 440 per game so far, and Morehead's longest gain was for only 15 yards.

Though tying it once in the second quarter for a 7-7 halftime score, UCLA was outplayed by Iowa in the second half, losing, 20-7. Iowa was no fluke and kept clearing its way through the season until landing in the Rose Bowl.

The Bruins slipped from the Top 10 all the way to number sixteen. They regained their equilibrium against Colorado, as Ramsey's arm got UCLA back into the swing of things, 258 passing yards and two touchdowns.

At first it seemed UCLA could only be foot-loose, as Johnson kicked four field goals in the first half, which tied the UCLA single-game field goal record. Then Ramsey found the end zone with a 10-yard scorer to Carney to put the Bruins up, 19-0.

Colorado scored at the end of the half, but a later Bruin touchdown put it to rest, bullish Tim Wrightman snaring a pass from Ramsey and carrying two Buffaloes on his back the last five yards on the 14-yard play. It was a timely 27-7 Bruin victory.

UCLA went on the road again to Palo Alto. Stanford was experiencing one of the most depressing downturns in their fortunes ever, opening 0-4 to enter conference competition.

As a sidelight, the team had lost its ''s.'' For some reason the board of trustees, still unable to come up with a team name to replace the fondly remembered ''Indians,'' had decided that if Harvard could be ''The Crimson'' and Cornell ''The Big Red,'' Stanford could be ''The Cardinal.''

270

All-America tight end Tim Wrightman on the go after a reception in the 1981 Colorado game, a 27-7 Bruin victory.

This game represented the one and only head-to-head collegiate meeting of the tailback brothers Nelson, Kevin the sophomore at UCLA and Darrin the senior at Stanford. Sanchez returned for the Blue defense, but quickly recracked the same broken arm and was lost for the season, an injury redshirt. It was also the second of three meetings between archrivals John Elway of Stanford and Tom Ramsey of UCLA. It was one more installment of "last one with the ball wins" between these two schools.

The game had more shifts than an 18-wheeler taking the coast route. UCLA scored first, Nelson tagging a touchdown from the three. Stanford's kicker Mark Harmon produced a field goal, then UCLA scored another touchdown, Wrightman pulling in a four-yard pass from Ramsey. The Bruins were up, 14-3, and looked to have the game moving in their direction.

Then Elway got hot. Continually shut down on first and second-down plays, he kept worming his team into the clear during this drive with three clutch third-down completions, all to his Nelson, and the Red scored a touchdown. On two more field goals, the last with no time remaining, Stanford assumed a remarkable 16-14 halftime lead.

In the third quarter UCLA and Stanford traded field goals. All in attendance were treated to some remarkable open-field running by Darrin Nelson, faking out his opponents with hip moves that would have impressed Gypsy Rose Lee.

In the fourth quarter, the Bruins put together a solid 83-yard drive, Bruno taking it in from the eight. But along the way they used two valuable time outs, one to clear their heads for a fourth-and-one from the Stanford 15, the other to correct a personnel mix-up in the two-point conversion attempt, which failed. Still, the Bruins led by four with just under seven minutes left.

Just over six minutes later, Stanford scored a touchdown, Darrin Nelson crashing over Plemmons from the two, the 63-yard drive initiated by a blocked 51-yard UCLA field goal attempt. With 46 seconds left, Ramsey took charge, jamming his team down the field as rapidly as he could, arriving on the Stanford 45 when the clock expired. The Bruin quarterback took off his helmet, defeated, 26-23, and spiked it into the ground in anguish and frustration. Elway had evened the score at a game apiece.

Traveling for still *another* road game, the Bruins traveled to Pullman to face revitalized Washington State. The Cinderella team of the Pac-10, the Cougars were 5-0 going into this game and were eyeing the Rose Bowl for their first visit in 50 years, and gained further credibility by having this game selected as the regional television game of the week.

The Bruins were again without the full services of Kevin Nelson, which more and more became a critical factor in UCLA's offensive efficiency.

So the Bruin defense began to assert itself as the dominant force on the team, though Washington State scored first in the second quarter, a 99-yard touchdown drive to go up 7-0. In the next 19 seconds, Ramsey in two plays drew the Bruins even, picking up 46 of the 73 yards on a scoring pass to Carney. Three minutes later, Johnson kicked a 31-yard field goal to give the Bruins a 10-7 halftime lead.

In the third quarter, as he was attempting a pass to Wrightman, Ramsey was hit by Cougar defender Mike Walker. The ball blooped into the arms of nose guard Matt Elisara, who managed to reach the end zone 42 yards away to score his team's second touchdown. Washington State picked up another field goal at the outset of the fourth quarter to make it 17-10.

Back-up quarterback sophomore Steve Bono came in for a slightly injured Ramsey and directed the Bruins to their second touchdown, and with six minutes remaining Donahue instructed Johnson to convert the PAT to tie the game, figuring there was enough time to get the ball back and score again.

UCLA did get the ball back and did move into scoring position, Johnson attempting a 35-yard field goal. As holder sophomore quarterback Rick Neuheisel put it, "I swear it was good by three or four feet. Norm has a little tail but not from that close." Even the fans behind the goalpost silently registered their disappointment in its success, until the man in the striped shirt waved that it was wide to the left.

The game ended at 17-17, and all over the West Coast pocket calculators were taken out to see what effect it would have on the Rose Bowl race.

The UCLA jet setters played at home for only the second time all season, hosting trouble-torn California. Head coach Roger Theder had attempted to install an aerial-type offense called the "Run and Shoot," employing impromptu pass routes run by two ends and two slotbacks plus occasionally the lone fullback flooding the secondary, attempting to clear into spots left uncovered by the defenders. It is triggered by the quarterback, who operates from the shotgun and rolls to either side in search of an open man.

Unfortunately, the quarterback that Cal had figured to make it work was injured in the first game that year, and his replacement, J Torchio, was more the drop-back passer than the gun-on-the-run artist it needed. Theder was quick to discover that to fans and alums there can be no excuse for losing.

UCLA had the game in hand by the start of the second quarter and cruised in from there. Nelson returned to play much of the first half, picking up 97 yards on 11 carries. His last carry hurt, as he reinjured his ankle on an 18-yard Statue of Liberty play. It was becoming obvious that the reserves who had begun to see action, Morehead and freshmen Burness Scott and Danny Andrews, would become important factors in any future Bruin efforts. The same situation was also hitting the fullback spot, as Bruno incurred a knee injury and sophomore Frank Cephous was called into service.

UCLA scored only in the first half, Cal mustering only one scoring drive in the third quarter to account for the 34-6 final. The Bruins now had defeated the Golden Bears 10 straight times.

There was, unbelievably, one more road trip to make. Oregon's fortunes, so bright in 1980, had turned bleak, as the team experienced a rash of close, close losses to accompany sheer devastation in its offensive arsenal. Four lineman including the center disappeared, three injury-laden quarterbacks were shuffled in and out during the season, and football life was miserable again in Eugene.

Oregon presented UCLA with the perfect situation to give the up-and-coming Bruin rushing backfield as much game experience as possible, and Donahue saw to it they got it. Against the number-two defense in the league, Donahue called 52 rushes vs. 14 passes, and his ballcarriers matured quickly, in bulk if not in bursts.

Andrews scored three touchdowns and rushed 22 times for 54 yards, Scott scored one touchdown through six carries and 52 yards, and Cephous picked up 35 yards in nine carries. As Donahue put it, "When you have a strength like we do, you should take advantage of it." The Bruins won, 28-11.

UCLA had now built itself up from the inside, its last two victories pulling an uncomfortable 1-1-1 conference start to 3-1-1. It now was retooled to meet three teams that were the cream of the conference—and playing at home was supposed to be a treat!

The first visitor was Washington. A great many Bruins remembered the thrashing they received from the Huskies in 1979. But 1981 was a different matter.

After a scoreless first quarter, the first Bruin score was set up when Husky quarterback Scott Pelluer fumbled the ball over to nose guard Karl Morgan on the Washington 14. Three plays later, Ramsey found Carney in the end zone and UCLA was off.

Ten minutes later cornerback junior Walter Lang intercepted Pelluer on the Bruin 49-yard line, and Ramsey lit up the scoreboard in six plays, capped by another touchdown pass to Carney. On the Huskies' first play after the kickoff, Morgan caused Ron Jackson to commit fumble number two, and Norm Johnson was called on to kick a gift 44-yard field goal as the half ended, lifting the Bruins to a pleasing 17-0 lead.

The same circumstances marked the second half. The third quarter went scoreless; then the Bruins scored touchdown number three at the start of the fourth, set up by long-snap center senior Russell Rowell's recovery of a fumbled punt by return specialist Anthony Allen on the Husky 10. Scott immediately scooted in for the score.

Nine minutes later, free safety freshman Neal Dellocono recovered a faulty Pelleur lateral on the Husky one, and sophomore Bono, inserted when Ramsey bruised his shoulder, popped through a beautiful hole to score. It was one of the most phenomenal Bruin blowouts in recent history, as UCLA defeated Washington, 31-0. Terry Donahue had now defeated Don James four out of five times.

Next up was Arizona State, still ineligible for the Rose Bowl because of NCAA sanctions. That did not prevent the Sun Devils from offensively ripping the conference, as they were tied for first with Southern Cal and sported the nation's number-four passer in Mike Pagel. They led the nation in yardage at 522 per game and also were ranked number eight in the AP poll.

Quietly, quietly, UCLA had through all the alleged offensive ineptitude created a passing force of its own in Tom Ramsey, who was actually the nation's number-nine passer himself. Though few expected it, this game turned out to be one of the finer two-pronged lessons in the power of the pass, and it was undoubtedly the high point of the 1981 Bruins' season.

Two Sun Devil touchdowns opened the scoring midway through the first quarter, the first after Ramsey fumbled the ball over on his own one-yard line, the other a five-play, 56-yard

Quarterback Tom Ramsey, at work against Washington in UCLA's 1981 blanking of the Huskies, 31-0.

drive as a balanced attack led by Pagel and a host of receivers and running back Willie Gittens made it look like clockwork.

Ramsey began to shine. In an 89-yard drive as the first quarter blended into the second, Ramsey nailed down passes to Carney, Curran, and Townsell, then handed the ball on the 28 to Nelson who took it in from there.

Then the Bruin defense began to assert itself. Later that period Dellocono recovered a Pagel fumble when outside linebacker "Mad Brad" Plemmons leveled the quarterback from behind in one of the most devastating tackles all season, and Ramsey instantly soared a pass to Jojo Townsell for the touchdown that brought the Bruins even at 14-14.

After Jimmy Turner returned a punt 59-yards to the 18,

the Arizona State defense stiffened, and UCLA settled for a 34-yard field goal and a 17-14 lead. As the half was about to end, Pagel pieced together a 61-yard drive resulting in a 38-yard field goal to knot it at the half, 17-17.

The dust settled for the third quarter, then both sides started to blast away again in the fourth. Rogers picked off a Pagel pass, and the Bruins sailed for 49 yards in 12 plays, Ramsey doing the honor from the one. Arizona State was held and had to punt, and Sullivan ran it back 19 yards to start the Bruins off at the 45. First moving backwards a few yards, like a catapult, Ramsey vaulted the ball to Carney for 46 yards and shortly thereafter Burness Scott punched it in from the two.

There was still some life left in Pagel, who drove his team 81 yards to score, though a pass interference call in the end zone accounted for 37 of those yards, Gerald Riggs scoring from the one. The Bruins had one more big defensive play left.

Arizona State got its hands back on the ball and Pagel let fly again, only to find nose guard Morgan rearing up almost out of nowhere to get a piece of it. The ball was deflected over to teammate Joe Gary, who started to lumber his way to the end zone from midfield, attempting a misguided lateral of the ball along the way to Morgan, who at least retained possession. Johnson was called upon to kick a 43-yard field goal in the final minute of the game, and that put the end to all Sun Devil hopes, the Bruins winning, 34-24.

That left only Southern Cal, who had dropped out of the Rose Bowl picture by losing its second conference game that same day against Washington, which served to also put the Huskies back *into* the race. It was 1977 all over again—if Southern Cal would defeat UCLA and Washington the Cougars, the Huskies would return to the Rose Bowl.

Bruins/Trojans 1981 was a game that will be long remembered as one Southern Cal kept trying to give away but seemingly could not. The Bruins received the ball and instantly took to the air, Ramsey connecting to Townsell, who upon being tackled fumbled the ball over to the Trojans. The Bruin defense was keyed up for this contest and kept Southern Cal from doing any more damage than a field goal by Steve Jordan, brother of ex-Trojan kicker Frank.

After an exchange, the Trojans' Heisman Trophy shoo-in

277

From the left, UCLA's noseguard Martin Moss, inside linebackers Gene Mewborn and Ron Butler, outside linebacker Ike Gordon and left tackle Joe Gary, on their way to joining teammate safety Tom Sullivan in tackling Southern Cal's Marcus Allen.

Marcus Allen, surprisingly fumble prone in the later goings of the season, turned the ball over to the Bruins' Mike Durden deep in Trojan territory. Two plays later, Nelson carried it in from the 11 for a 7-3 Bruin lead.

Though again stopping the Trojans, the Bruins were cited for a personal foul on a fourth-and-26 punt situation, enabling the Trojans to draw close enough on the subsequent fourth-and-11 to kick another field goal to cut the margin to one.

Troy assumed the lead on their next series, going the full 80 yards to score, charged by a brilliant flea-flicker pass by flanker Timmy White, who took the ball from Allen on a reverse, stopped short of the line on the right side, and angled the pass across the field to split end Jeff Simmons on the UCLA seven, a

48-yard completion. Allen scored on the next play to make it Southern Cal 12, UCLA 7, a two-point conversion try failing.

The Bruins turned it around to make it UCLA 15, Southern Cal 12, as the Trojans once again turned the ball over, this time on a bobbled punt by Joey Browner. Six plays later, Ramsey found Coffman in the end zone from the 23 and the Bruins were back in business, UCLA making good its two-pointer.

Allen fumbled the ball once again minutes later, received by inside linebacker sophomore Gene Mewborn, and Johnson cashed it in in the final minute of the half to send the teams into the locker rooms with UCLA on top, 18-12.

The Bruins padded their lead with another field goal in the third quarter, a 69-yard drive once kept alive by a personal foul called against the Trojans. Then the Bruins found themselves mired with poor field position for the rest of that quarter and in-to the fourth, unable to break off any big plays to get them into the clear.

The Trojans turned to their workhorse Allen in driving 77 yards to score a field goal to trim the margin to 21-15. The momentum began to shift back to the Bruins, as they began to see some daylight midfield, when Ramsey got off a bad pass that sailed right to Trojan defender Troy West. Like two battering rams, Allen and back-up Todd Spencer hammered their team the 39 yards needed to put it on top, 22-21.

At just over two minutes left, there was plenty of time for a Bruin comeback. The lights almost went out when Trojan Joe Turner intercepted a Ramsey pass, but overzealous teammate August Curley was cited for roughing the passer and the Bruins retained the ball. Ramsey hit Bruno for 12 yards, Nelson plugged away, and suddenly UCLA was on the Trojan 29, second-and-six with 28 seconds left.

The scoreboard incorrectly showed that UCLA had two time outs when instead there was only one, bringing on a case of hysterics in the stands and among some of the players. Though Ramsey would have liked to run another play, after calmly assessing the situation between the slow-to-return Trojans and his agitated teammates, he deemed it wise to back away from the melee and let the clock run down to four seconds before call-ing time out.

279

Johnson was called upon to kick what would be the winning field goal at 46 yards, well within his range. It was 1977 in reverse: UCLA was going to score with no time remaining and prove there was justice in the world, that given time things seem to balance out.

Not this time. Trojan nose guard George Achica burst through the Bruin line to block that Johnson kick, and the heart-stopping Bruin comeback was killed, the score frozen at 22–21 in USC's favor. Washington then went to the Rose Bowl, despite the radical loss to the Bruins, for the third time in five years, there to overwhelm Iowa, 28–0. Trojan Head Coach John Robinson, who admitted afterwards, "We almost drowned in our own mistakes," took his team for their first visit to the Fiesta Bowl in Tempe, Arizona, where they lost to Penn State, 26–10.

The Bruins, too, were not without a bowl, as they accepted a bid to play Michigan in Houston's Bluebonnet Bowl on December 31; this game marked the first time the Big 10 and the Pac-10 were opposed in a bowl other than the Rose, causing some consternation among the Rose

Elusive tailback Kevin Nelson, here scoring against Southern Cal to give the Bruins an early lead in the 1981 game, eventually won by the Trojans 22–21.

Bowl officials who feared this might distract from their prized event. It didn't.

Donahue's approach to this game was much the same as it was for the other bowls, "You approach every game to win. I do. I don't think a bowl game should be drudgery for the players. I think that the players should enjoy the bowl experience."

Across the field would be Glenn S. "Bo" Schembechler, a strict, obsessive taskmaster who would have none of the pregame fun and frolic that comes with a bowl for *his* team. For example, the Bruins took in an evening at Gilley's, the famous Country-Western nightclub. Bo's reaction? "It's a bar, isn't it? They've got bars everywhere, and we didn't come to Houston to go to a bar." (What would you do if you were 1–7 in bowl games?)

Unfortunately, when they got around to playing the game, the Bruins never seemed altogether there. It took almost the entire first quarter before Michigan's kicker, Ali Haji-Sheikh, broke the ice with a field goal after a 77-yard drive. The Wolverines scored but three minutes later on the first big play of the night, a 50-yard touchdown pass from quarterback Steve Smith to the great receiver Anthony Carter, and assumed a 10–0 lead.

Although the Bruin defense played up to its capabilities for the rest of the half, the offense couldn't get untracked. At one point, the Wolverines were up to 212 total yards to the Bruins' none. The one time Carney was clearly open with nothing but end zone in front of him, Ramsey's protection broke down, he was hit as he threw and the ball fluttered for an interception by Paul Girgash.

In a way, the roles reversed in the second half, the Bruin defense finally worn out by the excessive pressure of stopping a very good Wolverine attack. UCLA scored to open the third quarter, a 17-yard Ramsey-to-Townsell pass set up by Don Rogers' recovery of an Anthony Carter punt fumble on the Michigan 19, and trailing 10–7, the game was at least not out of reach.

Not for long. Michigan added a field goal a few minutes later, then stretched out the lead during the fourth quarter, scoring a touchdown on a 12-play, 74-yard drive. UCLA countered with an 80-yard scoring drive of its own, Wrightman catching the nine-yard pass in the end zone, Ramsey thus breaking Dennis Dummit's single-season touchdown record with 16 six-point tosses.

But in another time-consuming, defense-draining 80-yard march, Michigan scored the knockout with five minutes remaining for a 26–14 lead. The issue decided, Michigan still scored again in the game's final seconds to create the 33–14 final on the books. The Bruins finished out 7–4–1, a down-and-up season that unhappily ended with the team down for its finale.

As if turning a mental corner, both in terms of confidence in his program and confidence in himself, Terry Donahue had nothing but good feelings about his 1982 edition of Bruin football. Before fall practice began, he admitted, "I've liked every team, but as a group of kids, this team may be the most enjoyable. It may be the team that presents the fewest problems I've had as a head coach, so that's very encouraging."

There was a lot to be encouraged about. The defensive line was packed with seniors, right tackle Mike Barbee, nose guard Karl Morgan and left tackle Irv Eatman. The inside linebackers were headed by sophomore Tommy Taylor and senior Blanchard Montgomery, with the outside men junior Doug West and sophomore Neal Dellocono.

The defensive backfield was another strength. Junior Lupe Sanchez on the left corner, senior Jimmy Turner on the right, strong safety senior Tom Sullivan and free safety junior Don Rogers made it very difficult on opponents trying to gain ground through the air.

The offensive front lines became the only source of concern during this record-setting season. Tackles junior Don Mahlstedt and sophomore Dave Baran, guards junior Chris Yelich and senior Blake Wingle, and center senior Dan Dufour found it hard going to stay healthy as a unit. But the program was in sound shape, and a surprise mid-season shift of a star defensive lineman to the O-line had quite an impact on its success as the year wound down.

The running backs provided excellent balance to the ever-improving passing game. Junior Kevin Nelson and sophomore Danny Andrews were the primary tailbacks, and senior fullbacks Frank Bruno and junior Frank Cephous were valuable supports. The receiving corps was fabulously deep. Seniors Cormac Carney, Jojo Townsell and Dokie Williams would all factor-in, and from the tight-end ranks would emerge senior star Paul Bergmann.

Lastly, there were two individuals who would leave their cleat marks all over the Bruin record books, one a freshman, the other a senior. With junior Ken Potter asked to handle the kick-off chores (and continuously clearing the back of the end zone to make for painless special teams play), the point-kicking fell to Korean-born John Lee. A product of the Ben Agajanian kicking school, Lee would become the most incredibly accurate and point-generating kicker in school history.

And there was Tom Ramsey, who would become the most prolific quarterback in UCLA history. As Donahue wryly observed before the season began, "How can I, the most conservative coach since Attilla the Hun, have the all-time passer in the history of this great university? (My critics) say I don't pass enough, yet I'm about to have a quarterback who breaks every record. I can't figure that out!"

On July 23, 1982, UCLA's Chancellor Dr. Charles E. Young made an announcement that would have far-reaching effects on the Bruin football program. After a 52-year tenancy in the Los Angeles Coliseum, begun with the Pomona game of 1926, UCLA would instead play all its home games at the Rose Bowl in Pasadena, beginning that September. For the first time since leaving the old Vermont campus and Moore Field in 1929, the Bruins would have a field of their own.

From that first game in the 1982 season, the Rose Bowl proved to be the "home" for UCLA football the coaches and administration had hoped — and then some. In the six years that followed this move, the Bruins posted a 28–6–2 home record (53–15–4 overall), defeated rival USC four times and posted a bowl victory after each season. With the stands' close proximity to the playing field and the more than 70,000 seats between the end zones, it is the best place in all of southern California to watch and enjoy football. The Bruins' first home game in Pasadena, versus Long Beach State, rewrote school and conference passing records. Quarterback Tom Ramsey, 18 for 31 and four touchdowns, became UCLA's all-time touchdown passer, while all four scoring tosses went to flanker Jojo Townsell to tie a Pac-10 single game record and make him the career #1 point-receiver in UCLA history at 14 (with six more still to come).

It took a while for the Bruins to get untracked on their way to a 41–10 wipe-out. After UCLA jumped to a 10–0 first-quarter lead, talented Long Beach quarterback Todd Dillon supervised an 80-yard 14-play drive for a touchdown to narrow the gap to three as the quarter closed out. Three Ramsey scoring passes to Townsell in the second quarter quieted the contingent of 49er fans' dreams of a fabulous upset, and the second half was mop-up time.

Unfortunately, that second half did not go without a tragedy. Forty-niner reserve safety Todd Hart was involved in a mid-air collision in the third quarter with a teammate and a Bruin receiver. The resultant injury left him partially paralyzed. In 1988, Hart received a multi-million dollar award in a suit brought against the State of California and the maker of the helmet's face guard which dug into the turf but did not release.

The Bruins then faced three consecutive road games, trips that could increasingly tire and tax a team's stamina. The first was to pastoral Madison, Wisconsin, to take on the plucky Badgers in an arena, Camp Randall Stadium, where spirits flow freely — *very* freely. The Bruins quickly jumped to a 24–0 lead early in the second quarter and ran out the bench to an eventual 51–26 victory.

Start with a stadium deeply imbued with college football tradition, Maize-and-Blue style, called Michigan Stadium. Add to this a wonderfully irascible coach, Glenn S. "Bo" Schembechler, a scrambling quarterback named Steve Smith and a brilliant receiver in Anthony Carter. Top with an opponent like UCLA and you get one hell of a great game.

Sixty degree temperature, the sky overcast and misty, the 105,413 in the stands and a regional TV audience watched Smith, running back Lawrence Ricks, Carter, and a brutish Wolverine defense stake Michigan to a convincing 21–0 lead with less then 10 minutes left in the half. What followed was a comeback that ranks as one of the greatest in UCLA football history.

Getting the ball back on the 20, Ramsey briskly pieced together a 13-play drive, including a gutsy 4th-and-four completion to fullback Frank Bruno, that was capped by a gorgeous 46-yard pass to Dokie Williams that he gathered in at the seven and out-ran defender Marion Body for the score. Three plays and a Michigan punt later, Ramsey set up shop on the UCLA 35. With an 11 yard completion here to Williams, a couple of 25-yarders there to Townsell, Ramsey soon dove in from the one and suddenly it was 21–14 with 180 seconds to go in the half.

Michigan strived to get close enough for a field goal attempt, but when its receiver failed to get out of bounds as time ran out, the Bruins understandably headed off the field. Schembechler hurriedly threw one of his patented tantrums, claiming that the officials missed a time-out called by a Wolverine player, and shockingly they *bought it*, allowing one second to be returned to the clock. When an ensuing procedure call against UCLA drew them five yards closer, kicker Ali Haji-Sheikh cleared the crossbars from 47 yards out to put the Wolverines up 24–14. As Schembechler ran off the field he could be seen taunting Terry Donahue.

Needless to say, the UCLA players and coaches didn't take too highly to such shenanigans, and spent the longest 15 minutes of their lives chomping at the bit to get back out there and finish the comeback job they'd begun.

The second play of the second half resulted in a Don Rogers' interception, giving UCLA the ball on the Michigan 22. Five plays later, Ramsey hit Townsell in the end zone and suddenly it was Michigan 24,

UCLA 21. Later in the third quarter, a short punt gave Michigan the ball mid-field, but it was held at the 31 and could only generate a 48-yard field goal (Haji-Sheikh's career best). Coach Tom Hayes referred to this as ". . .the biggest series of the half."

On the ensuing kick-off, Dokie Williams ran back the ball 65 yards, and seven plays later Kevin Nelson scored from the two to finally put UCLA on top, 28–27. Freshman John Lee soon added a field goal to make it 31–27 with just over 11 minutes to go.

Although Smith was intercepted on Michigan's next two possessions Mike Durden and Neal Dellocono to keep it at bay, a botched pitch from Ramsey to fullback Frank Cephous gave Michigan one last chance on its own 48 with 93 seconds remaining. But Michigan *had* to get a touchdown, and although Smith drove his team down to the eight with 11 seconds left, his three end-zone passes went for naught.

The fear of an emotional letdown played on the minds of the Bruin coaches as the game against the Colorado Buffaloes approached. Sure enough, the Bruins struggled for 29 minutes to a mere 10–6 lead — that is, up until the closing minute, when Ramsey skied one to a streaking Dokie Williams, good for a 50 yard touchdown. The Bruins proceeded to roll in the second half to a 34–6 final score.

UCLA had finished its dangerous road swing undefeated and ranked #8, Ramsey leading the nation in passing efficiency. But the conference race now loomed directly ahead, and first up to face them in Pasadena was spoiler extraordinaire Arizona.

In this game, record after record was broken by Tom Ramsey: Single-game passing, all-time school passing, school attempts, school completions, school yardage, school touchdowns — and Cormac Carney also got into the act, tieing the school record for receptions and setting the career receiving yardage mark. Even so, this game ended in a tie, and UCLA was lucky to have it.

The Wildcats had broken a 21–21 tie in the fourth quarter with what appeared to be a game-winning field goal by freshman Max Zendejas. But with a mere 33 seconds left, Ramsey directed an astounding 61-yard drive with four passes and John Lee kicked what was the re-tieing field goal from 19 yards out with :02 left. At 24–24, this wasn't the way the Bruins had hoped to open their championship march, but a "T" was certainly better than an "L."

Fortunately, the three-game stretch of the conference schedule that followed was eminently march-throughable. First they chewed up Washington State, 42–17, scoring 28 points in a nine-minute span in the second half at the Rose Bowl to flatten a brief three-point Cougar lead. Then at Cal Berkeley they played trade-a-point until finally pulling away from a 31–31 fourth quarter tie to a 47–31 victory, Joe Kapp's first defeat to UCLA as the new Bear coach. Next back in rainy Pasadena came the slosh-happy Oregon Ducks, but the Bruins generated an effective rushing plan to complement "Air Donahue," and UCLA rocked to a 40–12 win.

Then came the Huskies, up in Washington. With this game came the disorienting, the bizarre, and perhaps to some minds the renewal of the infamous Seattle jinx. With the weather cold, windy and miserable, the kind Husky fans love to watch warm-weather teams suffer through, the Bruins contracted a case of fumblitis, coughing up the ball five times in Washington territory.

The most mind-boggling occurred when UCLA was down only 7–0 in the second quarter. Ramsey connected from the 47 to an uncovered Carney who, while loping down the center of the field for a sure touchdown 25 yards away, attempted to shift the ball from his left hand to his right, only his right hand wound up with air, the ball bounding away for another turnover. It was like that all day.

A third-quarter Husky field goal proved the winning margin, as UCLA could only muster a touchdown early in the fourth quarter, an 80-yard drive in three plays to provide the ultimate 10–7 score. Although another record fell by the wayside, as Ramsey surpassed the great Gary Beban's total offense mark, the loss seemed to spell doom for UCLA's Pac-10 Championship dreams.

But if strange things had happened there in Husky Stadium, stranger things were still to come in the Rose Bowl race that season. Bruins might call them miracles.

UCLA's road to recovery involved a spectacular tussle with Stanford back in the Rose Bowl, the last great conference match-up between Tom Ramsey and the Cardinal's John Elway. While Ramsey believes his counterpart would have agreed that ". . . it was never me against John, I never ran a play when he was on the other side of the line," it was still an opportunity for fans of Pac-10 football to see the league's two great leaders alternately direct their respective offenses in one memorable game.

Ramsey started by driving 91 yards to a touchdown with nothing but completions and a reawakened rushing offense. Elway then threw an interception in Stanford's first series, and 80 yards later sophomore Danny Andrews scored from the 7 to put the Bruins up, 14–0. It wasn't until the quarter drew to a close that the Cardinals got on the boards via a 40-yard field goal by kicker Mark Harmon.

After the teams exchanged touchdowns in the second quarter, Elway lightning struck in the last minute: two plays, two passes, the second a 47-yard touchdown. With a successful two point Cardinal conversion it was suddenly UCLA 21, Stanford 18 at the half. UCLA scored a lone touchdown in the otherwise quiet 3rd quarter to go up by 10.

The fourth quarter was another matter entirely. After both teams traded field goals (UCLA's Lee a 50 yarder), Stanford drove 80 yards for a touchdown, the two-point PAT pass incomplete, and UCLA's lead was four. Back came Ramsey for 77 yards in seven plays, including a 51-yard tie-up with Carney and a 16-yard quarterback scramble to the seven, Ramsey taking it in himself from the five for UCLA's final tally.

Four plays and 80 yards later, Elway found halfback Vincent White for an 11-yard score, and another successful two point conversion left UCLA ahead by only three with 3:52 left in the game. Knowing they faced potential disaster should Elway touch the ball again, the Bruins kept it the rest of the way and preserved the exhaustive 38–35 victory.

Finally, for first time home team UCLA faced USC in its new venue. In the weeks preceding this game, a petition had been circulated demanding that Trojan mascot horse Traveler III not be permitted to trot around the sidelines. Although it failed, the UCLA athletic department orchestrated some good-natured pre-game satire when student-costumed Joe Bruin came riding onto the field atop a massive Clydesdale.

Then the fun really started. UCLA scored via an 80-yard touchdown drive featuring the all-purpose talents of Danny Andrews, tight end Harper Howell gathering in a nine-yard pass for the score. The Trojans countered with a Steve Jordan field goal, then UCLA extended its lead with a 60-yard touchdown march, set up by Dokie Williams' kickoff return from the Bruin end zone to the 40. As the quarter closed it was UCLA 14, SC 3.

A Don Rogers interception led to a 45-yard field goal by Lee, and UCLA continued to dominate as it forced a Trojan turnover. But two plays later, a Ramsey fumble was recovered on the UCLA 16 by USC linebacker Joey Browner, and the Trojans didn't waste this golden opportunity. Five plays later tailback Todd Spenser carried it in from the three, cutting the UCLA lead at halftime to 17–10.

The stubborn Bruin defense took over the spotlight in the second half. Starting things off, lineman Mark Walen recovered Trojan quarterback Scott Tinsley's fumble on the Trojan 30, which was promptly cashed in for three points by John Lee, giving the Bruins a 10 point lead barely two minutes into the half. A punting war then ensued, and it wasn't until the fourth quarter was almost half gone when USC factored in another field goal after the Bruins held them at the four.

The final drive was pure "Big Game," and the final play of the entire game one of the most gripping of all.

Starting from the Trojan 34, Tinsley used 10 plays to drive his team to a first-and-goal at the UCLA four. The ball was handed to tailback Anthony Gibson, room was cleared up the middle, but he was met at the one by Bruin linebacker Blanchard Montgomery and was stopped. The collision had popped out Montgomery's left shoulder, but with everything on the line he wasn't about to come out. The next play got underway, and another rush by Gibson was met by another collision with Montgomery for another stop at the one.

There would be no taking Montgomery out now. Third-and-goal, the ball again handed to Gibson, he swung right, but along came Montgomery one more time to sweep him down for no gain. #27 for the Blue-and-Gold more than showed why this is the game of games for both teams each year.

Running the clock down to :03, the Trojans completed a gutty fourth-down pass to score, which thus drew them to one point of UCLA's lead. Head Coach John Robinson immediately decided to go for the two point conversion — it would be either victory or defeat. As he put it, "A tie was an alternative, but not an acceptable one."

As every fan stood in tense anticipation, the teams lined up for the absolute final play of the game. The ball was snapped, Tinsley back-peddled, cocked his arm, but couldn't see open receiver Jeff Simmons over the middle. In an instant, nose guard Karl Morgan stunted around center Tony Slaton, barreled into the Trojan backfield, wrapped his bear arms around Tinsley and down they went.

UCLA 20, USC 19.

Meanwhile, up in Pullman, the Washington State Cougars inaugurated their new stadium by beating the prohibitively-favored Huskies. This helped parlay UCLA into the Rose Bowl when Arizona upset next-in-line candidate ASU the following Saturday night in Tucson. Miracles? Maybe.

UCLA found itself inked in to play none other than Michigan, making it three times in 366 days the two teams were to meet. After Bo's behavior the last two games, Donahue tried to be as diplomatic as possible, but left little doubt in anyone's mind that beating the cantankerous

288

Michigan coach again would be more than just merely satisfying. For Schembechler, he characterized this "feud" as one of Donahue's making, and appeared to be more concerned over the fact he was 1–5 in the Rose Bowl.

While the course of this Rose Bowl game may have lacked the sort of wild swings and tension-filled heroics that make for memorable sports moments, it was one of the most sound, balanced and convincing victories ever constructed by UCLA. 181 yards rushing, 162 yards passing, only two penalties for 10 yards, it was hard fought and hard won. It was also a victory in the pure Ramsey mold, one in which it can be said, "When effective leadership is most required, effective leaders take charge." That moment came in the third quarter.

Qurterback Tom Ramsey, initiating line play against Michigan in the 1983 Rose Bowl.

UCLA had scored a touchdown in the first quarter and a field goal in the second to post a 10–0 half-time lead, with Bruin safety Don Rogers knocking quarterback Steve Smith out of the game with a shoulder separation during Michigan's second possession. When the Wolverines finally scored a touchdown almost 10 minutes into the second half to draw within three, it was as if, in a lumbering sort of way, the momentum was shifting in their favor.

With Ramsey starting from the 20 after the kick-off, pass #1 was batted away and pass #2, a swing-out to fullback Frank Bruno, netted zero yards as well. But the third was a 12-yard completion to Jojo Townsell, on a delayed out-pattern that worked to perfection. Unable to find a receiver on the next play, Ramsey made it back to the line of

289

scrimmage, and the next play was a keeper for five. Once again, Townsell's number was called, a pass off a planned quarterback bootleg that picked up 12 more yards. After Andrews rushed for two, Ramsey scrambled for 15, a run Coach Smith remarked "was probably the key play of the drive."

To continue: Cephous rushed for two, then Ramsey found reliable Cormac Carney and picked up 11 more yards, giving UCLA a first down on the Michigan 23. Danny Andrews broke up the middle for nine, Cephous struck for five, Andrews carried it in the final nine yards for the touchdown, and with this drive UCLA regained complete control of the game.

UCLA later would eschew an easy field goal from the one, failing on a fourth-and-goal Andrews plunge up the middle, but two plays later Montgomery intercepted a pass from Wolverine back-up David Hall for an easy 11-yard touchdown return, and that locked it up. A Wolverine touchdown three minutes later ended the scoring for the day, making for a 24–14 final.

Ramsey and Rogers were named Co-Players of the Game, Rogers becoming the first defender so honored since 1967. Ramsey appropriately closed his Bruin career in record-setting fashion, namely: for the season, 219 completions, 366 attempts, 2,986 yards, 21 touchdowns; for career, 451 completions, 751 attempts, 6,168 yards, 50 touchdowns, all for UCLA records.

Although as a pro it was inevitable that he, like many other quarterbacks throughout professional football, would be overshadowed by Conference Co-MVP John Elway, it's a fact that it was UCLA's Tom Ramsey who led the nation in passing efficiency during their final college year. He truly was one of the important Bruin stars in UCLA history.

During the interim between seasons, athletic director Robert Fischer decided to retire. To replace him, Chancellor Charles Young selected one of the most capable men from within his own administration, Peter T. Dalis. A life-long Bruin, Dalis had been a manager for four UCLA football teams ('55–'58), and his comprehensive and wide-ranging 20-year career at UCLA had provided him with one of the best perspectives in how to coordinate such a complicated department with the rest of the university and beyond. His steady and calming manner has certainly been a factor in the stability and growth of the UCLA football program during his tenure.

As the 1983 season approached, instead of using the cliche to refer to this as a "rebuilding" year, Terry Donahue cleverly called it "restructuring." Towards that end, he planned to merely take the talented components annually developed within his program and simply put them in their proper slots.

On defense, the main component was senior free safety Don Rogers, whose secondary territory was aptly dubbed "Mr. Rogers' Neighborhood." Rogers was teamed with cornerbacks senior Lupe Sanchez and junior Ron Pitts, with sophomore Joe Gasser handling the strong safety turf, JC transfer junior Herb Welch subbing there and at left corner.

At linebackers, the inside chores were handled by junior Lee Knowles, the intense sophomore Tommy Taylor, seniors Ron Butler, Mike Mahan, and the dependable Gene Mewborn. The outside mainly featured senior Doug West, junior Neal Dellocono (also an inside man) and soph Tony Phillips.

The D-line required a complete overhaul from 1982. Junior Chris Block enjoyed a complete year at nose guard, with both tackles spots involving the interchangeable talents of seniors Jeff Chaffin and Kenny Page and junior Dave Randle.

The other side of the ball posed the same sort of problem. At right tackle junior Duval Love became a solid mainstay, while right guard featured sophomore Jim McCullough switching over from the defensive line, with senior Chris Yelich the #2 man. Junior Dave Baran was the primary anchor at center, junior Mark Mannon a spot starter there as well. Left guard was filled by Mannon and talented sophomore Mark Hartmeier, and left tackle was locked in by senior Scott Gordon, classmate Steve Gemza the sub behind him.

Stellar tight end Paul Bergmann was back for his final season, as was back-up Harper Howell. The flankers and wide-outs included the ultra-dependable junior Mike Young and sophomores Karl Dorrell and Mike Sherrard. Fullback featured the bullish senior Frank Cephous, plus sophomore Bryan Wiley and freshman Derek Tennell, and the tailback spot belonged to senior Kevin Nelson, although junior Danny Andrews pressed him as best he could.

Having established himself as the premier field-goal kicker not only on the team but soon in the nation, sophomore John Lee had a hammerlock on that position. The punting was handled by Kevin Buenafe, and kick-offs by deep-footed Ken Potter.

Then there was the quarterback.

As if never again to face the dark no-backup-to-Bashore days of the late 70's, Terry Donahue began stockpiling some of the finest passing prospects in the nation, and once three-year starter Tom Ramsey

291

had graduated, that string began to play out. First up in this heavily recruited roster he had junior Steve Bono, Pennsylvania product, tall, strong-armed. Then, from Oregon, there was sophomore David Norrie, even taller, very accurate. Next to make his case was hustler freshman Matt Stevens, a prep star from nearby La Canada-Flintridge.

Oh yes, there was also this fifth-year senior walk-on from Arizona named Rick Neuheisel, who over the years had dutifully fulfilled his role as scrub-team QB, long-snap holder, sideline clipboard carrier — in other words, he had *patience*. As the seasons rolled by, he developed a strong sense of humor while going about his business, absorbing the intricacies and every nuance of the offensive system as dictated by Homer Smith.

Then, like an eye-rolling Hollywood clich, yes, the humble understudy got the star on his dressing room door, opening night, Sept. 3, 1983. Rick Neuheisel started for UCLA when the team took the rain-clogged field in Athens, Georgia against Vince Dooley's Bulldogs. But if his ordeal was over, fate still had a few dirty tricks to pull on him.

Neuheisel, coping as he was with a blatantly juiced crowd (82,122 in a downpour, mind you) and a national TV audience, managed to throw for 219 yards and earn Chevrolet Player of the Game honors. There was never a point until the last seconds of the game when it didn't seem he was going to pull out a victory.

Georgia, on the strength of two field goals and an unconverted touchdown, led 12–0 as the half was running out. John Lee provided two field goals within the last 1:15 of the half to cut the Georgia lead in half. With all quiet through almost the entire second half, UCLA was presented with two more points when the Bulldogs smartly took a safety with 1:06 left in the game to free-kick themselves out of danger.

UCLA's final drive had all the earmarks of a game-breaker, as Neuheisel sharply passed his team into Georgia territory. Then safety Charlie Dean stepped in front of a sideline pass at the 31 and ran it back for a touchdown to seal it up, Georgia winning it, 19–8.

A tough beginning, and the harbinger of tougher things to come, UCLA burdened as it was with the hardest schedule in the nation that year. UCLA's home opener two weeks later was also its conference opener, as Darryl Rogers' ASU team came to play. The Sun Devils had the year before defeated Oklahoma in the Fiesta Bowl, and were one of the heavy contenders for the league championship.

They looked like one, too, with 12 of their 26 points coming from four field goals by their superb kicker Luis Zendejas. With the score

26–10 with 11+ minutes to play, it looked like UCLA's Pac-10 title defense was doomed from the start. It would take a spectacular comeback for the Bruins to salvage this game. So they came back.

Starting on their own 20, for the first time all game they successfully generated a ground game with Kevin Nelson and Danny Andrews. 13 plays later, on a 4th-and-goal from the seven, Neuheisel connected with Karl Dorrell, and with Nelson's two-point conversion run, the Bruins drew within eight.

Brazenly going to the air, ASU quarterback Todd Hons was intercepted by Bruin safety Joe Gasser on the 47. Eight plays later, UCLA tallied touchdown #2, a 19-yard pass to Mike Young, and when Nelson scored another two-point PAT UCLA had miraculously tied the game, 26–26.

In spite of having 1:36 left and a phenomenal kicker at his disposal, Darryl Rogers ordered his troops to run out the clock and be thankful to come away with the tie. As the Los Angeles Times' brilliant columnist Scott Ostler put it, "People knock L.A. fans for leaving ballgames early to beat the traffic, but this is the first known instance of a team leaving a game early."

If those first two games were rough, along came the monster game against #1 Nebraska, in sunshiny Lincoln. The Bruins did manage to put a little scare into the early-fumbling Cornhuskers, jumping to a snappy 10–0 lead. But the Huskers scored two touchdowns by halftime, thanks in part to a wild sideline-to-sideline run by escape artist Mike Rozier for five yards and the go-ahead points, and proceeded to wallop UCLA from there, 42–10.

Battered, bruised, their linebacker corps almost completely wiped out, the 0–2–1 Bruins next faced Brigham Young University, its freewheeling passing attack led by Steve Young, a great-great-great-grandson of the university's founder. With the pre-season tendinitis in Steve Bono's shoulder finally healed, Coach Donahue decided to let him start instead of the win-less Neuheisel.

Unfortunately, Bono didn't win either, although he did surpass Tom Ramsey's single-game passing yardage record with an incredible 399 yards. Nevertheless, it wound up a 37–35 loss, UCLA's final score coming with :16 left to play and no further possibility for more. With Bono subsequently named the permanent starter for the rest of the season, Neuheisel graciously said, "Even if all I do the rest of the year is hold for kicks. . .those three games made the whole five years worth it."

But Hollywood wasn't through with him yet.

293

Against Stanford on a gorgeous day in Palo Alto, Neuheisel's sideline sojourn lasted a mere quarter. Bono was lost for the season with a shoulder separation, and in came Neuheisel to take his place for good. However, the difference in this game was the Bruin defense, and safety Don Rogers in particular.

For three quarters it was a typical UCLA/Stanford see-saw game. The pass-happy Cardinals, now coached by Jack Elway (graduated John's father), was co-quarterbacked by freshman John Paye and senior Steve Cottrell. Trailing 21-13, UCLA scored a touchdown to begin the fourth quarter, Neuheisel having driven his team 74 yards to score and pull within two (tying-run PAT failed).

Then the defensive boom was lowered. Stanford's first play after UCLA's kickoff was intercepted by Rogers which he returned for an easy 29-yard score; this was followed soon after by two John Lee field goals and yet another interception/touchdown, this by cornerback Lupe Sanchez, and UCLA cleared out a vital 39-21 win.

This victory started UCLA on a conference-cleansing roll, including a second-quarter comeback to defeat Washington State in Pullman 24-12 and a fourth-quarter 14-point comeback to beat Cal in the Rose Bowl 20-16 (its consecutive-game win streak over the Bears at 12).

Next came Washington to Pasadena, where in a wild passing show staged by Neuheisel and the Huskie's Steve Pelleur, Rick set an NCAA record by completing 25 of 27 passes (92.6%!) and almost another NCAA mark with 17 straight completions. As the final seconds ticked off, the defense was asked to protect UCLA's slight lead against the accurate Pelleur, who had thrown 137 times without an interception (a Washington record) and today had gone 19 of 24 and two touchdowns. Don Rogers finally picked him off and preserved this victory for UCLA, 27-24.

For the first time all season, UCLA's "Cardiac Kids" didn't need a comeback to defeat Oregon in Eugene, 24-13. Tailback Kevin Nelson scored three TD's to regain some attention for the Bruin rushing attack. Suddenly, the once hapless 0-3-1 Bruins had amazingly gelled to 5-3-1 and were leading the conference for the Rose Bowl.

But once again, plucky Arizona staged a little upset to seemingly crash UCLA back down to earth. Although there were moments in this no-lead-is-safe game in the hot sun of Tucson that kept both sides on tenterhooks, the focus of the day went to John Lee: With the game on the line, he *missed*, a game-ending chip-shot field goal and so UCLA absorbed a 27-24 loss.

UCLA's Rose Bowl hopes evaporated, Washington now expected

to roll over Washington State and advance to Pasadena. No one could realistically expect the Huskies to lose *two* years in a row, not to the Cougars, and especially not in Seattle.

Oh, but they did! It was halftime at the Coliseum, UCLA down 10–6 to a here-to-fore struggling USC under new coach Ted Tollner, when the word filtered into the Bruin locker room that the Cougars were upsetting the Huskies and putting UCLA a victory away from the Rose Bowl. Armed with this knowledge, the Bruins took the kickoff and exploded for 21 unanswered points in just over 11 minutes to smother the Trojans, who scored a lone touchdown in the fourth quarter to account for the 27–17 final. For the first time in school history, UCLA was going to back-to-back Rose Bowls.

Meanwhile, Illinois became the first team in Big-10 history to beat all nine of its opponents. This in turn set the psychological stage for one of the most remarkable return engagements in college football history.

Back in the Rose Bowl of 1947, a heavily-favored UCLA met lightly regarded Illinois, the Bruins going so far as to publicly express disdain for their opponents because they wanted to play top-ranked Army instead. The insulted Fighting Illini smashed their way to a 45–14 victory, leaving no doubt as to the folly of thumbing one's nose at a bowl opponent.

37 years later, along came a heavily-favored Illinois team, 10–1 and feeling invincible, wanting to be tested by only the best the Pac-10 has to offer. But instead of Washington, it's a UCLA team with the worst record in Rose Bowl history and *wasn't even ranked*. When players from both teams happened to bump into each other while visiting Disneyland, the Illini were pointedly aloof and condescending.

The insulted Bruins smashed their way to a 45–9 victory, leaving no doubt as to the folly of not only thumbing one's nose at a bowl opponent but ignoring a valuable history lesson as well.

Although the morning of January 2, 1984, dawned clear and bright (January 1 being a Sunday, no bowl games were played), such was not the state of Rick Neuheisel's innards. He'd awakened at four in the morning with a horrendous stomach ache, one of seven players stricken by a case of food poisoning that actually kept two of them out of the game entirely.

But Neuheisel would not be denied. Forcing himself to play, he somehow managed to throw for 298 yards (22 of 31, 71%), four touchdowns (tying school and Rose Bowl records), helped generate 511 total offensive yards, and was voted player of the game.

Once again, Don Rogers paved the way, intercepting Illini quarterback Jack Trudeau on only the third play of the game. When John

Lee's subsequent try for a field goal from the 26 was blocked, Illini defensive back Craig Swoop tried to carry it forward, fumbled it when tackled by Harper Howell, and UCLA's Steve Gemza recovered it on the 14 to give UCLA a second chance to score. Four plays later, Neuheisel threw his first touchdown pass, three yards to tight end Paul Bergmann, and UCLA was off and scoring.

For the most part, UCLA picked on Illinois freshman d-back Keith Taylor, who proved incapable of handling UCLA's array of experienced receivers. Although the Illini did score a field goal to narrow the gap to 7–3 at 1:01 into the second quarter, 30 minutes clicked off the game clock before they finally scored again, a touchdown with a failed two-point conversion attempt. In the interim, UCLA had racked up 31 unanswered points to turn it into a laugher, with one final touchdown tallied by Bryan Wiley from eight yards out in the fourth quarter to account for UCLA's 45-point total.

1984 Rose Bowl MVP quarterback Rick Neuheisal, setting up for a pass against Illinois.

UCLA held Illinois to 0 yards rushing, the Rose Bowl record. As the game ticked down a grinning Neuheisel mugged for the camera, wondering on-air was UCLA now good enough to be ranked in the Top-20? Sure, 13th in UPI, 17th in AP. Not a bad finish for a team starting out 0–3–1 with a quarterback self-described as slow, fat, small . . . and with a weak arm to boot!

Between seasons, a Pandora's Box of sorts was opened when the Universities of Oklahoma and Georgia succeeded in legally wresting control of their television rights away from the NCAA, which gave them and every other school the "freedom" to strike their own contracts with the networks and syndicators. But instead of the expected bonanza of riches they'd hoped to reap, the rights fees plunged from the over-saturation of games suddenly available throughout the nation. With each school scrambling to obtain as many airings and TV dollars as possible, all semblance of order disappeared, as game dates and starting times changed at a moment's notice.

At the outset of the 1984 campaign, there were high expectations in some camps for that year's Bruin team, based in part on the 47 lettermen returning as two-time Pac-10 and Rose Bowl Champions. Not only had AP and UPI made UCLA #5 on both polls, Sports Illustrated even went so far as to rank it #1! However, there was one voice crying in the wilderness for one and all not to get too carried away with this pre-season hoopla and fanfare. That voice, of course, belonged to Terry Donahue.

Even so, it was tough to deny this team was talent-laden. Fifth-year senior Steve Bono started at quarterback, having already set the single-game passing yardage record in the BYU game. There was senior Danny Andrews and freshmen Gaston Green and James Primus at tailback, and senior Bryan Wiley at full.

The offensive line was meaty, with right tackle senior Duval Love (6-2¾, 265 lbs), junior right guard Jim McCullough (263), senior center Dave Baran (262), senior left guard Mark Mannon (250) and junior left tackle Mike Hartmeier (263) hardly "gutty little Bruins." The fact that these five players improved on their 47 of 60 individual line position starts possible from the previous year, suggests this was one of the best Bruin offensive lines ever, posting a 56-of-60 starts record.

Able efforts at tight end were delivered by junior Derek Tennell, freshman Russ Warnick and senior Greg Bolin. senior Mike Young, juniors Mike Sherrard and Al Wilson, and sophomore Karl Dorrell were supreme pass-catching artists; the year before, Sherrard set the UCLA single-season reception record at 48 catches.

Youth became more prevalent on defense. Free safety became the unchallenged province of red-shirt freshman James Washington. Sophomore Craig Rutledge was moved over to strong safety, with junior Joe Gasser and sophomore Dennis Price filling in when needed. One corner was covered by dependable senior Herb Welch or the intense sophomore Chuckie Miller, and the other by senior leader Ron Pitts.

Outside linebackers for 1984 included junior Tony Phillips and senior Ron Butler on the right and seniors Neal Dellocono and back-up Terry Moore on the left. Stuffing the middle went to the always-aggressive senior Lee Knowles and junior Tommy "Freight Train" Taylor.

The down linemen were senior left tackle Dave Randle, nose guards senior Chris Block and sophomore Tory Pankopf, and right tackles junior Mark Walen and sophomore Doug Wassel, Block the only player to have started every game the previous year.

Senior Kevin Buenafe was back for the punting chores and senior Ken Potter was returning to handle the kickoffs. Lastly, UCLA was blessed with a field-goal and PAT kicker with no collegiate equal in junior John Lee.

Regardless of all the identifiable talent one might analyze before a season begins, the 1984 Bruins remained virtually indecipherable from the first game forward, proving to be one of the more complicated and hard-to-mesh assemblages to date, perhaps not coming into their own until January 1, 1985.

The first game was a "renewal" between UCLA and San Diego State, having last played each other in 1934. The Aztecs had long waited for the chance to play a team so close to home of the caliber of UCLA, and were hoping to make an upset of it. They came close.

The game was played in San Diego's Jack Murphy Stadium, shared with the Padres baseball team, which meant that a good portion of the playing surface was crusty infield dirt. It was also a hot, muggy night, and into the stadium during the pre-game festivities dropped the Navy's Blue Angels sky divers, thick smoke trails in tow. This fog hung around the field to make most of the first quarter look like action in no-man's land.

UCLA managed a lot of running and passing between the 20's but its entire scoring output depended on John Lee's prodigious right foot. The six successful field goals he kicked may have tied an NCAA and set a UCLA record, but the team's inability to score a touchdown sent nervous tremors throughout the Bruin coaching staff.

Two Aztec miscues in the fourth quarter (ergo a good Bruin defense), each killing a possible go-ahead touchdown drive, preserved this dicey and penalty-ridden UCLA 18–15 win. After UCLA's 380-yards-but-no-TD's performance, Mike Sherrard understated, "I think it's pretty obvious we have a lot of work to do."

Whatever they lacked, it wasn't found in time before they played expected-gimme Long Beach State the following week in the Rose Bowl. The pass-happy 49'ers gave the Bruin defense fits, and the still-stumbling Bruin offense, scoring only two touchdowns, barely squeezed out a win, 23–17.

To make matters worse, Steve Bono sprained his right ankle in the fourth quarter, and could not start against Nebraska the next Saturday in the Rose Bowl. Donahue under-stated, "At this time it's difficult to feel good about the prospects. We're a team that's obviously struggling."

Unfortunately, the last team that a foundering club like the Bruins needed to face was the beefy Cornhuskers. With sophomore Matt Stevens starting for the hurt Bono, UCLA was battered to the tune of 42–3, only the inestimable John Lee able to maintain UCLA's continuous game scoring streak begun in 1971. Injuries? Wiped out for the season was receiver Dorrell and safety Gasser, with defenders Price, Walen, Phillips and offensive starters Young and Andrews needing two weeks to recover. The Bruins' ranking plunged to the mid-teens in both polls.

The Bruins next gutted it out against Colorado in Boulder, displaying some of the offensive spark that had been expected those first two games. At least Stevens had a 33–16 victory this time out to show for his efforts. With his four field goals and three PATs, John Lee exceeded Gary Beban by one notch as UCLA's all-time leading point generator at 615.

In the two previous conference openers, UCLA relied on radical fourth-quarter rallies to achieve at least face-saving ties. Against Stanford, that well was dry. Under coach Jack Elway the Cardinals had developed, of all things, a running game, featuring fullback freshman Brad Muster. Signal-caller Fred Buckley, who subbed for the injured John Paye, led Stanford to a speedy 20–0 lead mid-way through the second quarter. UCLA starter Stevens finally located Mike Young for a touchdown with barely a minute left to make the half-time score 20–7. Stanford then extended its lead in an otherwise dull third quarter to 23–7 via the third Mark Harmon field goal of the game.

UCLA's over-taxed fourth-quarter magic began with an interception by cornerback Ron Pitts, and the resulting 46 yard drive ended when fullback Bryan Wiley scored from the six. A Gaston Green run for two put UCLA down by eight, with visions of ASU '83 suddenly looming large.

Stanford returned the ensuing kickoff 89 yards, but Buckley was then intercepted in the end zone by Washington which he brought out to the UCLA four, six points a mere 96 yards away. Stevens got them, linking up with Sherrard on a 60-yard pass play — but Green failed in his attempt to sweep his way right for the tying two pointer.

Still, with 6:47 left to play, there appeared plenty of time for UCLA to score again. It was also plenty of time which Stanford managed to eat up, UCLA not getting the ball back on its own 22 until 2:27 showed on the clock. The Bruins fizzled out, losing 23–21.

Regrouping for Washington State the next week, it took the ultimate in freak plays for the Cougars to lose in the Rose Bowl. As its sardonic Coach Jim Walden put it, "Why did God decide to help Terry Donahue? He should know I've helped him enough!"

As if borrowing a page from UCLA's Standard Operating Procedure playbook, the Cougars furiously rallied from a 24–7 third-quarter deficit to score 17 fourth-quarter points to achieve a 24–24 tie. Then, with 52 seconds left, they were positioned on the UCLA 25, a kick away from a possible three-point victory. But the center snap inconceivably caromed away from holder Ed Blount and skittered pass kicker John Traut, who had no recourse but to fall on it at the UCLA 49. With no time-outs left, returning starter Steve Bono sharply drove his team to the WSU 30, and as time ran out John Lee kicked a 47-yarder to flip what would have been a flop, and UCLA miraculously won, 27–24.

Traveling the next week to Memorial Stadium in Berkeley, Bono and the Bruins played a somewhat lackluster game offensively, but the defense came to the fore and helped make it 13 wins in a row against the Bears. The bona fide star of the game was freshman linebacker Ken Norton, Jr., son of boxing's former heavyweight champ, who with an interception and a recovered fumble wound up as ABC's Player-of-the-Game. The defense of the day held Cal to a minus 13 yards rushing.

Cal was ahead 14–7 just into the fourth quarter. Ten unanswered points later, UCLA had rallied to a 17–14 victory. The tempestuous Coach Joe Kapp thus found himself losing for the third time in a row to UCLA.

Although conference undefeateds USC and Washington led the Rose Bowl race, UCLA was at least still in the hunt as it flew over to Tempe to play ASU. The Bruins may have relied on a jet to get them there, but it was a "Freight Train" in the form of linebacker Tommy Taylor that made the difference in their 21–13 victory. He achieved a quarterback sack for a safety and almost single-handedly held ASU at bay in the closing moments of the game to secure UCLA's 21–13 victory.

Unfortunately, in the next game against Oregon in Pasadena, a flat and lifeless UCLA offense repeated its conference-opening performance, letting an opponent get too far out in front before making a desperate comeback try. Although both UCLA and Oregon only scored three points apiece in the first half, the Ducks then generated two touchdowns via the passing of quarterback Chris Miller to go up 17–3. UCLA stormed back for two Bono-tossed fourth-quarter scores, but they were sandwiched by an Oregon field goal that kept the Bruins from climbing over the Duck lead. Coming up a 20–18 loser, UCLA's shot at a third-consecutive trip to the Rose Bowl was ignominiously wiped out.

In the following week's game against Oregon State in the Rose Bowl, UCLA journeyed its way to a 26–17 victory after leading at the half 20–3. Of greater interest was the jockeying going on for a bowl berth, the Bruins being courted by the Fiesta Bowl (now on January 1) and Christmas Day's Aloha Bowl. Only one team in the conference that day knew where they were going: The Trojans.

USC knocked off #1-ranked Washington to clinch the Rose Bowl berth. But hyper Trojan quarterback senior Tim Green did a most unwise thing — he popped off, and bragged that he and his team would give the Bruins "a whipping" the next Saturday at the Rose Bowl.

Xerox machines all over Westwood worked overtime that week. Tim Green ate those words seven days later.

Badgered and pummeled, he threw three interceptions and lost his composure to the point of near-embarrassment. For a while, UCLA's game was all John Lee, as his four first-half field goals secured a 12–3 UCLA lead that seemed extremely surmountable, especially as Bruin tailback Danny Andrews suffered a broken leg. Thankfully, late in the half, Bono and freshman tailback Gaston Green teamed to drive the Bruins into scoring range, Mike Sherrard taking in a pass from the five to extend the lead to 19–3.

Then mid-way through the third quarter, Dennis Price had a Bruin cornerback's dream come true when he intercepted a Trojan pass and ran it back 63 yards for a touchdown and a now-insurmountable 23-point lead. Tim Green did score a touchdown for USC on a two-yard rollout, but that was it. UCLA's Lee added one more field goal to up his total for the year to 29 and set the NCAA single season field goal record. For his part, Gaston Green finished with 134 yards, fourth best against USC in UCLA history, at 7.44 yards a carry. The final score 27–17, for only the second time in history UCLA had won three straight from "them."

When the shuffling of bowl line-ups finally ended, UCLA found itself playing in the Fiesta Bowl on January 1, there to face Miami of Florida, the previous year's National Champion. On the strength of Hurricane senior quarterback Bernie Kosar's ability to rack up yardage and touchdowns, plus the prospects of UCLA enjoying a healed and healthy Steve Bono as well as freshman phenomenon Gaston Green, it was expected to be a high-scoring affair.

First to score was UCLA, a touchdown after a snappy 51-yard drive to take a brief 7–0 lead. When, wham, the 'Canes scored on a 34-yard run by Darryl Oliver on a 4-play 62-yard drive. Then, Miami receiver Eddie Brown returned a UCLA punt 68 yards for a touchdown; Kosar connected from 48-yards out to Brian Blades, 10 plays, 86 yards, and suddenly it was Miami 21, UCLA 7 with just over 10 minutes left in the half.

Then it was UCLA's turn, Gaston Green burst into a run on a misdirected off-right tackle, veered to his right and kicked into overdrive, a 72 yard score, a two-play touchdown drive. Next, UCLA nailed Kosar for a safety, then, scored on a Lee field goal set up after the ensuing Miami free kick. In the waning moments of the half after a Kosar-to-Washington interception, UCLA scored another Lee field goal, and suddenly the score was UCLA 22, Miami 21 at the half.

Miami scored to open the second half for a brief 24–22 lead via a Greg Cox field goal. When, wham, Bono teamed with Sherrard from the 10 for a touchdown; wham, Bono connected with Young from the 33, this a 76-yard drive; and UCLA took an almost comfortable 36–24 lead just seconds into the fourth quarter. Back came Miami, 60 yards and a 19-yard scoring rush by fullback Melvin Bratton (2-point PAT failed); still back came Miami, as Bratton took in a Kosar pass from the three to cap a 79-yard drive; and with 3:58 to play, Miami assumed a 37–36 lead.

Once again, the incomparable John Lee came through, as UCLA took the ensuing kick, used 10 plays to reach the 22, and with 51 seconds to play scored the go-ahead field goal. But back came Kosar, zap-zap, two plays, mid-field, only to be sacked by Bruin nose guard Terry Tumey, causing a fumble recovered by teammate Eric Smith, and the scoreboard finally had a chance to cool down. Final score: UCLA 39, Miami 37.

As if saving the very best for the very last: Steve Bono completed 18 of 27 passes for 243 yards and two touchdowns; the Bruins scored four touchdowns — having never scored more than three in any game all season long; and the 404 total yards was a season high, all of which helped propel UCLA to #9 on the AP and #10 on the UPI final polls. Although Steve Bono never achieved the heights of glory that seemed possible after his record-setting single-game performance against BYU in 1983, this one game helped to appease some of the critics who'd labeled him a great field-goal orchestrator. A relieved Bono said it quite plainly, "This was the best game of my life." Amen.

In 1985, for the third year in a row Terry Donahue faced the prospect of starting a fifth-year senior at quarterback, David Norrie. Although at season's start hustling junior Matt Stevens would initially form a two-man alternate unit with him, the good sense of sticking with a player well-versed in the Donahue-Smith offensive system won out, and it wasn't long until the job was solely Norrie's.

Thanks to the annual restocking of talent as masterminded by recruiting coordinator par excellence Bill Rees, the Donahue program was capable of filling vacated positions with players of strength and experience. Youth marked the tailback squad, the accelerating sophomore Gaston Green at the fore, followed by redshirt freshman Eric Ball and sophomore James Primus. Fullback was a season-long battle between junior Marcus Greenwood and sophomore Mel Farr, Jr., son of the great Bruin and All-Pro running back for the Detroit Lions, Mel Farr, Sr.

With seniors Mike Sherrard and Al Wilson and sophomore Willie "Flipper" Anderson at split end, plus junior Karl Dorrell and sophomore Paco Craig at flanker, UCLA boasted some of the best long-range pass catchers in the nation. The tight ends were manned by juniors Bob Garibaldi and Derek Tennell, with seniors Earl Smith, Jeff Nowiski and sophomore Joe Pickert the players inserted for the double-tight end calls.

The offensive line was stocked by right tackle junior Onno Zwaneveld, right guard senior Jim McCullough, center junior Joe Goebel, senior Mike Hartmeier moved from left tackle to left guard, and left tackle senior Robert Cox. There was justifiable concern over the depth across the board, but with versatile players such as sophomores Russ Warnick and John Kidder and junior Eric Rogers at tackle, guards junior Jim Alexander and sophomore Steve Davis, and junior center Tory Pankopf, that problem was solved.

The defensive side of the trench featured senior right tackle Mark Walen, sophomore nose guard Terry Tumey and gonzo junior left tackle Frank Batchkoff. UCLA's legacy of great linebackers continued with Tommy Taylor, back for his final stint at the weak inside spot, senior classmate Steve Jarecki fighting off sophomore Ken Norton Jr. for the right to line up on the strong side beside him.

On the outside, lone senior Tony Phillips suffered a practice injury which put him on the sidelines for the entire season. He was replaced by sophomore Eric Smith, who promptly established himself as one of the finer up-and-coming outsidemen in the nation, with redshirt freshman Chance Johnson acting as super-sub. The other outside spot went to sophomore Melvin Jackson, who proved to be a fixture there for the next three years.

The Bruin secondary returned a host of young but experienced players, led by sophomore free safety James Washington, while strong safety was dominated by junior Craig Rutledge. The corners were well protected, on the left by junior Chuckie Miller and on the right by redshirt freshman Darryl Henley and sophomore Dennis Price.

The punting chores went to senior Ted Henderson, kick-offs to senior James Bray, and the long-snappers were seniors Terry Theodore and Scott Franklin. And, lastly there was senior John Lee, UCLA's point kicker for the ages, who would lay waste to virtually every Bruin kick-and point-scoring record on the books, including 108 consecutive PAT's and an astounding 390 total points scored.

The Bruins opened the season by playing defending National Champion Brigham Young University, in Provo, Utah. BYU was sitting on top of a 25-game winning streak, at the time the nation's longest, and with back-to-back games with UCLA and Washington was determined to prove its #1 ranking the previous year, in light of its less-than-demanding schedule, was no fluke.

But stellar defensive plays aren't flukes, and UCLA used them to promptly unseat BYU. With two interceptions, a blocked punt and three out of four fumbles recovered, the Bruins exacted a dramatic victory as televised on ESPN.

Norrie started, but couldn't seem to put it all together to counteract the stellar passing performance of BYU's Robbie Bosco, who threw for 340 yards and two touchdowns. Two John Lee field goals were all UCLA could offensively produce in the first half, the defense coming through with the Bruins' only touchdown, Craig Rutledge getting a pick and returning it 65 yards for the score. BYU led after the first 30 minutes, 17–13; Norrie for his half had gone 6-for-11, but netted only 29 yards and was intercepted once.

Matt Stevens took over after Norrie couldn't manage a first down to open the second half, and although he too went 6 for 11, he amassed 117 yards and displayed a team-rallying spirit that made the difference. BYU was held scoreless while Lee tacked on two more field goals in each quarter to put the Bruins on top, 19–17. But with just under three minutes to play, Bosco completed an 80-yard drive, sneaking it over from the one and with the PAT the Cougars enjoyed a five point lead.

Then Stevens shocked the spectators by connecting with Mike Sherrard for 62 yards on the first play of the return series, then totally stunned them as he completed the drive of 84 yards to score in just six plays, Gaston Green taking it in from the two, adding a two-point conversion for good measure to lead by three. With less than a minute left, Bosco attempted to fight long-bomb fire with fire, but was intercepted by freshman right cornerback Marcus Turner to lock up the 27–24 Bruin victory.

The defensive player of the game was left cornerback Chuckie Miller, who blocked a punt (that led to three points), caused a fumble (another field goal), and was instrumental throughout the game in frustrating the Cougar receivers. The defense, in its way responsible for 13 points, kept the Bruins in the game when it counted most.

Game #2 was another road game, this to the 91,249 capacity madhouse called Neyland Stadium, home of the very orange-and-white Tennessee Volunteers. Regionally televised on ABC, this game secured the UCLA-Tennessee rivalry as one of the most exciting in the country. Volunteer quarterback Tony Robinson merely amassed a Tennessee single-game passing and total-yards record (387 and 510 respectively), with both teams racking up a combined 965 yards!

Stevens started for the Bruins, and behind the explosive running of Gaston Green (including a 72-yard scoring burst, part of his 194 yards total, the fifth-best rushing day in UCLA history to that point), the Bruins surged to a 10–0 first quarter lead. Then Stevens threw three straight interceptions, and Tennessee dominated the scoring in the second and third quarters until it stretched out to a 26–10 lead.

But after Norrie was inserted in the fourth, shades of the '83 ASU game emerged, as he led UCLA to two clutch touchdowns in the last five minutes (the first a 97-yard drive), and with the two successful 2-point PATs brought about an incredibly beautiful 26–26 tie game. As Donahue succinctly put it, "I've said all along that we are going to need both quarterbacks."

The tie still left Terry one win away from surpassing the all-time UCLA victory record held by the venerable Bill Spaulding during his 14 seasons at the helm, but that was easily achieved in the home opener against San Diego State, UCLA overwhelming the Aztecs, 34–16. It was altogether a busy night in UCLA football history: Freshman Eric Ball scored a UCLA record-tying four TD's, split end Mike Sherrard became

305

the Bruins' all-time receiver with 110 catches, John Lee kicked his 75th consecutive PAT to tie the Pac-10 record, and in less than 10 seasons Terry Donahue posted a 73–29–6 record to become UCLA's winningest coach.

If the 2–0–1 Bruins were riding high on their way up to damp and blustery Seattle to face Washington, the multi-injured Huskies were down, struggling through a 1–2 season, having lost to the same BYU team UCLA had previously beaten. And UCLA played like it, dominating for almost all of the first half to build a 14–3 lead behind starter Norrie. But then Washington scored as time ran out on an incredibly obvious long-bomb situation, added a two-point conversion, and carried that momentum shift into the second half, shutting off the Bruins for a 21–14 upset on regional TV.

For the fourth year in a row, the Bruins failed to win their conference opener. Not only that, Stevens had suffered an injury against the Huskies, sidelining him from backing up Norrie as UCLA went up against Arizona State in the Rose Bowl, again on regional TV. The new ASU coach was John Cooper, a man who'd been instrumental in keeping Terry Donahue in coaching during some rough times in his early days as an assistant.

Although UCLA anticipated a tough contest, ASU having just come off back-to-back shutouts against Pacific and USC, it was anything but, as the Bruins crushed the Sun Devils, 40–17. Norrie clicked for 14 of 24 and two touchdowns, Lee added four more field goals to his credit, and fullbacks Farr and Marcus Greenwood each added a six-pointer to make for a well-rounded rout. The only negative on the day was, shortly after breaking the all-time receiving yardage record with 1,921 yards, Mike Sherrard suffered a broken clavicle, sidelining him until the bowl season arrived.

With Sherrard and Green both out, visiting UCLA faced the prospect of coping with unpredictable Stanford, 1–3 but fronted by quarterback John Paye, who led the nation in total offense. But for the second game in a row, the overall Bruin talent was too deep to not take up the slack, and UCLA overwhelmed the Cardinals, 34–9 in a game regionally televised by CBS. Paye was sacked five times (four by right tackle Mark Walen alone), the Bruins' Flipper Anderson scored on a 51-yard pass play from Norrie, James Primus tacked on a 40-yard scoring run of his own, and Tod Spieker's classic post-game party for all visiting Bruins had a lot to celebrate.

Washington State coach Jim Walden had emphasized the wishbone in his team's repertoire the game before meeting UCLA, making Terry Donahue worry about the myriad possibilities that might be offensively sprung on his team up at the ol' Palouse. The additional fact that WSU always seemed to rush well against UCLA increased his almost manic penchant for worry even more.

Walden, sharp-witted, wily and a master of promotion, clad his team in their rarely-used crimson pants (saved primarily for the hated Huskies) for this homecoming game, syndicated on Lorimar Television, and things started out right when WSU's Kitrick Taylor ran back UCLA's opening punt 69 yards for a touchdown. Then, instead of running the ball at the nation's #2 rushing defense, Walden sprang a passing attack that bolted his team to a 24–10 second quarter lead. The Bruins managed to shear it to 24–17 by the half, then after a pointless third quarter scored two touchdowns to lead by seven.

WSU scored a touchdown with 3:44 remaining in the game, and Walden chose to go for two and regain the lead. Quarterback Mark Rypien peeled off to the right, threw for Taylor, but the pass was batted away by lineman Batchkoff, and although the Cougars had one last chance with the ball two minutes later, linebacker Tommy Taylor smashed into and stopped fullback Kerry Porter's midfield dive on 4th-and-1 to seal up another Bruin victory, 31–30.

That same afternoon across the state, previously unbeaten in conference play Washington fell out of the league's co-lead when lowly Oregon State, posted as a 37-point underdog and unmercifully ridiculed that week by the Seattle media, shot-gunned the Huskies with an reverberating 21–20 upset. UCLA suddenly found itself firmly back in the Rose Bowl race, next hosting Cal and then able to enjoy a bye before traveling to meet Arizona, the only remaining undefeated team left on the Pac-10 books.

But if 2–4 Oregon State could beat 4–2 Washington, why couldn't 1–5 Stanford upset 5–1 Arizona too? Amazingly enough, while UCLA was making it 14 straight against Cal to the tune of 34–7, Stanford did just that, 28–17, and created a massive five-way tie of teams with one loss all vying for the conference championship: UCLA, Washington, USC, Arizona and ASU. When none of the other four suffered a setback the following week during the Bruins' bye, it was all going to come down to the final three weeks of the season to thin out the Rose Bowl ranks for good.

A healthy Gaston Green returned to the Bruin lineup the night of November 9th in Tucson, and his three touchdowns made it possible

307

for UCLA to knock Arizona out of the picture. UCLA was in control for most of the game, scoring first after a bad snap on a Wildcat punt situation turned the ball over to the Bruins on the Arizona 27, Green taking it in from the seven. UCLA added 10 more points to lead 17–0 at the half, and maintained that difference when the two schools exchanged touchdowns in third quarter.

Arizona tried to wrest control of the game away from UCLA in the final period, first scoring a touchdown midway through the quarter in a drive interrupted by cornerback Dennis Price's interception that was fumbled back to the Wildcats. The try for a two-point PAT failed, as did the one following Arizona's 61-yard scoring interception with just over three minutes remaining. Although Arizona got its hands on the ball two more times after that, the Bruin defense rose to the occasion and kept the score 24–19 in UCLA's favor.

When ASU knocked off Washington and Cal upset USC, the Rose Bowl race was narrowed to just two teams: UCLA, 5–1 in conference play, controlled its own destiny; 4–1 Arizona State clung to its hopes that the Bruins would somehow slip along the way. But Donahue said it wouldn't surprise him, given the strong parity in the league, if the champion wound up with *two* conference losses.

As if to prove his conjecture, UCLA breezed pass Oregon State, 41–0, leaving just USC to create that two-loss parlay. And in that game against the Trojans, the Bruins just about did everything they needed to win except score enough points. Virtually every time they neared the USC end zone, something would go haywire; one such play, needing but one yard to score, Eric Ball dove over the top, but without a finger touching him the ball squirted out of his hands and plopped into the surprised arms of Trojan linebacker Marcus Cotton, who moved it out to the 11 yard line.

Led by the irrepressible freshman Rodney Peete, the Trojans, thrashed for well over three quarters, sucked it up and drove 56 yards for the game-winning touchdown, scoring with just 1:13 left on the clock to knock the Bruins out of the Rose Bowl picture, 17–13. Even so, Arizona State had to avoid losing to arch-rival Arizona to make it permanent.

It didn't. Arizona Coach Larry Smith, long a friend of Donahue's, once again came through with an impressive win over ASU. As it happened in '82 and '83, only after all the conference games had been factored-in did UCLA become the Pac-10's Rose Bowl representative.

UCLA's opponent on New Year's Day was Iowa, 10–1, #3 in the nation after having been ranked #1 for several weeks in succession until suffering its only loss to Ohio State. The Bruins, ranked #13, were posted as slight underdogs, but Hawkeye Coach Hayden Fry did all he could to dispel any notions that the Bruins weren't as dangerous as they come.

A sad note going into the sun-drenched game was that David Norrie had not been able to recover from a post-season quadriceps muscle injury in his right leg as the game drew near. Taking his place would be Matt Stevens, long recovered from his own injury but who had been seldom used once Norrie had assumed the uncontested starter's role.

Iowa's last trip to Pasadena, against Washington in 1982, was a disastrous 28–0 loss. Adding to their sense of mission were the letters "ANF" stenciled on their helmets, signifying "America Needs Farmers," honoring the plight of those fans throughout the midwest who were struggling through some harsh times. Lastly, quarterback Chuck Long, eligible the previous year for the NFL draft, opted for one last year of college play specifically in order to lead his team to victory in the Rose Bowl.

But a football game is a football game, and on January 1, 1986, UCLA absolutely creamed Iowa, 45–28.

The unheralded hero of the game proved to be freshman tailback Eric Ball, himself a midwesterner out of Ypsilanti, Michigan, who entered the game early in the second quarter after Gaston Green was lost for the afternoon due to a hamstring injury. Ball tied the Rose Bowl record for most touchdowns at four, and would have been allowed to score the record-breaking fifth on an inches-to-go call had the Bruin coaching staff known it was in the offing. As it was, he rushed for 227 yards, second best in Rose Bowl history, and tied four other records, becoming only the second freshman to ever earn MVP honors.

After Iowa scored first, needing only 29 yards after Stevens was intercepted, UCLA snapped back for 10 points, Ball scoring on a 30-yard rush to cap a 79-yard drive and John Lee nailing one from the 42 after heretofore clutch-handed Hawkeye tailback Ronnie Harmon suffered one of his four first-half fumbles. Iowa managed to tie it at 10–10 midway through the second quarter; then UCLA cut loose with two Ball-bearing scores, the first from 40 yards out, and closed out the half leading, 24–10.

Iowa drew within a touchdown early in the second half, but a 9-yard scoring pass to Sherrard to tag a 73-yard drive and an additional Ball touchdown, this cruised in from the 32 less than two minutes into the fourth quarter, put the game effectively out of reach at 38–17, as Stevens scored one last Bruin touchdown to make for UCLA's 45 point total.

UCLA had thus become only the third school in history to win four January 1 bowl games in a row, and by finishing ranked #6 (UPI) and #7 (AP) was the only Pac-10 team to finish in the Top 10 three out of the past four years. Plus as a post-season attraction, it had scored 153 points in these last four bowls, for an average of more than 38 points a game.

1986 Rose Bowl MVP freshman tailback Eric Ball, breaking away from a would-be Iowa tackler.

Although this Rose Bowl belonged to Eric Ball, the Fiesta Bowl to Green, and the two previous Rose Bowls to Neuheisel and Ramsey, the significant contribution made by John Lee during this four year skein cannot be under-estimated. His accumulated game-saving heroics made the quiet difference in UCLA's achievements during this period, and without him it's doubtful UCLA would have advanced into such heady post-season opportunities.

Terry Donahue barely got a chance to blink after this tremendous victory when attention was focused on the next season. And against what school would UCLA be opening the 1986 season? None other than defending National Champion Oklahoma, in Norman no less. As Terry pleaded in the locker room, "I want to enjoy (the Rose Bowl win) for several months before I start to worry about those guys!"

For the fourth year in a row, still another 5th-year senior was tagged for the starting quarterback job. But in this case, Matt Stevens didn't have another upperclassman breathing down his neck. The job was his, for the entire season, no platooning, no threat, no problem. There was sophomore Brendan McCracken in the system, as was red-shirt freshman Ron Caragher, but unless Stevens went down with an injury they wouldn't be factored-in.

There was another Bruin quarterback practicing in Westwood that fall, Troy Aikman, a transfer who would be ineligible to play until 1987. In fact, by mutual consent between his former coach and Donahue, he had to wait until after UCLA's first game before reporting. This was because he was *Oklahoma's* ex-quarterback, a golden-armed gem who had started as a sophomore the previous season only to be injured four undefeated games into the season. He was replaced by freshman Jamelle Hollieway, an option artist for whom the wishbone was reinstalled, permanently. When Aikman asked head coach Barry Switzer for help in finding a pass-oriented school, Switzer called Terry Donahue, who was happy indeed to provide Mr. Aikman with a new home.

UCLA was rich in running backs. Both junior Gaston Green and sophomore Eric Ball were bowl MVPs at tailback, with junior James Primus, freshman Brian Brown and sophomore Danny Thompson filling out the depth chart. At fullback, senior Marcus Greenwood vied with junior Mel Farr Jr. for playing time, with Primus also logging some hours there as the season came to a close.

The receiving corps featured split ends junior Flipper Anderson, senior (and place-kick holder) David Clinton, junior Paco Craig, and flankers seniors Karl Dorrell, Bob Garibaldi, and freshman Mike Farr (brother of Mel Jr.). Coming back for his final year at tight end was senior Derek Tennell, with junior Joe Pickert picking up a couple of starting assignments as well.

The offensive line was another edition of beefed-up Bruin excellence. At left tackle, junior Russ Warnick eventually lost his starting role to senior Eric Rogers, but wound up switched to the right side and started there at season's end. The left guard position was filled by senior

Jim Alexander, whose broken hand allowed sophomore Frank Cornish to start the final four games of the regular season.

The center's role belonged to personable Joe Goebel, moved to right guard for only the post-season game, senior back-up Tory Pankopf then getting his first and only start as snapper. Senior Onno Zwaneveld was the season-long fixture at right guard, as was junior John Kidder at right tackle.

Taking the heat as John Lee's replacement was David Franey, a most amiable and competent point kicker, who made 16 of his 21 FG attempts. The punting duties were divided between sophomore Wes Denton and freshman Kirk Maggio, who specialized in short "pooch" punting.

At free safety there was junior James Washington, who had led the team in tackles for two years running, junior Alan Dial his able sub. Teamed with strong safety senior Craig Rutledge, they made most deep threats against the Bruins a doubtful prospect. The right cornerback position proved to be a season-long skirmish between the effervescent sophomore Darryl Henley, junior Dennis Price and sophomore Marcus Turner, with only senior Chuckie Miller maintaining permanence on the left side.

Glory days at linebacker returned with junior Ken Norton, Jr. and sophomore Chance Johnson on the inside and juniors Eric Smith and Melvin Jackson on the outside, with sophomore Carnell Lake also adding some brilliance on the fringe. The interior line was nicely experienced, sophomore Jim Wahler at right tackle, junior Terry Tumey at nose guard, and the fiery senior Frank Batchkoff at left tackle.

As might be expected, the buildup for the UCLA-Oklahoma game was tremendous, especially with the pre-season Bruins tabbed at #4 and the Sooners carried over as #1, and this game was appropriately a national telecast on ABC. Although it slightly drizzled before the game and was overcast most of the day in Norman, it was shirt-sleeve weather all the way, 76 degrees and intensely humid.

Both teams played warily as the game began, the Sooners only good for a field goal in the first quarter. UCLA put a real scare into them to begin the second quarter when cornerback Darryl Henley almost returned an interception for a score, but after he was pulled down from behind (by an offensive lineman, no less) the Bruins could only muster a Franey field goal. Not unlike the 1984 Nebraska game, this field goal made all the difference between a complete disaster and a complete *shut-out* disaster.

The expected rash of wishbone fumbles historically typical of past

Sooner early-season games never materialized, as the Oklahoma wishbone began to rip off large chunks of turf on its way to 470 total yards and a sickening romp over UCLA. Any hopes of stuffing what he snidely referred to as a "pastel blue" Bruin jersey into the mouth of the Sooners' rude linebacker Brian Bosworth fell by the wayside, as UCLA suffered a humiliating 38-3 defeat.

Although the Bruins had an extra week to regroup and heal before the next game, it also meant an extra week to dwell on the ignominy and debilitation that game brought. UCLA dropped from #4 in the AP poll to #19, and disappeared entirely from the UPI. Although snapping back with easy victories against San Diego State (in San Diego) and Long Beach State (at the Rose Bowl) — there was a haunting need to put everything in perspective relating to the Oklahoma game.

With its subsequent loss to Arizona State, UCLA again failed to win its fifth-straight Pac-10 opener, and it combined with the Oklahoma failure to cast a shadow over the rest of the Bruin season, a relatively disappointing year that was only salvaged by two awesome season-ending performances by Gaston Green.

The Sun Devils had never defeated the Bruins, a psychological edge UCLA hoped would continue to work in its favor. But when a team proves only capable of producing points via field goals as UCLA did this regionally-televised afternoon, that edge can wear thin — or disappear entirely.

The Bruins held a mere 6-3 half time lead, and an exchange of three-pointers in the third quarter maintained that difference, but under the leadership of quarterback Jeff Van Raaphorst, the Sun Devils scored the game's only touchdown seconds into the fourth, and an added field goal provided them with the 16-9 final score, finally breaking the "Bruin jinx" that had pestered them for seven previous contests.

The "backs against the wall" balance of the season began with a brilliant game against previously unbeaten Arizona, again in the Rose Bowl. After the Wildcats skunked the inept and stumbling Bruins in the first half taking the lead, the turnaround-of-the-year began two minutes into the third quarter. An interception by safety James Washington was knocked free but squirted mid-air into the arms of teammate Darryl Henley, and 54 yards later he arrived in the end zone to put his team finally on the boards.

Arizona valiantly struggled to maintain its advantage through the rest of that quarter, but with 17 unanswered points, including a soaring 78-yard Stevens-to-Craig pass, UCLA swung itself into a 24-18 lead.

Arizona then staged it's own comeback, finally scoring some second-half points on a tailback-pass play from the 15 to take a 25–24 lead with just under 3+ minutes left.

With the next possession, Stevens led the team down to the Arizona 32. On his next carry, all Green was supposed to do was keep the ball near the middle to set up a game-ending Franey field goal, but his instincts took over and three broken tackles later he scored, and with it provided UCLA with its 32–25 victory.

The Bruins then traveled to Strawberry Canyon to face a Bear team struggling under volatile coach Joe Kapp, destined to lose his job by the end of the year. His team seemed to reflect the unsettled state of affairs, as it turned the ball over three times and played shakily all afternoon, losing for the 15th straight time to UCLA, 31–10.

Returning to the Rose Bowl, UCLA faced a Washington State team with hopes of continuing a string of upsets that included a tie against Arizona State and a 20-point victory over USC; a loss by either team would mean sure expulsion from the Rose Bowl race. In spite of his bunion-sore left foot, Gaston Green ran for 162 yards, scored twice; the Bruins as a team amassed 345 total yards, 198 yards through the air, and eliminated the Cougars, 54–16.

UCLA continued in stride through Oregon State in Portland. The Bruin secondary was attacked by 57 passes, of which eight were picked off, two returned for touchdowns, one by Alan Dial for the maximum 100 yards, and none good for any Beaver points. Henley and Rutledge each made three interceptions, doubly tying the Bruin record for most in a game set by Ron Carver vs. Texas in 1971; and including a fumble recovered by Eric Smith for a touchdown, the defense alone scored almost half of UCLA's 49–0 victory points.

Then Stanford made its bi-annual trek to the Rose Bowl. In an almost carbon-copy repeat of its upset staged on its previous visit, the Cardinals immediately put the Bruins in a hole, scoring two touchdowns in the first quarter, and with that was never headed. Stanford primarily relied upon the strength of bullish tailback junior Brad Muster, 6'3", 226 lbs., good for 38 carries (the Stanford record), 183 yards, two touchdowns, Pac-10 player of the week award, and perhaps solely responsible for his school's 28–23 victory over UCLA.

Not only did this loss eliminate UCLA's Rose Bowl hopes (ASU clinching the championship later that evening with its 49–0 win over Cal), it virtually canceled whatever thoughts it might have of landing in a January 1 bowl anywhere else, too. Only one slim chance remained for Terry Donahue to pass Paul "Bear" Bryant and achieve what no other coach in history had done, appear in and win five straight New Year's Day bowls. His 6–3 team had to beat Washington in Seattle to keep that chance alive.

Washington, too, had made preliminary plans to go major bowling, it's 7–2 record definitely a desirable commodity. But on this cold and windy afternoon in the Great Northwest, neither team was able to put away the other.

Midway through the second quarter, the Bruins struck first, Stevens bootlegging it in from the 25. Shortly thereafter, the Huskies returned the favor, a rare Green fumble setting them up on the UCLA 19, punching it in from there in three plays. The third quarter rolled around, and again the Bruins scored a touchdown, a seven-play 30-yard drive after Rutledge intercepted Husky passer Chris Chandler at the Washington 35. Thanks to a short kickoff, the Huskies promptly snapped back for a matching score in but three plays.

It all came down to a wild fourth-quarter finish. With 91 seconds left, UCLA finally broke the tie with a Franey field goal, but just as it had in the two previous instances, back sprang Washington, able to make some exceptional connections in spite of the knee-jerk Bruin "prevent" defense. Camped on UCLA's 27 with time running out, Husky coach Don James opted for the face-saving (but fan-displeasing) field goal, and when Jeff Jaeger's kick cleared the uprights with no time left, the 17–17 tie left both teams in a bowl quandary, with neither then attractive enough to be tabbed for a January 1 date.

UCLA accepted an invitation to Freedom Bowl III, played in close-at-hand Anaheim, eventually to be matched up with Brigham Young. But there was still one game left in the schedule, against USC. The 7–2 Trojans were bound for the January 1 Citrus Bowl, which made the Bruins' nonNew Year's Day circumstances even harder to stomach, feeling as they did that the wrong team in town was being accorded that honor. Played in the Rose Bowl on an incredibly blustery day, they more than hammered home that point.

Hammered? Make that *bludgeoned*. Gaston Green alone scored four touchdowns and ran for 224 yards, the most ever against USC by any single player in its history, while the Trojans as a whole were held to a scant 45 yards rushing. UCLA punted once to USC's six. Green scored twice in the first quarter on runs of 46 and 27 yards, again in the second quarter from the two shortly after a Franey field goal, and with the score 24–0 the game was all over but the shouting. Then the Bruins administered the *coups de grace*.

As the half neared to a close, USC attempted to block a punt but roughed the kicker. Time for only one more play, the ball on the SC 39. Flooding the end zone with receivers, Stevens let one fly. Sure enough, two Trojans tipped the ball into the hands of Karl Dorrell, and with no time remaining the insult increased by another touchdown to 31–0.

Lest there be *any* doubt, UCLA promptly took the second half kickoff and marched 80 yards in 10 plays to make it 38–0, Green picking up his UCLA record-tying fourth touchdown from the one. USC finally scored a touchdown to avert a shutout, then UCLA engineered still another 80 yard touch-down drive. The thrill long gone, the Trojans picked up 18 fourth quarter points to account for the 45–25 final score.

Ted Tollner's third loss to UCLA in four years, plus USC's fourth straight loss to Notre Dame the following week and a subsequent loss to Auburn in the Citrus Bowl, got him fired shortly into the new year. Considering that only two years

Tailback Gaston Green during his one-man demolition of the Trojan defense in the 1986 UCLA-USC game.

earlier he'd taken his team to victory in the Rose Bowl and was named Pac-10 Coach of the Year, this was quite a slide down the razor blade of life. His replacement would be Arizona's Larry Smith, who like Arizona State's John Cooper was one of Terry Donahue's close friends — at least for 51 weeks of the year.

The only remaining business for the 1986 Bruins was the Freedom Bowl, played on the night of December 30th.

With the gelling of what finally resolved itself into a potent UCLA team, and a somewhat less-than-challenging opponent in a BYU team that failed to win some part of the WAC championship for the first time in 10 years, the prospects of this being anything more than a Bruin bash were slim. On this warmish southern California evening, UCLA waltzed its way to consecutive bowl win #5 in a game that gave Green, the seniors and the unsung one last chance to strut their stuff.

BYU did have the nation's Outland Award winner on defense, nose tackle Jason Buck, which made Gaston Green's all-time bowl record-setting 266 yards rushing performance somewhat surprising. And to BYU's credit, the high-drive UCLA offense was held to only seven first half points, the Cougars actually scoring first on kicker Leonard Chitty's 32-yard field goal almost 3+ minutes into the game. Touchdown #1 for Gaston Green, a three-yard carry scored as the first quarter came to a close, was sparked by an inspiring 49 yard reverse run by Karl Dorrell, but that was it for both teams in the first half.

The second half, however, was all UCLA. Green bookended a David Franey 49-yard field goal with two third quarter touchdown runs, the second from the BYU 21, at 79 yards easily the longest in Freedom Bowl history. Then, for the first time in his collegiate career Gaston threw a pass, complete to Karl Dorrell for a 13 yard touchdown. A last-ditch touchdown was scored by BYU, but UCLA culminated its 1986 season with a solid 31–10 victory.

On top of Green's records set against USC and BYU, he also set the UCLA single-season rushing record at 1,405 yards, the single-season touchdown record with 17, and his 266-yards this night was the second best in single-game UCLA history. These two games helped propel him into the front-ranks of the Heisman Trophy race for the following year.

Of several factors that figure into the continued success of any football program, that of coaching continuity is often cited as a primary one. The shuttling in-and-out of assistants through the early years of Donahue's tenure was stilled for the most part after the 1979 season. In fact, for the years running 1982–1986, except for a new strength coach, Donahue's staff remained completely intact. That changed with the 1987 season.

First and foremost was the departure of offensive coordinator Homer Smith, who must be credited for having followed to the letter Terry Donahue's request to jazz up the Bruin offense. Smith spent a year in the pros, but returned to the collegiate ranks in 1988 as the offensive coordinator for the University of Alabama. His replacement was Steve Axman, who was Larry Smith's offensive coordinator while at Arizona.

Other changes included the departure of the hip running back coach, Norm Andersen, as the former UCLA receiver moved on to join Jim

Walden's new staff at Iowa State, inside linebacker coach Ted Williams moving over to handle the ball carriers in his stead. Williams' old slot was filled by Larry Coyer, who had years of coaching experience at both the collegiate and USFL levels.

Also, a familiar face began appearing at practices and on the sidelines, former Bruin quarterback Rick Neuheisel. Starting as an intermittent volunteer assistant coach helping the Bruin quarterbacks, he would be hired outright as a full-timer soon after the end of the 1987 campaign.

Once again, UCLA was accorded a high pre-season national ranking, #4 in the UPI, #3 in the AP, right behind the one-two punch of Oklahoma and Nebraska. With the Cornhuskers slated as the Bruins' second opponent that year, part of this logjam at the top would be quickly shaken out. On paper, UCLA's ranking seemed well founded.

Defensively, the Bruins returned 2/3's of the starting line, 3/4's of the starting linebackers, and a backfield featuring senior free safety James Washington and a slew of experienced players. At strong safety, senior Alan Dial would start every game, with the corners covered by senior Dennis Price and junior Darryl Henley. The outside linebackers included junior Carnell Lake and seniors Melvin Jackson and SMU transfer David Hummel; senior Eric Smith, of All-America caliber, was unfortunately sidelined for the entire season with a back problem, but would return for 1988, a year's eligibility still remaining for him.

The inside linebacking chores went to senior pre-season All-American Ken Norton, Jr, and junior Chance Johnson, with junior Doug Kline, sophomore Craig Davis and freshman Randy Austin taking up the slack. On the line, the left tackle slot was filled by senior Jeff Glasser, backed up by sophomore Mike Lodish, while right tackle was secured by junior Jim Wahler, and the nose guard for the year was steady senior Terry Tumey.

Flipping to the offense, left tackle senior Russ Warnick, left guard sophomore Rick Meyer, sophomore center Frank Cornish, right guard senior John Kidder, and right tackle senior David Richards (another transfer from SMU), started every game for the Bruins, providing an entire season's worth of offensive line stability that topped the mark set by the O-line of '84. At tight end, sophomore Charles Arbuckle vied all season with senior Joe Pickert and freshman Corwin Anthony for the starter's job.

The fine art of catching Bruin passes was carried on by senior wideout Flipper Anderson and flanker senior Paco Craig. *The* tailback was senior Gaston Green, with injury-plagued junior Eric Ball and sophomore sensation Brian Brown the stringers behind him. Fullback duties went to seniors Mel Farr, Jr. and James Primus.

Taking over the point-kicking from graduated David Franey was sophomore Alfredo Velasco, who went on to All Pac-10 honors. Velasco shared kick-off duties with fellow sophomore Wes Denton, and the other kickers included deep punter junior Harold Barkate and "pooch" master sophomore Kirk Maggio.

What quarterback controversy existed was between juniors Brendan McCracken, who had gained much of his playing time the previous season by running the wishbone in any short-yardage situations, and Troy Aikman, transfer extraordinaire from Oklahoma. Either way, for the first time in seven years, a fifth-year senior would not be the starting signal caller for UCLA. Aikman won the job, and went on to lead the entire nation for all but the final week of the season in passing efficiency, throwing for over 2,500 yards and posting a .652 percentage.

The schedule provided UCLA with what might be considered a tune-up before the encounter with Nebraska, as up-and-coming San Diego State, fresh from its WAC championship the previous year, returned to the Rose Bowl. The Aztecs, who barely lost to Iowa in the Holiday Bowl in December, still enjoyed the talents of senior quarterback Todd Santos, a Heisman candidate in his own right, but many of the players that helped the team bounce back from the previous year's loss to the Bruins were gone.

On this pleasantly hazy Saturday afternoon over the Labor Day weekend, Santos' very first pass was picked off by Carnell Lake. Worse things were to come for the Aztecs. Santos was picked for a second time shortly thereafter by Ken Norton, Jr., which led to UCLA's first touchdown. When Darryl Henley returned a punt 74 yards for a touchdown, incredibly the first such return for UCLA in 21 years, the worse things finally came. Five different backs were to score for the Bruins, and Green ripped off a nice 61-yard run to keep the Heisman eyes focused on him.

Aikman threw only 10 passes, completing eight for 166 yards, but with a rushing game good for 334 yards his skills were somewhat left on the shelf. Even so, he admitted, "It felt great to finally get back on the field after sitting out for nearly two years. I still felt 'rusty,' but things were looking bright once again." That brightness was exemplified by the final score: UCLA 47, SDSU 14.

One week later, the Bruins traveled to Lincoln to face Nebraska. (On game days, Husker Stadium becomes the state's third-largest "population area." Honest.) UCLA did exactly what it thought it had to do to win the game. It shut down the Nebraska running game, holding the Huskers to 117 yards.

Unfortunately, Nebraska more than returned the favor, holding UCLA to only 94 rushing yards, Green's Heisman hopes dissipating from only 46 yards on 19 carries, although he did score three touchdowns and two two-point carries for 22 total points. More unfortunately, Cornhusker quarterback Steve Taylor resorted to an unheralded passing attack that resulted in 217 yards and the Nebraska single-game record for touchdowns at five, tying the Big-8 record as well.

Perhaps most unfortunate was the breakdown of UCLA's special team play: poor punts, shabby protection, a bungled placement, low kickoffs and weak coverage that gave Nebraska good field position and/or easy points all day. Add to that an arguable fumble by Aikman, an easy catch dropped here and there, and the mistakes mounted up until the game simply got away from the Bruins in the second half, losing 42–33.

To the good was Aikman's emergence, throwing for 211 yards on 22 attempts and 14 completions, as well as the Bruins finally scoring some real points against a Big-8 power for the first time in history — the most ever by UCLA against Nebraska. Perhaps most important was the respect earned by the Bruins in comparison to the last two debacles. As Aikman put it, "We have closed the gap with the Nebraskas and Oklahomas. . . but we're not satisfied!"

In spite of the protestations by the players that they wouldn't suffer a let-down when facing lightly regarded Fresno State the next Saturday afternoon, 10 sacks of Aikman and only a 17–0 victory didn't seem to jibe with them. Defensively the Bruins did hold the Bulldogs to minus 26 yards rushing, recorded eight sacks, and kept the only scoring threat to a missed 54-yard field goal attempt, causing the first shutout against Fresno State in 64 games.

The last time UCLA had won a Pac-10 opener was in 1981. The Bruins finally broke that string and put into motion an almost-undefeated march to the conference co-championship when they hosted Arizona the following week. UA was now coached by Dick Tomey, formerly of Hawaii and, yes, yet another friend of Donahue's, having been on Terry's 1976 staff after assisting together under Rodgers and Vermeil.

Maybe it took two more quarters of uninspired play to finally shake the Nebraska willies out of UCLA's system, plodding along as it did to trail Arizona at the half, 17–7. But oh, that second half, and oh, that Troy Aikman! After the Bruins scored 10 points to tie mid-way through the third quarter, the Wildcats posted another touchdown to lead 24–17. A

320

61 yard Bruin drive carried over into the fourth quarter, Aikman passing for his second touchdown of the day to retie the score at 24–24. Marcus Turner then intercepted Arizona quarterback Bobby Watters, the momentum swung entirely UCLA's way, and 10 points later the Bruins locked up conference game #1, 34–24.

Aikman was the primary influence, going 19-of-25 for 256 yards, two touchdowns, rushing for a third, and firmly establishing himself as the team leader. As he saw it, "For the first time this season, I felt poised and relaxed. Our football team showed some character coming from behind, and we all realized at that point that we were destined and committed to being a good football team."

Traveling to the Farm to play Stanford on a sweaty day the following Saturday afternoon, the Bruins were confident they would overwhelm a decidedly weaker Cardinal team, but given the eccentricities of games past there was no way they could have imagined winning 49–0. A complete victory in every way possible, the defense scored two interception-touchdowns, Velasco kicked four field goals, and Green surpassed the great Freeman McNeil as UCLA's most gainful ball carrier. Adding even a fourth quarter safety, the players eventually joined in with the traveling fans in the stands to echo the famous "U-C-L-A Fight Fight Fight!" throughout otherwise-stilled Stanford Stadium.

UCLA next played an impressively resilient Oregon team, the Bruins unable to administer any sort of knock-out punch through the entire first half, leading by only 17–7. Then, recalling some of the classic trick plays from the annals of football history, Donahue permitted his team to spring something called "The Bumerooski."

As created by pro coach Bum Phillips, it's a punt-formation sneaker in which the ball is snapped not to the kicker but to the blocking up-back, in this case Mel Farr Jr. As kicker Harold Barkate first distracted the Duck defenders by faking a high uncatchable snap, Farr handed the ball up between the legs of linebacker Randy Austin, who held it out of sight while maintaining steady eye contact with the opponent in front of him; Farr then spun, faked a hand-off to by-passing linebacker Doug Cline, and all the Bruins shouted "reverse!" while the line blocked as if that was being run. Austin palpitatingly counted to three to allow the opposition time to bite and chase after the decoy, then took off for an unmolested 38-yard touchdown.

This daring fourth-down play put the Bruins up 24–7, and they never looked back until the final score read 41–10. With this game, with the first score, a one-yard touchdown run by Brian Brown, UCLA established the all-time NCAA consecutive game scoring record of 187 straight games. This broke the record originally established by USC, with a shutout of 24–0 at Washington in 1983.

Sensing his star back needed some heavy p.r. in the Heisman race, Donahue decided to turn Green loose the following week against Cal, calling on #44 to carry the ball 28 times out of the 72 plays run. Green more than responded. He tallied three scores, the first a 79-yard rush, the third on a pass reception for the first receiving touchdown in his Bruin career, and blasted through the Bears for 220 yards, averaging 7.86 yards per carry.

Aikman, too, had a successful day, throwing 22 passes and completing 15, good for 236 yards and three touchdowns.

New Cal Coach Bruce Snyder joined the long list of Bear coaches unable to beat the Bruins, as UCLA triumphed for the 16th straight year, 42–18.

Early in the first quarter in the pivotal Pac-10 game against Arizona State in Tempe, on national TV, Gaston Green incurred a pinched nerve in his neck; out he came, and when he missed the subsequent game against Oregon State and then sparingly played the week later against Washington, he was no longer a major factor in the Heisman race. But out of the ashes of this failed campaign in the rain-laced Arizona desert two new heroes emerged, one the known commodity in quarterback Troy Aikman, who threw for a season-high 328 yards, the other the unexposed tailback Brian Brown.

The Bruin defense held ASU to just three first half field goals, but the UCLA offense went scoreless. In the second half, UCLA turned things around: The Bruins received the kickoff, Aikman starting slinging, and they drove 84 yards in eight plays, the last a 35-yard Aikman-to-Craig connection, and the comeback was on. Bruin linebacker Melvin Jackson then intercepted a pass, which led to a Velasco 32-yard field goal.

After forcing an ASU punt, return-man Henley surprised the Sun Devils with a reverse hand-off to David Keating good for 39 yards to their 28. Aikman soon hooked up with Craig for a score and a 17–9 lead. ASU successfully ran its own reverse at UCLA on the ensuing kickoff, then closed out the quarter with its first touchdown but failed in its two-point tying attempt. It was then Brown's turn to shine, scoring from the eight to cap a 74-yard seven play drive, and on the next possession ripping off a beautiful 74-yard scoring run to put a lock on the game. ASU added eight last-minute points to account for the 31–23 final count.

A prescient Terry Donahue said, "Obviously we're on a collision course with USC." The Trojans had suffered only one conference loss, that to Oregon the week prior to the Duck-Bruin game, and having previously disposed of Washington and not facing ASU that season had two relatively easy games leading to the season finale with UCLA at the Coliseum. In a way, so did UCLA.

The first game was such going in, against air-minded Oregon State. Played in Corvallis, the Bruins typically rumbled their way to a 52–17 victory, but this game was devastating, both in terms of the winning margin and in two key injuries suffered. Utterly valuable reserve quarterback Brendan McCracken broke his collarbone on a fourth-quarter touchdown run and was out until bowl-time, and linebacker Melvin Jackson tore up his knee and was lost for everything.

The second soft game, however, was against historically tough Washington. Played in the Rose Bowl, the Bruins at first see-sawed with the Huskies, UCLA scoring two first quarter touchdowns (one PAT failed), UW scoring two second quarter touchdowns to go up by one. . .only to be never heard from again. A field goal, the half-time break, another field goal, and then four unanswered touchdowns absolutely wiped out the Huskies, 47–14, — the greatest point total ever scored against a Don James team in Pac-10 play.

UCLA had thus won all seven of its conference games, tying the school record set in 1946, and with a win over USC could have been the first Pac-10 team to win eight league games on its way to the Rose Bowl. It was not to be. UCLA appeared to have the game well in hand throughout most of the first half, blanking the Trojans while painstakingly building a 10–0 lead, Gaston Green scoring from the six in the first quarter and Velasco adding three in the second. Furthermore, SC lost the services of its star tailback Steve Webster mid-way through the half with a season-ending knee injury. USC bungled its two major scoring opportunities late in the half: Tailback Ryan Knight lost the ball on a fourth-and-goal from the one, then junior quarterback Rodney Peete was intercepted at the goal, the ball almost returned the length of the field by safety Eric Turner, only to be tackled as time ran out by Peete himself at the 11, a game-saver if there ever was one.

In the third quarter, UCLA increased its lead to 13-0 on still another Trojan miscue, this a weak 18-yard punt by Chris Sperle, but then everything seemed to fall out of whack for the Bruins. Aikman, having thrown only three interceptions through 10 games, was uncharacteristically picked off three more times in this second half alone; on the other hand,

Peete turned in the game of his life, continually eluding Bruin defenders and throwing for 304 yards, the first-ever 300+ performance in his career.

Finally scoring a field goal later in the third period, USC then proceeded to control the rest of the game. The Trojans scored just 51 seconds into the fourth quarter on a six-yard Roscoe Tanner reception to end a 76-yard drive to draw within three. Then, after Trojan safety Mark Carrier picked off his first of two interceptions, Peete threw the game-winning 33-yard pass to receiver Eric Anholter, who juggled the ball while falling out of the end zone but was adjudged in possession for the score.

Sperle later made up for his earlier punting gaffe by kicking a 47-yarder to pin UCLA on its own one. When Aikman's last pass of the regular season proved to be an interception, the Bruins were finished.

UCLA's quarterback put it mildly: "The game with USC was a nightmare in every sense of the word. We had worked extremely hard to get into that position, and to lose was very devastating. It's a game we'll never forget, and the feeling after it will serve as motivation for me and our team going into and throughout the '88 season."

The Bruins accepted a bid to play in the Aloha Bowl on Christmas Day. The opponent was Florida, sporting a deceptive 6–5 record after having survived a grueling schedule that included eventual National Champion Miami, highly-ranked Florida State and most of the good ol' boys that make up the Southeastern Conference. The Gators had two exceptional offensive players, senior quarterback Kerwin Bell and frosh wonderback Emmitt Smith, who had just set the Florida single-season rushing record.

On the strength of their considerable talents alone, the Bruins managed to prevail over the Gators, 20–16. These talents were hampered by the absence of a thigh-sore Gaston Green, plus tight end Charles Arbuckle and fullback Mel Farr Jr. were also stuck on the sidelines. With virtually no home fans in the stands, with a crowd total of 24,839 that only bettered that of the Oregon State game in Corvallis, UCLA went through most of the game without emotion, only putting up when it had to to post a 10-point fourth quarter margin then withstood the pestering Gators for over 11 minutes to preserve the win.

It took a wee bit of luck, too. Down 10–3 in the closing moments of the first half, Aikman moved the Bruins 81 yards to tie the game on a one-yard Brown score, highlighted by a one-armed catch by tight end Joe Pickert on a third-down play to keep it alive. In the same vein, UCLA scored its second touchdown late in the third quarter when Gator defender

Kerry Watkins batted away Aikman's end zone pass, only to have it drop into intended receiver tailback Danny Thompson's arms — while he was lying on the ground, having stumbled while running his route.

Record-breaking quarterback Troy Aikman, in action during the 1987 season.

The last Bruin score of the year amounted to a unique 7-play stand-still drive: UCLA got the ball on a Chance Johnson-created turnover on the Florida 15, moved it to the one, then with a penalty and a sack later wound up back on the 15, Velasco's successful field goal then making it 20–10. To sum it all up, Troy Aikman said, "It was a bittersweet ending to what was a great season in spite of not reaching the Rose Bowl."

On the day, Flipper Anderson snagged four passes to tie Mike Sherrard's UCLA single-season reception record at 48, and his 52 yards set him as UCLA's single-season receiver at 903 yards and all-timer at 2,023 yards. Although he didn't play, Gaston Green nevertheless finished the 1987 season as UCLA's greatest back in history, having set or tied 12 records, including control of career rushing yards (3,731), career carries (708) and career touchdowns (40). Lastly, the team was able to reflect on the fact that with this victory it tied a consecutive bowl win record for Terry Donahue shared with two legendary coaches, Georgia Tech's Bobby Dodd and Alabama's Bear Bryant — and as the only one still alive he had a much better chance of winning #7.

1988 found the UCLA Sports Information Department exchanging one Heisman campaign for another, as the push for quarterback Troy Aikman got underway. But, as the season approached, Aikman was typically more concerned with the team than with personal honors, "We are optimistic about 1988. A lot of hard work is left to be done, but we are encouraged by how we have grown. 1987 was a great year, but we fell short of the mark. We plan to spend New Year's '89 where we belong. . .at home. . .in the Rose Bowl!"

On top of that, coach Terry Donahue began to intimate that this edition of Bruin football was the best he'd ever had to challenge for the top spot in the nation. So it was that the 13th coach in his 13th year at UCLA continued on his way to over 100 victories and over 25% of UCLA's wins overall.

UCLA GAME-BY-GAME RECORD
1919-1987

(Home Games Indicated By (*) Asterisk)

1919: Fred W. Cozens

0 Manual Arts HS	74
6 Hollywood HS	19
12 Bakersfield HS	27
*7 Occidental Frosh	2
*7 Los Angeles JC	0
*0 USS Idaho	20
*7 Los Angeles JC	21
13 Occidental Frosh	30
52 Season totals	193

W—2, L—6, T—0: Pct 250

1920: Harry Trotter

0 Pomona	41
*0 Occidental	21
21 Redlands	27
*0 Caltech	32
0 Whittier	103
21 Season totals	224

W—0, L—5, T—0: Pct 000

1921: Harry Trotter

*7 Redlands	35
*7 Pomona	55
0 Occidental	35
*0 Whittier	62
0 Caltech	27
14 Season totals	214

W—0, L—5, T—0: Pct 000

1922: Harry Trotter

24 San Diego State	6
34 Redlands	9
*7 Occidental	14
6 Whittier	6
6 Pomona	20
*6 Caltech	7
83 Season totals	62

W—2, L—3, T—1: Pct 417

1923: James Cline

*12 San Diego State	0
*6 Loyola	0
*12 Whittier	14
*6 Pomona	27
*6 Redlands	12
6 Occidental	20
6 Caltech	59
54 Season totals	132

W—2, L—5, T—0: Pct 286

1924: James Cline

*0 Loyola	0
*13 La Verne	14
0 Whittier	6
*7 Occidental	20
7 Pomona	50

0 Redlands	0
13 San Diego State	13
*0 Caltech	6
40 Season totals	109

W—0, L—5, T—3: Pct 188

1925: Wm. H. Spaulding

*7 San Diego State	0
*16 La Verne	3
*26 Pomona	0
*0 Whittier	7
9 Occidental	0
0 St. Mary's	28
*23 Redlands	0
0 Stanford	82
10 Caltech	10
91 Season totals	130

W—5, L—3, T—1: Pct 611

1926: Wm. H. Spaulding

*25 Santa Barbara State	0
*42 San Diego State	7
6 Whittier	16
27 Pomona	7
*24 Occidental	7
26 Redlands	3
*3 Caltech	7
*0 Iowa State	20
153 Season totals	67

W—5, L—3, T—0: Pct 625

1927: Wm. H. Spaulding

*33 Santa Barbara State	0
*7 Fresno State	0
*25 Whittier	6
*8 Occidental	0
*32 Redlands	0
*7 Pomona	7
13 Caltech	0
13 Arizona	16
*6 Drake	25
144 Season totals	54

W—6, L—2, T—1: Pct 722

1928: Joined PCC
Coach: Wm. H. Spaulding

*19 Santa Barbara State	0
*7 Arizona	7
32 Caltech	0
7 Stanford	45
*29 Pomona	0
6 Idaho	20
0 Washington State	38
*65 La Verne	0
*6 Oregon	26
171 Season totals	136

W—4, L—4, T—1: Pct 500
9th in PCC

1929: Wm. H. Spaulding

*0 USC	76
*56 Fresno State	6
*0 Stanford	57
31 Caltech	0
*20 Pomona	0
0 Oregon	27
*0 St. Mary's	24
*14 Montana	0
121 Season totals	190

W—4, L—4, T—0: Pct 500
6th in PCC

1930: Wm. H. Spaulding

*0 USC	52
*21 Pomona	0
*6 St. Mary's	21
30 Caltech	0
*0 Stanford	20
0 Oregon	7
*0 Oregon State	19
*20 Idaho	6
77 Season totals	125

W—3, L—5, T—0: Pct 375
Tied for 8th in PCC

1931: Wm. H. Spaulding

*0 Occidental	0
0 Washington State	13
0 Northwestern	19
*46 Pomona	0
6 Stanford	12
*12 St. Mary's	0
*6 Oregon	13
*13 Florida	0
83 Season totals	57

W—3, L—4, T—1: Pct. 438
9th in PCC

1932: Wm. H. Spaulding

*26 Calif. Aggies	0
*6 Idaho	0
12 Oregon	7
*51 Caltech	0
*13 Stanford	6
*7 St. Mary's	14
*32 Montana	0
*0 Washington State	3
*0 Washington	19
2 Florida	12
149 Season totals	61

W—6, L—4, T—0: Pct 600
3rd in PCC

1933: Wm. H. Spaulding

*34 Los Angeles JC	0
*13 San Diego State	0
0 Stanford	3
*22 Utah	0
*20 Loyola	7

*0 Oregon 7
*0 California 0
14 San Diego Marines 13
0 Washington 10
*14 St. Mary's 22
*7 Washington State 0
123 Season totals 62
W—6, L—4, T—1: Pct 591
5th in PCC

1934: Wm. H. Spaulding
*14 Pomona 0
*20 San Diego State 0
3 Oregon 26
*16 Montana 0
0 California 3
*49 California Aggies 0
*0 Stanford 27
*6 St. Mary's 0
*25 Oregon State 7
*13 Loyola 6
146 Season totals 69
W—7, L—3, T—0: Pct 700
6th in PCC

1935: Wm. H. Spaulding
*39 Utah State 0
20 Oregon State 7
7 Stanford 6
*33 Oregon 6
*2 California 14
*0 So. Methodist 21
*19 Hawaii 6
*14 Loyola 6
*13 Idaho 6
13 St. Mary's 7
160 Season totals 79
W—8, L—2, T—0: Pct 800
Tied for 1st in PCC

1936: Wm. H. Spaulding
*21 Occidental 0
*26 Pomona 0
*30 Montana 0
*0 Washington 14
17 California 6
*22 Oregon State 13
*6 Stanford 19
7 Oregon 0
*7 Washington State 32
7 USC 7
143 Season totals . . . . : 91
W—6, L—3, T—1: Pct 650
5th in PCC

1937: Wm. H. Spaulding
*26 Oregon 13
7 Stanford 12
7 Oregon State 7
*0 Washington State 3
*14 California 27
0 Washington 26
*13 So. Methodist 26
*13 Missouri 0
*13 USC 19

93 Season totals 133
W—2, L—6, T—1: Pct 278
8th in PCC

1938: Wm. H. Spaulding
*27 Iowa 3
12 Oregon 14
*13 Washington 0
7 California 20
*33 Idaho 0
*6 Stanford 0
21 Washington State 0
*7 Wisconsin 14
7 USC 42
*6 Oregon State 6
46 Honolulu Town Team 0
32 Hawaii 7
217 Season totals 106
W—7, L—4, T—1: Pct 625
4th in PCC

1939: Edwin C. Horrell
*6 Texas Christian 2
14 Washington 7
14 Stanford 14
*20 Montana 6
*16 Oregon 6
*20 California 7
*0 Santa Clara 0
*13 Oregon State 13
*24 Washington State 7
0 USC 0
127 Season totals 62
W—6, L—0, T—4: Pct 800
Tied for 1st in PCC
Ranked 7th by AP

1940: Edwin C. Horrell
*6 So. Methodist 9
*6 Santa Clara 9
*0 Texas A&M 7
7 California 9
*0 Oregon State 7
*14 Stanford 20
0 Oregon 18
*34 Washington State 26
*0 Washington 41
12 USC 28
79 Season totals 174
W—1, L—9, T—0: Pct 100
8th in PCC

1941: Edwin C. Horrell
*7 Washington State 6
0 Stanford 33
*14 Montana 7
7 Washington 14
*14 Oregon 7
*7 California 27
0 Oregon State 19
*29 Camp Haan 0
*13 Santa Clara 31
*7 USC 7
30 Florida 27

128 Season totals 178
W—5, L—5, T—1: Pct 500
Tied for 5th in PCC

1942: Edwin C. Horrell
*6 Texas Christian 7
*7 St. Mary's Pre-Flight 18
*30 Oregon State 7
21 California 0
*14 Santa Clara 6
*20 Stanford 7
7 Oregon 14
*14 Washington 10
*40 Idaho 13
14 USC 7
0 Georgia 9
(Rose Bowl)
173 Season totals 98
W—7, L—4, T—0: Pct 636
1st in PCC

1943: Edwin C. Horrell
*0 USC 20
*7 College of Pacific 19
7 March Field 47
*0 California 13
0 San Diego Navy 28
*7 Del Monte Pre-Flight 26
6 California 13
*19 St. Mary's 7
13 USC 26
59 Season totals 199
W—1, L—8, T—0: Pct 111
4th in PCC

1944: Edwin C. Horrell
13 USC 13
0 California 6
12 San Diego Navy 14
*39 St. Mary's 0
*12 St. Mary's Pre-Flight 21
*26 Alameda Coast Guard . . . 13
13 March Field 35
*7 California 0
*54 College of Pacific 7
*13 USC 40
189 Season totals 149
W—4, L—5, T—1: Pct 450
3rd in PCC

1945: Bert LaBrucherie
*6 USC 13
*20 San Diego Navy 14
*50 College of Pacific 0
*13 California 0
*6 St. Mary's Pre-Flight 13
*12 Oregon 0
*13 St. Mary's 7
0 California 6
15 USC 26
135 Season totals 79
W—5, L—4, T—0: Pct 555
5th in PCC

1946: Bert LaBrucherie

*50 Oregon State 7
39 Washington 13
*26 Stanford 6
13 California 6
*33 Santa Clara 7
*46 St. Mary's 20
14 Oregon 0
*61 Montana 7
*13 USC 6
*18 Nebraska 0
14 Illinois 45
(Rose Bowl)
327 Season totals 117
W—10, L—1, T—0: Pct 909
1st in PCC
Ranked 4th by AP

1947: Bert LaBrucherie

*22 Iowa 7
26 Northwestern 27
*24 Oregon 7
39 Stanford 6
*0 So. Methodist 7
*0 California 6
27 Oregon State 7
*34 Washington 7
0 USC 6
172 Season totals 80
W—5, L—4, T—0: Pct 555
4th in PCC

1948: Bert LaBrucherie

*48 Washington State 26
*0 Northwestern 19
*28 Idaho 12
6 Washington 27
*14 Stanford 34
*0 Oregon State 28
27 Nebraska 15
13 California 28
*7 Oregon 26
*13 USC 20
156 Season totals 235
W—3, L—7, T—0: Pct 300
8th in PCC

1949: Red Sanders

*35 Oregon State 13
41 Iowa 25
35 Oregon 27
14 Stanford 7
*0 Santa Clara 14
27 Washington State 20
*21 California 35
*47 Washington 26
7 USC 21
227 Season totals 188
W—6, L—3, T—0: Pct 667
2nd in PCC

1950: Red Sanders

*28 Oregon 0
*42 Washington State 0
20 Washington 21
*6 Illinois 14
*21 Stanford 7
20 Purdue 6
*20 Oregon State 13
0 California 35
*39 USC 0
196 Season totals 96
W—6, L—3, T—0: Pct 667
3rd in PCC

1951: Red Sanders

*14 Texas A&M 21
13 Illinois 27
*44 Santa Clara 17
7 Stanford 21
*41 Oregon 0
*21 California 7
7 Oregon State 0
*20 Washington 20
21 USC 7
188 Season totals 120
W—5, L—3, T—1: Pct 611
2nd in PCC

1952: Red Sanders

*13 Oregon 6
*14 Texas Christian 0
32 Washington 7
*20 Rice Institute 0
*24 Stanford 14
20 Wisconsin 7
28 California 7
*57 Oregon State 0
*12 USC 14
220 Season totals 55
W—8, L—1, T—0: Pct 889
2nd in PCC
Ranked 6th by AP, UPI

1953: Red Sanders

*41 Oregon State 0
*19 Kansas 7
12 Oregon 0
*13 Wisconsin 0
20 Stanford 21
44 Washington State 7
*20 California 7
*22 Washington 6
13 USC 0
20 Michigan State 28
(Rose Bowl)
224 Season totals 76
W—8, L—2, T—0: Pct 800
1st in PCC
Ranked 4th by UPI, 5th by AP

1954: Red Sanders

*67 San Diego NTC 0
32 Kansas 7

*12 Maryland 7
21 Washington 20
*72 Stanford 0
61 Oregon State 0
27 California 6
*41 Oregon 0
*34 USC 0
367 Season totals 40
W—9, L—0, T—0: Pct . . . 1.000
1st in PCC
NATIONAL CHAMPIONS (UPI)
Ranked 1st by UPI, 2nd by AP

1955: Red Sanders

*21 Texas A&M 0
0 Maryland 7
55 Washington State 0
*38 Oregon State 0
21 Stanford 13
*33 Iowa 13
*47 California 0
34 College of Pacific 0
*19 Washington 17
17 USC 7
14 Michigan State 17
(Rose Bowl)
299 Season totals 74
W—9, L—2, T—0: Pct 818
1st in PCC
Ranked 4th by AP, UPI

1956: Red Sanders

*13 Utah 7
13 Michigan 42
*6 Oregon 0
*28 Washington State 0
34 California 20
7 Oregon State 21
*14 Stanford 13
13 Washington 9
*13 Kansas 0
*7 USC 10
148 Season totals 122
W—7, L—3, T—0: Pct 700
Tied for 2nd in PCC

1957: Red Sanders

*47 Air Force Academy 0
*16 Illinois 6
0 Oregon 21
*19 Washington 0
*26 Oregon State 7
6 Stanford 20
*16 California 14
19 Washington State 13
21 College of Pacific 0
20 USC 9
190 Season totals 90
W—8, L—2, T—0: Pct 800
3rd in PCC

1958: George Dickerson

*6 Pittsburgh 27
18 Illinois 14
0 Oregon State 14

Bill Barnes, acting coach

*14 Florida 21
20 Washington 0
*19 Stanford. 21
*20 Washington State 38
17 California 20
*7 Oregon. 3
*15 USC 15
136 Season totals 173
W—3, L—6, T—1: Pct 350
6th in PCC

1959: Joined AAWU
Coach: Bill Barnes

*0 Purdue 0
21 Pittsburgh 25
*19 California 12
*7 Air Force Academy 20
*7 Washington 23
55 Stanford 13
*21 No. Carolina State 12
10 USC 3
*21 Utah 6
*8 Syracuse 36
169 Season totals 150
W—5, L—4, T—1: Pct 550
Tied for 1st in AAWU

1960: Bill Barnes

*8 Pittsburgh 7
27 Purdue 27
8 Washington 10
*26 Stanford. 8
*7 No. Carolina State 0
28 California 0
*22 Air Force Academy 0
*6 USC 17
16 Utah 9
*27 Duke 6
175 Season totals 84
W—7, L—2, T—1: Pct 750
3rd in AAWU

1961: Bill Barnes

19 Air Force Academy 6
6 Michigan 29
3 Ohio State 13
*28 Vanderbilt 21
*20 Pittsburgh 6
20 Stanford 0
*35 California 15
*28 Texas Christian 7
*13 Washington 17
10 USC 7
3 Minnesota 21
(Rose Bowl)
185 Season totals 142
W—7, L—4, T—0: Pct 636
1st in AAWU

1962: Bill Barnes

*9 Ohio State 7
*35 Colorado State 7
6 Pittsburgh 8
*7 Stanford. 17
26 California 16
*11 Air Force Academy 17

0 Washington 30
*3 USC 14
14 Utah 11
*7 Syracuse 12
118 Season totals 139
W—4, L—6, T—0: Pct 400
5th in AAWU

1963: Bill Barnes

*0 Pittsburgh 20
14 Penn State 17
10 Stanford 9
*7 Syracuse 29
12 Notre Dame 27
*12 Illinois 18
*0 California 25
21 Air Force Academy 48
*14 Washington 0
6 USC 26
96 Season totals 219
W—2, L—8, T—0: Pct 200
3rd in AAWU

1964: Bill Barnes

17 Pittsburgh 12
*21 Penn State 14
*27 Stanford 20
0 Syracuse 39
0 Notre Dame 24
7 Illinois 26
25 California 21
*15 Air Force Academy 24
20 Washington 22
*13 USC 34
145 Season totals 236
W—4, L—6, T—0: Pct 400
4th in AAWU

1965: Tommy Prothro

3 Michigan State 13
24 Penn State 22
*24 Syracuse 14
14 Missouri 14
*56 California 3
10 Air Force Academy 0
*28 Washington 24
30 Stanford 13
20 USC 16
34 Tennessee 37
14 Michigan State 12
(Rose Bowl)
257 Season totals 168
W—8, L—2, T—1: Pct 773
1st in AAWU
Ranked 4th by AP, 5th by UPI

1966: Tommy Prothro

*57 Pittsburgh 14
31 Syracuse 12
*24 Missouri 15
27 Rice 24
*49 Penn State 11
28 California 15
*38 Air Force Academy 13
3 Washington 16
*10 Stanford 0
*14 USC 7

281 Season totals 127
W—9, L—1, T—0: Pct 900
Tied for 2nd in AAWU
Ranked 5th by AP, UPI

1967: Tommy Prothro

*20 Tennessee 16
40 Pittsburgh 8
51 Washington State 23
17 Penn State 15
*37 California 14
21 Stanford 16
*16 Oregon State 16
*48 Washington 0
20 USC 21
*14 Syracuse 32
284 Season totals 161
W—7, L—2, T—1: Pct 750
Tied for 2nd in AAWU
Ranked 10th by UPI

1968: Tommy Prothro

*63 Pittsburgh 7
*31 Washington State 21
7 Syracuse 20
*6 Penn State 21
15 California 39
*20 Stanford 17
18 Tennessee 42
21 Oregon State 45
0 Washington 6
*16 USC 28
197 Season totals 246
W—3, L—7, T—0: Pct 300
Tied for 5th in Pacific-8

1969: Tommy Prothro

*37 Oregon State 0
*42 Pittsburgh 8
34 Wisconsin 23
36 Northwestern 0
46 Washington State 14
*32 California 0
20 Stanford 20
*57 Washington 14
13 Oregon 10
12 USC 14
329 Season totals 103
W—8, L—1, T—1: Pct 850
Tied for 2nd in Pacific-8
Ranked 10th by UPI

1970: Tommy Prothro

14 Oregon State 9
24 Pittsburgh 15
*12 Northwestern 7
17 Texas 20
*40 Oregon. 41
24 California 21
*7 Stanford 9
*54 Washington State 9
20 Washington 61
*45 USC 20
17 Tennessee 28
274 Season totals 240
W—6, L—5, T—0: Pct 545
Tied for 2nd in Pacific-8

1971: Pepper Rodgers

*25 Pittsburgh	29
*10 Texas	28
0 Michigan	38
*17 Oregon State	34
34 Washington State	21
28 Arizona	12
*24 California	31
*12 Washington	23
9 Stanford	20
7 USC	7

166 Season totals 243
W—2, L—7, T—1: Pct 250
7th in Pacific-8

1972: Pepper Rodgers

*20 Nebraska	17
38 Pittsburgh	28
*9 Michigan	26
*65 Oregon	20
*42 Arizona	31
37 Oregon State	7
49 California	13
*35 Washington State	20
*28 Stanford	23
21 Washington	30
*7 USC	24

351 Season totals 239
W—8, L—3, T—0: Pct 727
2nd in Pacific-8

1973: Pepper Rodgers

13 Nebraska	40
*55 Iowa	18
34 Michigan State	21
*66 Utah	16
59 Stanford	13
24 Washington State	13
*61 California	21
*62 Washington	13
27 Oregon	7
*56 Oregon State	14
13 USC	23

470 Season totals 199
W—9, L—2, T—0: Pct 818
2nd in Pacific-8
Ranked 9th by UPI

1974: Dick Vermeil

17 Tennessee	17
10 Iowa	21
*56 Michigan State	14
27 Utah	14
*13 Stanford	13
*17 Washington State	13
28 California	3
9 Washington	31
*21 Oregon	0
33 Oregon State	14
*9 USC	34

240 Season totals 174
W—6, L—3, T—2: Pct 636
Tied for 3rd in Pacific-8

1975: Dick Vermeil

*37 Iowa State	21
*34 Tennessee	28
20 Air Force	20
*20 Ohio State	41
31 Stanford	21
37 Washington State	23
*28 California	14
*13 Washington	17
50 Oregon	17
*31 Oregon State	9
25 USC	22
23 Ohio State	10
(Rose Bowl)	

349 Season totals 243
W—9, L—2, T—1: Pct 792
Tied for 1st in Pacific-8
Ranked 5th by AP, UPI

1976: Terry Donahue

28 Arizona State	10
*37 Arizona	9
*40 Air Force	7
10 Ohio State	10
*38 Stanford	20
*62 Washington State	3
35 California	19
30 Washington	21
*46 Oregon	0
45 Oregon State	14
*14 USC	24
6 Alabama	36
(Liberty Bowl)	

391 Season totals 173
W—9, L—2, T—1: Pct 792
2nd in Pacific-8

1977: Terry Donahue

13 Houston	17
†*17 Kansas	7
13 Minnesota	27
†*34 Iowa	16
28 Stanford	32
† 27 Washington State	16
†*21 California	19
†*20 Washington	12
†† 21 Oregon	3
††*48 Oregon State	18
27 USC	29

269 Season totals 196
W—7, L—4, T—0: Pct 636
Tied for 2nd in Pacific-8

†indicates games later forfeited
††no contest

1978: Terry Donahue

10 Washington	7
13 Tennessee	0
24 Kansas	28
*17 Minnesota	3
*27 Stanford	26
*45 Washington State	31
45 California	0

*24 Arizona	14
*23 Oregon	21
13 Oregon State	15
*10 USC	17
10 Arkansas	10
(Fiesta Bowl)	

261 Season totals 172
W—8, L—3, T—1: Pct 708
2nd in Pacific-10

1979: Terry Donahue

*16 Houston	24
*31 Purdue	21
37 Wisconsin	12
*13 Ohio State	17
24 Stanford	27
14 Washington State	17
*28 California	27
*14 Washington	34
*31 Arizona State	28
35 Oregon	0
14 USC	49

257 Season totals 256
W—5, L—6, T—0: Pct 455
7th in Pacific-10

1980: Terry Donahue

*56 Colorado	14
23 Purdue	14
*35 Wisconsin	0
17 Ohio State	0
*35 Stanford	21
32 California	9
17 Arizona	23
*14 Oregon	20
23 Arizona State	14
*20 USC	17
34 Oregon State	3

306 Season totals 135
W—9, L—2, T—0: Pct 818
2nd in Pacific-10

1981: Terry Donahue

35 Arizona	18
31 Wisconsin	13
7 Iowa	20
*27 Colorado	7
23 Stanford	26
17 Washington State	17
*34 California	6
28 Oregon	11
*31 Washington	0
*34 Arizona State	24
21 USC	22
14 Michigan	33
(Bluebonnet Bowl)	

302 Season totals 197
W—7, L—4, T—1: Pct. 625
Tied for 4th in Pacific-10

1982: Terry Donahue

*41 Long Beach State 10
51 Wisconsin 26
31 Michigan 27
34 Colorado 6
*24 Arizona............... 24
*42 Washington State 17
47 California............. 31
*40 Oregon............... 12
7 Washington 10
*38 Stanford.............. 35
*20 USC 19
24 Michigan 14
(Rose Bowl)
399 Season Totals 231
W—10, L—1, T—1: Pct. ...875
1st in Pacific-10
Ranked 5th by AP, UPI

1983: Terry Donahue

8 Georgia 19
*26 Arizona State 26
10 Nebraska 42
*35 Brigham Young 37
39 Stanford.............. 21
24 Washington State 14
*20 California............. 16
*27 Washington 24
24 Oregon............... 13
24 Arizona............... 27
27 USC 17
45 Illinois 9
(Rose Bowl)
309 Season Totals 265
W—7, L—4, T—1: Pct. 625
1st in Pacific-10

1984: Terry Donahue

18 San Diego State........ 15
*23 Long Beach State 17
* 3 Nebraska 42
33 Colorado 16
*21 Stanford.............. 23
*27 Washington State 24
17 California............. 14
21 Arizona State 13
*18 Oregon............... 20
*26 Oregon State 17
*29 USC 10
39 Miami (Fla) 37
(Fiesta Bowl)
275 Season Totals 248
W—9, L—3, T—0: Pct 750
Tied for 3rd in Pacific-10
Ranked 9th by AP, 10th by UPI

1985: Terry Donahue

27 Brigham Young 24
26 Tennessee 26
*34 San Diego State........ 16
14 Washington 21
*40 Arizona State 17
34 Stanford.............. 9
31 Washington State 30
*34 California............. 7
24 Arizona............... 19
*41 Oregon State 0
13 USC 17
45 Iowa................. 28
(Rose Bowl)
363 Season Totals 214
W—9, L—2, T—1; Pct 792
1st in Pacific-10
Ranked 6th by UPI, 7th by AP

1986: Terry Donahue

3 Oklahoma............. 38
45 San Diego State........ 14
*41 Long Beach State 23
* 9 Arizona State 16
*32 Arizona............... 25
36 California............. 10
*54 Washington State 16
49 Oregon State 0
*23 Stanford.............. 28
17 Washington 17
*45 USC 25
31 Brigham Young 10
(Freedom Bowl)
385 Season Totals 222
W—8, L—3, T—1; Pct 708
Tied for 2nd in Pacific-10

1987: Terry Donahue

*47 San Diego State........ 14
33 Nebraska 42
*17 Fresno State............ 0
*34 Arizona............... 24
49 Stanford.............. 0
*41 Oregon............... 10
*42 California............. 18
31 Arizona State 23
52 Oregon State 17
*47 Washington 14
13 USC 17
20 Florida 16
(Aloha Bowl)
426 Season Totals 195
W—10, L—2, T—0; Pct ... 833
Tied for 1st in Pacific-10
Ranked 9th by AP

UCLA FOOTBALL LETTERMEN

Here, in alphabetical order, is UCLA's list of football lettermen dating back to 1919.

— A —

Abrams, Leslie '20
Adams, Chuck '86
Adams, Tom '55
Adkins, Bryce '76-77
Adkins, James '28
Agajanian, Larry '66-67-68
Agnew, James '43
Aikman, Troy '87
Akers, Arthur '77-78-79-80
Albany, Tony '60
Alder, Eugene '39-40-41
Alexander, Jim '84-85-86
Alexander, Kelton '84-86-87
Alexander, Kermit '60-61-62
Alexander, Kirk '83-84-85-86
Allen, Dick '60-61-62
Allen, Jimmy '72-73
Allington, Robert '34
Almquist, Glen '57-58-59
Altenberg, Kurt '63-64-65
Alumbaugh, Dennis '68-69
Andersen, Foster '59-60-61
Andersen, Norm '73-74-75
Anderson, Art '40-41
Anderson, Dave '48
Anderson, Wilbert '56
Anderson, Willie '84-85-86-87
Andrews, Bob '43
Andrews, Danny '81-82-83-84
Andrews, Fred '52
Andrusyshyn, Zenon '67-68-69
Angle, Robert '26-27-28
Anthony, Corwin '87
Arbuckle, Charles '86-87
Arceneaux, Whitney '50-52
Armstrong, Bill '40-41-42
Armstrong, James '26
Armstrong, Levi '75-76-77
Armstrong, Ray '64-65-66
Armstrong, Sean '83
Arnold, Mike '67
Asher, Tom '44-45-46
Austin, Edward '31-32-34
Austin, Randy '87
Avery, Tom '56-57
Ayers, Eddie '73-74-75

— B —

Baaden, Steve '83
Baggott, Bill '74-75
Baggott, Brian '76-77-78-79
Baida, John '36-37-38
Bailie, Ed '30
Bajema, Ken '67
Baldwin, Burr '41-42-46
Baldwin, Clarence '32-33-35
Baldwin, Harry '58-59-60
Ball, Eric '85-86-87
Ball, Russell '74
Ballard, Bob '54-55
Ballou, Mike '67-68-69
Banducci, Russ '63-64-65
Banning, Wayne '19-21
Baran, Dave '81-82-83-84
Barbee, Mike '79-80-81-82
Barber, Charles '36
Barkate, Harold '86-87
Barnhill, Gordon '36
Barnes, Bruce '70-71-72
Barr, Robert '34-35-36
Barta, Charles '26-27-28

Bartlett, Bob '68-69-70
Bartlett, Ray '39-40
Bashore, Rick '76-77-78-79
Bashore, Ted '64
Baska, Rick '71-72-73
Batchkoff, Frank '83-84-85-86
Bauwens, Joe '60-61-62
Bauwens, Steve '59-60-61
Beamon, Willie '74-75
Beardsley, Harold '46-47
Beban, Gary '65-66-67
Beck, Julius '25-26-27
Beling, Willard '43
Bell, Raymond '75-76-77
Benjamin, Warner '52-53-54
Bennett, Tom '63
Benstead, Roy '58
Benton, Carl '46-47
Berg, Jim '70-71
Bergdahl, Bob '54-55-56
Bergdahl, Lenny '30-31-32
Bergdahl, Mike '66
Bergey, Bruce '68-69-70
Bergman, Jim '60-61-62
Bergmann, Paul '82-83
Berliner, Myron '51-52-53
Bernstein, Gary '67
Berry, Joe '32
Betts, Dean '58-59
Beverly, Randy '86-87
Bickers, Gary '64
Biddle, Brooks '44-45
Billington, Barry '56-57
Binney, John '19-20
Birlenbach, Scrib '25-26-27
Birren, Don '55-56
Bischof, Vince '67-68-69
Bishop, George '23-24-25-26
Bishop, Harold '27-28-29
Bleymaier, Gene '72-74
Block, Chris '83-84
Blower, Albert '44
Boermeester, Peter '77-78-79
Boghosian, Sam '52-53-54
Bolden, Bill '67-68-69
Bolin, Greg '83-84-85-86
Bono, Steve '80-81-83-84
Boom, Herbert '44-45-46
Borden, Don '43-46
Bosserman, Gordon '67-68-69
Boyd, Brent '75-77-79
Boyd, Jack '43-44-45
Boyer, Verdi '32-33-34
Boze, Dave '73-74
Bradley, Doug '54-55-56
Braly, Harold '48-49
Brant, Michael '77-78-79-80
Braunbeck, Dick '54
Bray, James '85
Breeding, Ed '42-46
Breeland, Oran '51
Breiniman, Ansel '29
Bresee, Horace '23-24-25
Bright, Jim '71-72-73
Briley, Dave '73
Brisbin, Kent '76-77-78
Britten, Larry '51-52-53
Broadwell, Brewster '36-37-38
Brockington, Fred '77
Brown, Brian '87
Brown, Carl '27-28-29
Brown, Dave '43
Brown, Don '36
Brown, George '47

Brown, Jack '46-47-48
Brown, Jefferson '23-24
Brown, Jim '54-55
Brown, Jim '74-75-76
Brown, Joe '38
Brown, John '56-57-58
Brown, Sam '53-54-55
Brown, Theotis '76-77-78
Browne, Henry '86
Bruno, Frank '80-81-82
Bryan, Jack '29
Bryson, Brad '86-87
Buchanan, Jim '49-50
Buenafe, Kevin '81-82-83-84
Bukich, Steve '74-76-77-78
Burkley, Laurence '87
Burks, Raymond '73-74-75-76
Burnett, Anthony '87
Busby, Harold '66-67-68
Bussell, Elmer '22
Butler, Dick '57-58
Butler, Homer '76-77
Butler, Ron '80-81-82-84
Butler, Steve '63-64-65

— C —

Caldwell, Jack '33
Callies, Gary '62-63-64
Cameron, Paul '51-52-53
Campbell, Craig '70-71
Campbell, Gary '70-71-72
Campbell, Merle '43
Campbell, William '45
Cannon, Glenn '77-78-79-80
Cantor, Izzy '36-37-38
Cantor, Leo '39-40-41
Capp, Don '46-47
Caragher, Ron '86-87
Cargo, Dave '73-74
Carney, Cormac '80-81-82
Carroll, Frank '38-39
Carver, Ron '69-70-71
Cascales, Charles, '38-39
Case, Ernie '41-45-46
Cashon, Charles, '24-25
Cephous, Frank '80-81-82-83
Chaffin, Jeff '81-83
Chambers, Bill '46-47
Champion, Cornell '64-66
Champion, John '66
Charles, Russel '72-73-74
Chavoor, Sherman '34-35-36
Cheshire, Chuck '33-34-35
Childers, Marion '45
Christiansen, Bob '69-70-71
Christiansen, Gregg '78-79-80
Chudy, Craig '57-59-60
Claman, Alan '65-66-67
Clark, Gene '71-73-74
Clark, Kenneth '24-25-26
Clark, Walter '32-33
Clayton, Mike '70-71
Clements, Bill '45-46-47-48
Clinton, David '83-84-85-86
Coats, Lee '31-32-33
Cochran, Mike '71
Cochran, Rod '57-58-59
Coffman, Ricky '78-79-80-81
Cogswell, Don '49-50
Cohen, Jack '39-40
Coleman, Dick '43

Colletto, Jim '63-64-65
Collins, Donald '19-20
Collins, Vernon '23-24
Collins, Willie '53
Compton, Lynn '41-42
Cooper, Gwen '67-68-69
Cope, Bill '51
Copeland, Ron '67-68
Coppens, Gus '75-76-77
Cornish, Frank '86-87
Corral, Frank '76-77
Cory, Frank '36
Coulter, Michael '75-76-77
Cox, Chris '84
Cox, Larry '64-65-66
Cox, Robert '84-85
Craig, Paco '84-85-86-87
Crawford, Bob '74-75-76
Crawford, Lyndon '80-81-82-83
Crestman, John '68
Cress, Robert '38
Cronin, Kevin '84
Cross, Randy '73-74-75
Cureton, Hardiman '53-54-55
Cureton, Mickey '68-69
Curran, Willie '78-79-80-81
Curry, Dale '73-74-75
Curti, Noah '40-41

— D —

Dabov, Dave '59-60
Dailey, Pete '51-52-53
Dalby, Dave '69-70-71
Damron, Jeff '85-86-87
Daniels, Tom '70-72
Dankworth, Jeff '74-75-76
Dathe, Walt '61-62-63
Davenport, Bob '53-54-55
Davidson, Dick '68
Davis, Bruce '75-76-77-78
Davis, Chuck '62-63-64
Davis, Craig '86-87
Davis, Elvin '26-27
Davis, John '57-58
Davis, Milt '52-53
Davis, Richard '26
Davis, Ron '77-78-79
Davis, Steve '84
Dawson, Jim '56-57-58
Deakers, Rich '64-65-66
Debay, Terry '51-52-53-54
DeBose, Ronnie '78-79-80
Decker, Jim '54-55
Decker, Robert '30-31-32
DeFrancisco, Nate '39-40-41
Dellocono, Neal '81-82-83-84
DeMartinis, Jack '74-75
Denis, Joe '34
Dennis, Ted '28-29
Denton, Wes '86-87
Derflinger, Paul '67
Devlin, Thomas '25-26
DeWitt, Bret '80
Dial, Alan '84-85-86-87
Dias, Bob '83
Dickerson, George '34-35-36
Diebolt, Doug '69
Diehl, Ralph '22
Dills, Preston '54-56
Dimas, Mike '31
Dimitro, Mike '46-47-48
Dimkich, Mitch '60-61-62
Dinaberg, Bob '57
DiPoalo, Carmen '61-62
Debrow, David '46-47-48
Donahue, Terry '65-66

Donald, Dick '65-66
Donatelli, Doug '82-83
Dorrell, Karl '82-83-85-86
Doud, Chuck '52-53
Dougherty, James '41-42
Dow, Norm '65-66
Dressel, Dennis '56-57
Duddleston, Tom '43
Duffy, Ted '28-29
Duffy, Bill '48
Dufour, Dan '79-80-81-82
Dummit, Dennis '69-70
Duncan, Don '56-57
Duncan, John '29-30-31
Duncan, Norm '29-30-31
Durbin, Steve '64-65-66
Durden, Mike '79-80-81-82
Dutcher, Bob '53-56
Dutcher, Erwin '64-65-66
Dye, Cecil '39-40

— E —

Easley, Kenny '77-78-79-80
Eatman, Irv '79-80-81-82
Eaton, Edward '47-48-49
Echols, Reggie '70-71-72
Eck, Keith '74-75-76
Edgar, Anthony '78-79
Edwards, Oscar '75-76
Ehrlich, Lyman '51
Elias, Chris '77-78-79-80
Elias, Lou '56
Ellena, Jack '52-53-54
Elliott, Stacey '87
Ellis, Alan '70-71-72
Enger, Bob '55
Ennen, Henry '47
Epstein, Herman '26-27-28
Erlich, Mickey '65
Erquiaga, John '65-66-67
Escher, Erik '78
Escher, Werner '50-51
Estwick, Mark '87
Evans, Mike '70
Evans, Ron '86-87

— F —

Fade, Bill '44-45
Fagerholm, Rod '58
Fahl, Matt '73-74-75
Farber, Stu '56
Farmer, George '67-68-69
Farr, Mel '64-65-66
Farr Jr., Mel '84-85-86-87
Farr, Mike '86-87
Fears, Charles '40-41-42
Fears, Tom '46-47
Feldman, Rudy '51-52-53
Fenenbock, Charles '38-39
Ferguson, Donvel '35-36-37
Ferguson, Mark '79-81-82
Ferrell, Bobby '72
Fields, Earl '26-27-28
Fields, Jerry '49
Finlay, Jack '40-41-42
Finn, Charles '19
Finstad, Jim '62
Fiorentino, Tony '60-61-62
Fleming, Joe '26-27-28
Fletcher, John '31-32
Florence, John '50-51
Flores, Mike '71
Flynn, Ed '50-51-52
Forbes, Ted '40-41
Ford, Jim '68-69
Forge, James '77-78-79-81
Forster, George '28-29-30
Foster, Don '51-53
Fowler, John '75-76-77

Francis, Don '62-63-64
Francisco, Kent '62-63-64
Francois, Greg '83-84-85
Franey, David '86
Frankel, Lorry '71
Franklin, Scott '83-84-85
Frankovich, Lee '36-37
Frankovich, Mike '32-33-34
Frawley, John '36-38-39
Fraychineaud, Chuck '50-51
Frazier, Cliff '74-75
Freedman, Morris '65
Freitas, Steve '68-70
French, Marion '27-28-29
Frost, Wallace '22-24-25-26
Fry, Art '72
Frye, Stuart '36
Fryer, Mike '72-73
Funk, Fred '34-35-36
Funke, Sigfried '33-34
Fyson, Ed '45

— G —

Gaines, Gene '58-59-60
Galigher, Ed '70-71
Gallagher, Clay '72
Gardner, Earle '23-24-25
Garibaldi, Bob '83-84-85-86
Garratt, Mike '67-68-69
Gary, Joe '78-79-80-81
Gary, Richard '34
Gaschler, Randy '70-71-72
Gasser, Joe '82-83-84-85
Gaston, Dave '40-41
Geddes, Bob '68-69
Gelfand, Chuck '55
Gemza, Steve '80-81-82-83
Gertsman, Steve '56-57-58
Geverink, Al '61-62-63
Ghormley, Dan '62
Gibbs, Dave '61-62-63
Gibbs, Johnny '77-78-79
Gibson, Alfred '28-29
Gilbert, Dan '72
Gilmore, Dale '37-38-39
Glasser, Jeff '84-85-86-87
Goebel, Joe '83-84-85-86
Gomer, Dave '78
Goodman, Brian '70-71
Goodrich, Paul '67
Goodstein, Maurice '28-29-30
Gordon, Ike '78-79-80-81
Gordon, Scott '82-83
Gould, Stanley '26-27-28
Goynes, Chester '80
Graham, Danny '68-69
Graham, Doug '44
Grant, Wes '68-69
Gray, Rex '81-82
Green, Gaston '84-85-86-87
Green, Sandy '65-66-67
Greenwood, Marcus '84-85-86
Grider, Dallas, '65-66
Griffin, Edison '56
Griffin, Harold '66-67-68
Griffith, Kim '67-68
Griswold, Hoxie '42-46
Grossman, Aubrey '29-31
Grounds, Randy '77
Grubb, Gerald '40-41
Gueringer, Ron '77
Gueringer, Tony '78
Gunther, Rich '72
Gustafson, Mark '66-67-68
Gutman, Tom '60-61

— H —

Hackett, Kyle '83
Haffner, Mike '61-63-64
Haight, Leslie '30
Hale, Lynn '49
Hall, Larry '79-80
Hampton, Kerns '30-32
Hampton, Russ '54-55
Hansen, Howard '48-49-50
Hanson, Bob '44-45
Haralson, Burnett '19-20-22-23
Haradon, Howard '34
Harden, Wilbur '75-76
Hardin, Harold '74-75-76
Harmon, Mark '72-73
Harper, Joe '56-57-58
Harris, Earl '35-36-37
Harris, Esker '55-56
Harris, Merle '36-38
Harrison, Morrie '42
Hartmeier, Mike '82-83-84-85
Harvey, Clarence '43
Haslam, Fred '31-32-33
Haslam, Warren '38
Hassler, Edgar '31-32-33
Hastings, Charles '24-25-26
Hastings, John '34-35-36
Hatcher, Orville '46
Hauck, Bill '61-62-63
Helm, John '78-79
Henderson, Bob '25-26-27
Henderson, Scott '71
Henderson, Ted '85
Hendricks, Phil '70
Hendry, Robert '31-32-33
Henley, Darryl '85-86-87
Henry, Wally '74-75-76
Hermann, Johnny '53-54-55
Herrera, Andy '65-66-67
Herrera, Efren '71-72-73
Herrera, Mike '75
Hershman, Leo '49-50
Hesse, Don '39
Heydenfeldt, Bob '52-53-54
Hickman, Gale '62-63
Hicks, Chuck '59-60-61
Hill, Ernest '37-38-39
Hinshaw, Lynn '67
Hirshon, Hal '36-37-38
Hohl, Mason '43
Hoisch, Alan '46-47
Hollaway, Chuck '55-56
Hollingsworth, Cece '23-24-25
Holman, H. R. '43
Hookano, Steve '71-72
Hopwood, Don '77-78
Horgan, Paul '63-64-65
Horta, Joe '50
Horton, Myke '73-74
Horton, Troy '43
Hosea, Bobby '77-78
Howard, Bob '52
Howard, Jack '43
Howell, Harper '80-81-82-83
Hoyt, Bill '46-47
Hubbard, Phil '76-77-78-79
Hudson, James '25-26-27
Hudspeth, Marcus '84-85-86
Huff, Doug '68-69-70
Huff, Robert '20
Hull, Ron '59-60-61
Hummel, Ben '87
Hunt, Howard '41-46
Hunt, Don '47-48-49
Huse, Russell '28-29

Hutchins, Adam '83-86
Hutt, Eddie '64-65-66

— I —

Inglis, Bill '52
Irvine, Gifford '84-85-86
Irwin, Ed '40-41
Izmirian, Albert '42

— J —

Jacobson, Abe '19
Jacobson, Don '28-29-31
Jacoby, Mike '74
Jackson, Billy Don '77-78-79
Jackson, John '24-25-26
Jackson, Melvin '84-85-86-87
Jackson, Warren '62-63
James, Gary '73
James, Stewart '20
Jarecki, Steve '82-83-84-85
Jarvis, William '24
Jaso, Jerry '69-70
Jennings, Charles '23-24-25
Jensen, Keith '61
Jensen, Roy '48-49-50
Jessup, Morris '25
Johns, Gerald '63-64
Johnson, Chance '85-86-87
Johnson, Ernie '46-47-48-49
Johnson, Jim '58-59-60
Johnson, John '41-46
Johnson, Kermit '71-72-73
Johnson, Mitch '62-63-64
Johnson, Mitch '85
Johnson, Norm '78-79-80-81
Johnston, Dan '67
Jones, Arthur '22-23-24-25
Jones, Brian '86
Jones, Carl '62-63
Jones, Dick '45
Jones, Eugene '72-73
Jones, Frank '69-70
Jones, Gerald '78
Jones, Gordon, '30-31-32
Jones, Greg '67-68-69
Jones, Ike '50-51-52
Jones, Ivory '59-60
Jones, Jimmie '72-73
Jones, Ted '39-40
Jordan, Fritz '86-87
Jordan, Wes '83
Jorgensen, Bruce '68-69

— K —

Kahn, Mitch '74-75-76
Kealey, Pat '72
Keating, David '86-87
Keeble, Joseph '31-32-33
Keefer, Robert '44-46-47
Keeton, Rocen '87
Keim, Paul '22
Kendall, Chuck '57-58
Kendricks, Marv '70-71
Key, R. F. (Ted) '34
Keyes, Luther '50-51
Kezirian, Ed '72-73
Kezirian, Rob '75-76
Kibbe, George '26
Kidder, John '84-85-86-87
Kiefer, Ken '44-45-46
Kilmer, Bill '58-59-60
Kimble, Phil '74
King, Bob '57-58
King, Nelson '44-45

Petrie, Roger '86
Pfeiffer, George '36-37-38
Phifer, Roman '87
Phillips, Art '57-58-59
Phillips, George '41-42-44
Phillips, Tony '82-83-84-85
Phinny, Sherm '37-38
Pickert, Joe '85-86-87
Pierovich, John '57-58-59
Pierson, Ray '41-42
Pifferini, Bob '69-70-71
Pike, Charles '34-35-36
Pinkston, Pat '56
Pitts, Ron '81-82-83-84
Piver, Arthur '32
Plemmons, Brad '77-78-80-81
Polizzi, Ignatius '46-48
Porter, Jack '45
Potter, Ken '82-83-84
Preston, Steve '68-69
Price, Dennis '84-85-86-87
Primus, James '84-85-86-87
Profit, Mel '61-62-63
Pryor, Jon '86-87
Purdy, Rick '66-67-68
Putnam, Bill '44

— Q —

Quinby, Roy '21
Quarles, Bernard '79

— R —

Raffee, Alan '51
Rafferty, Thomas '31-32-33
Ramsey, Herschel '72-73-74
Ramsey, Tom '79-80-81-82
Randle, David '82-83-84
Raney, Jack '33
Rasmus, Bob '27-28-29
Ray, Billy '85-86-87
Ray, George '25
Ray, Joe '52-53-54
Record, Clayton '70
Reece, Severn '75-76-77-78
Reed, Jack '62
Reel, Stanley '32-33
Reese, Floyd '67-68-69
Reeves, Doug '80
Reichle, Art '35-36
Reid, Scott '77-78
Reiges, Ben '46-47
Reinhard, Robert '29
Reilly, Paul '86
Remsberg, John '29
Reyes, Bob '73-74-75
Rice, Dan '71
Richards, David '87
Richardson, Bob '63-64-65
Richardson, John '64-65-66
Riddle, Everett '41-42
Riggs, Darrell '48-49-50
Rile, Glen '35-36
Riley, Avon '79-80
Riskas, Mike '57-58
Roberts, Dick '45
Roberts, Gerry '72-73
Roberts, Howard '29-30-31
Robinson, George '35-36
Robinson, G. H. '43
Robinson, Jackie '39-40
Robinson, Jerry '75-76-77-78
Robinson, Raymond '78-79
Robotham, George '42-45
Roesch, Johnny '43-44-46-47

Rogers, Don '80-81-82-83
Rogers, Eric '83-85-86
Rohrer, Robert '43
Roof, Mike '64-65-66
Rosenkrans, Joe '59-60-61
Ross, Ben '34
Rossell, Eddie '20-21
Rossi, Cal '44-45-46-47
Rosskopf, Bob '23
Rowell, Russell '80-81
Rowland, Gene '45-46-47-48
Ruddy, Lorenz '22
Ruettgers, Joe '38-39
Rumbaoa, Phil '79
Russell, Bob '44-45-46-47
Russo, Mario '41
Russom, Jerry '27-28-29
Rutledge, Craig '83-84-85-86
Ryland, John '36-37-38

— S —

Sabol, Joe '50-51-52
Saenz, Ernie '77
Saipale, Toa '78-79-81-82
Salsbury, Jim '51-52-53-54
Sanchez, Lupe '79-80-82-83
Sandifer, Bill '72-73
San Jose, Bobby '87
Sargent, Earl '35-36
Sarpy, James '75-76-77
Sarver, Joe '33
Schell, Walt '35-36-37
Schexnayder, Anthony '87
Schmidt, Mark '86-87
Schmidt, Pat '75-76
Schneider, Bert '46
Schoner, Bob '63
Schroeder, Cliff '48-49
Schroeder, Jay '80
Schroeder, Robert '34-35-36
Schuhmann, Charlie '72-73-74
Schwartz, Randy '62
Schwenk, Vic '46
Sciarra, John '72-73-74-75
Scribner, Rob '70-71-72
Scott, Burness '81-82
Selecky, Mark '87
Senteno, Rick '78-79
Sergel, Jack '22
Settles, Gene '72-73-74
Sharpe, Luis '78-79-80-81
Sheley, Dale '74
Sheller, Henry '44-46
Sherrard, Mike '82-83-84-85
Shinnick, Don '54-55-56
Shinnick, Josh '82-83-84-85
Shipkey, Jerry '44-46-47
Shirk, Marshall '59-60-61
Shoemaker, Steve '75
Short, Dick '48-49-50
Shubin, John '37
Shubin, William '39
Simons, John '44
Simpson, Clifton '27-28-29
Simpson, David '85
Simpson, Robert '39-40-41
Simpson, Sherwood '49
Sims, Arthur '70
Sindell, Steve '63-64
Singler, Jake '26-27-28
Singleton, Ezell '60-61-62
Slagle, Larry '65-66-67
Smalley, Steve '67-68
Smith, Arthur '26-29
Smith, Bobby '59-60-61

Smith, Brian '79
Smith, Charles '30-31
Smith, Chester '29
Smith, Dave '57
Smith, Earl '59-60
Smith, Earl '84-85
Smith, Eric '84-85-86
Smith, Frank '43
Smith, Hal '55-56
Smith, Jeff '74-75
Smith, John '45
Smith, John (Cappy) '50-51-52
Smith, John '53-55
Smith, Julian '33-34
Smith, Lee '77
Smith, Mark '76
Smith, Martin '19
Smith, Milt '40-41-42
Smith, Nathan (Skip) '58-59-60
Smith, Ray '57-58-59
Smith, Rob '61-62
Smith, Vic '41-42-44
Smith, Willie '65-67
Snelling, Ken '41-42
Snyder, Greg '69-70-71
Solari, Al '41-42
Solid, Ken '44-45
Solomon, Edward '27-29-30
Sommers, Jack '38-39-40
Sosnowski, Steve '76-77
Sparlis, Al '41-42-45
Spaulding, William '34-36
Spielman, Art '42
Spindler, Rich '65-66-67
Spurling, Dennis '68-69
Stalwick, Don '51-52-53
Stamper, Bill '45-48
Stanley, Charles '26
Stanley, Jim '60-62-63
Stanley, Steve '65-66-67
Stauch, Scott '77-78-79-80
Stawisky, Sam '33-34-35
Steel, Greg '73
Steele, Scott '68
Steffen, Art '45-46-47-48
Steffen, Jim '57-58
Steiner, Les '46-47-48
Stephens, Frank '75-76-77
Steponovich, Tony '67
Stevens, Bob '59-60-61
Stevens, Matt '83-84-85-86
Stevens, William '19-20
Stevenson, Scott '86-87
Stickel, Walter '31-32
Stiers, William '43
Stiles, Bob '65
Stits, Bill '51-52-53
Stockert, Ernie '50-51-52
Stoeffen, Howard '29
Story, Al '59
Storey, Sam '33-34
Stout, Dave '60-61-62
Strawn, Dean '44
Strode, Woody '37-38-39
Stroschein, Breck '48-49-50
Sullivan, John '73-74-75
Sullivan, Tom '79-80-81-82
Sutherland, Lester '36-37-38
Svensgaard, Ira '45
Sweetland, Pat '73-74
Swick, Jim '73-74
Sykes, Jim '64

— T —

Taber, Norman '35-36
Tamborski, Steve '70
Tandy, John '26

Tauscheck, Russell '44-45
Tautolo, John '77-78-79-80
Tautolo, Ray '79
Tautolo, Terry '74-75
Taylor, Eric '64
Taylor, Greg '74-75-76
Taylor, Tommy '82-83-84-85
Tennell, Derek '83-84-85-86
Tenningkeit, Tim '74-75-76
Terry, John '26
Tetrick, Steve '75-76-77
Theodore, Terry '82-83-84-85
Thoe, Rueben '28-29-30
Thomas, Cliff '78-79
Thomas, Jewerl '75-76
Thomas, Jim '51-52
Thomas, Larry '80-81-82
Thompson, Almose '60-61
Thompson, Danny '85-86-87
Thompson, Harry '48-49
Thursby, Scott '23-24
Tibbs, Burt '51
Tiedemann, Bill '63
Tiesing, Scot '79-81
Timmons, George '24
Tinsley, Phil '46-47-48
Titensor, Glen '76-77
Toland, Don '40
Townsell, Jojo '79-80-81-82
Treadaway, Jim '82
Treat, Ben '58
Trembley, Vic '72
Tretter, Ron '66-68-69
Tritt, Bill '45
Trotter, Harry '33-34
Troxel, William '37
Truesdell, Steve '61-62-63
Tuiasosopo, Manu '75-76-77-78
Tuinei, Mark '78-79
Tumey, Terry '84-85-86-87
Turner, Eric '87
Turner, Jimmy '78-80-81-82
Turner, Marcus '85-86-87
Turney, Grayson '24-25
Tyler, Ed '42
Tyler, Randy '70-71-72
Tyler, Wendell '73-74-75-76

— V —

Vannatta, Chuck '43-44
Vassar, Brad '75
Veal, Zeno '71
Velasco, Alfredo '86-87
Velasco, Louis '28
Vena, Dan '59-60-61
Vernoy, Terry '70-71-72
Versen, Walter '46
Viger, Joe '38-39
Villalobos, Ray '86-87
Villanueva, Primo '53-54
Vlack, Russ '46
Von Sonn, Andy '60-61-62
Vujovich, Roy '48-49

— W —

Waddell, Tom '72-73-74
Wahler, Jim '85-86-87
Wai, Francis '37-38-40
Walen, Mark '82-83-84-85
Walker, John '61-62-63
Walker, Ken '76-77-78